九日世剋をうち小信頼卿数百騎乃重

参りてを院御所三条殿へ参て信頼

をうちへきよと承れハ東國七方へまうら

催ふむさ年乗ちうく給て川つき続御に

催ふむき人不ぬ君に

ら給ろく忍て都をうらふん事も恐う

催へと申をく量なに弟れふ体う仰

THE BOOK OF THE
Samurai
THE WARRIOR CLASS OF JAPAN

THE BOOK OF THE
Samurai
THE WARRIOR CLASS OF JAPAN

STEPHEN R TURNBULL

Bison Books

Published by
Bison Books Ltd.
176 Old Brompton Road
London, SW 5
England

Copyright © 1982 Bison Books Ltd.

Produced by
Bison Books Ltd.
176 Old Brompton Road
London, SW 5
England

Printed in Hong Kong
Reprinted 1986.

Page 1: *A mounted samurai
from the Heiji Monogatari
Emaki.*

Page 2–3: *A scene from the
Osaka Natsu-no-jin Scroll
which Kuroda Nagamasa had
painted as a memorial.*

Page 4–5: *A scene from* The
Seven Samurai.

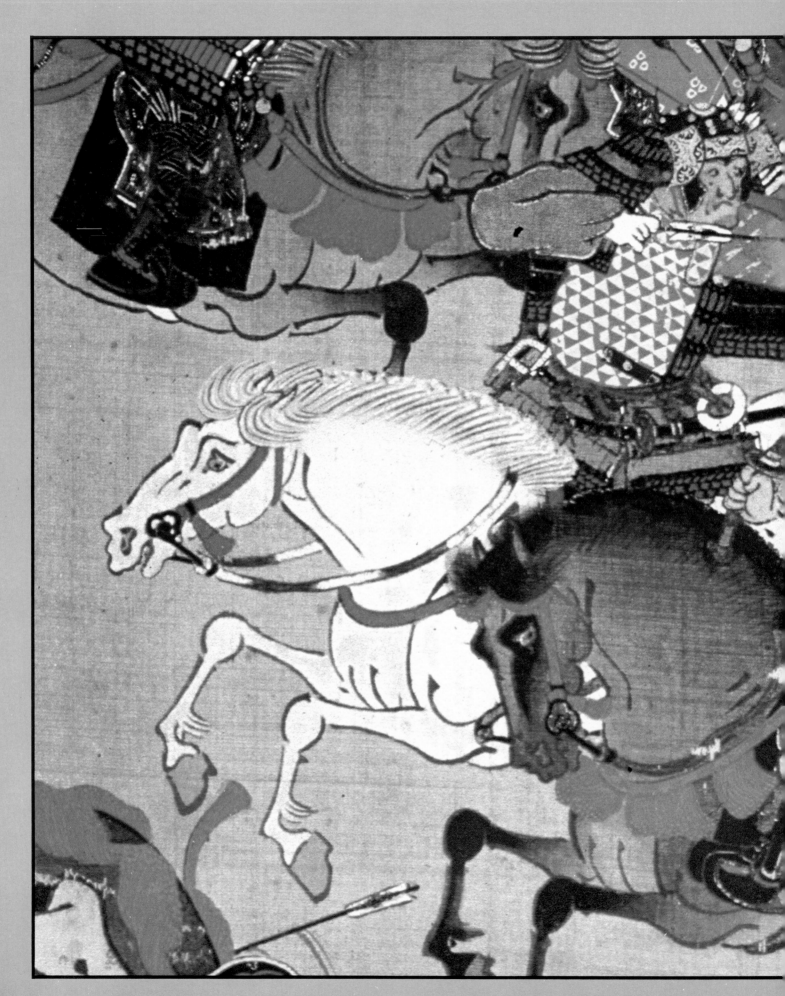

The Way of the Horse and Bow

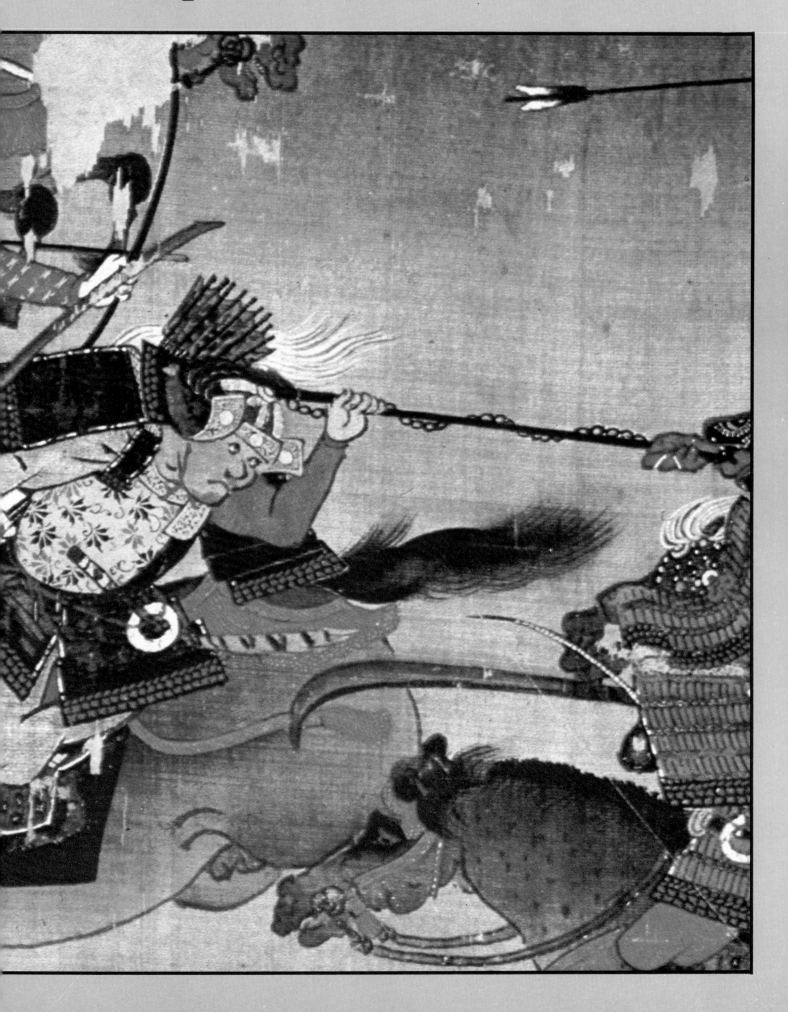

Few countries have a warrior tradition as long and as exciting as that of Japan. It is a tradition found particularly in the person of the romantic, loyal and self-sacrificing knight of old Japan, the samurai. He is the valiant lone swordsman, the ultimate individual warrior. He is the esthete, appreciating the beauty of cherry blossom, and seeing in its brief career his own short and glorious life. He is the commander of a host on the battlefield, the assassin in the night, the keeper of peace, the aristocratic administrator and the avenger of his master.

At various times in Japanese history the samurai fulfilled all these roles. As a military elite they began as tribal warriors, were relegated briefly to the background during the zenith of power of the Imperial family, then slowly grew to dominate the civil bureaucracy the emperors had maintained. It is at this time, between the ninth and eleventh centuries AD, that the word 'samurai,' literally 'those who serve,' comes to be used. There follows six centuries of war, when we meet the samurai as commander in battle and as esthete in brief moments of rest, followed by three centuries of peace, with the samurai as administrator and keeper of peace. The time of war is almost exclusively a catalogue of civil war, characterized by the rise of one group of samurai to national hegemony, only to decline and be supplanted by another. Even the time of peace, the Tokugawa period from 1603–1868, is one of peace forced upon the nation by a samurai regime, a peace that is more the absence of war.

This later period is largely responsible for the romantic image of the samurai hero and his code of conduct, bushido, that is so familiar today. Both aspects of samurai life were fostered by the government of the age as a means of supporting its own legitimacy as a purely samurai government, and ensuring the stability of a class system with the samurai firmly established as an aristocracy. At the same time the spread of literacy and learning among all levels of Japanese society produced an awareness of an earlier military tradition, when the samurai was a mounted knight, a fighter rather than the administrator. Knowledge of the brave deeds of their ancestors had long been enshrined in the samurai tradition, and samurai were used to seeing such exploits enacted in the stylized *noh* drama. However, in peacetime the tales could be told more widely, in the lively *kabuki* theater, the wood-block print, and in reprints of early classics of *Gunkimono*, the military chronicles.

Such stories, of which the greatest, *Heike Monogatari*, the 'Tales of the Taira family,' deals with the great civil wars of the twelfth century, paint a vivid picture of the early samurai as those warriors saw themselves. Moving back a further two centuries we can examine such works as the *Konjaku Monogatari*, compiled about 1080, which gives us perhaps the earliest account of the world of the samurai as viewed by the first of the warrior elite to use that name. To understand the origins of the samurai it is necessary to go back even further than these written sources to see the historical and geographical setting in which the samurai evolved.

The key to understanding much of Japanese history is an appreciation of the struggle for land. It is so important that the student of samurai history has to spend at least as much time trying to understand land surveys, grants of land, tax systems, fief distribution and the like as he does following military campaigns and battles. In part this is due to Japan's geographical nature. Four-fifths of the land surface of the Japanese islands is mountainous. The remaining fifth of good agricultural land is distributed unevenly, with large concentrations in the three great alluvial plains on the main island of Honshu, where today are found the major urban areas such as Tokyo and Osaka. However, Japan cannot be said to have a real shortage of land at any time during the history of the samurai, because in terms of productivity the method of agriculture, which was largely the intensive cultivation of rice by efficient irrigation and considerable manpower, was sufficient to feed a large population. In the late eighteenth century, for example, Japan was feeding nearly 30,000,000 people in a country closed to imports.

Below: A map showing the general outline of Japan, its main islands, and its position in relation to the Asiatic mainland.

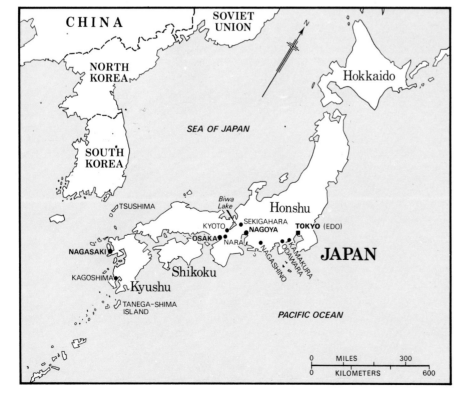

9

England at that time had a population of 7,500,000 supported to some extent by oceanic trade.

Yet in common with many other Asiatic countries, Japanese society was characterized by a huge peasant farmer base, bearing a ruling class on its shoulders. In Japan's case this class was the samurai, whose wealth, until modern times, was to be assessed in terms of land and the rice that land produced by the sweat of the farmers' brows. (The unit of measurement of wealth, incidentally, was the *koku* [about 180 liters] which was regarded as the amount of rice necessary to feed one man for one year.) It is the land where this rice grew, land jealously held and bitterly contested, for which the samurai were fighting.

Another factor of consequence for a study of the samurai is Japan's geographical isolation. The four islands are spread out along the edge of the Asiatic mainland, close enough to make travel possible, but not close enough to make it easy, so that Japan has always been able to absorb what it wants from other countries, and to reject what it does not need. This is not to say that foreigners have had no impact on Japan. Different countries have dominated the cultural scene at different times in the history of the samurai. Sometimes it was China. In the sixteenth century it was Spain and Portugal. In the nineteenth it was the United States and the colonial powers of western Europe. From all of these Japan absorbed ideas and technology, showing that remarkable talent for a quick assimilation and the perfection of another's original idea that has characterized Japanese craftsmanship to this day.

The forerunners of the samurai are the military elite of the tribes that formed the first Japanese state, the Yamato, in the early centuries of the Christian era. The most dramatic evidence of a ruling class at this time are the huge burial mounds called *kofun*, which are larger in mass than the better-known pyramids of Egypt. From these tombs we find the first artistic representation of a Japanese warrior. These are the *haniwa*, pottery figures, showing in some detail the appearance of the ancestors of the samurai. They wear armor and helmets, carry iron swords and ride horses. They are armed with long bows and use stirrups.

The elite that lie buried within such tombs are the early emperors, who can be seen as the leaders of the dominant *uji*, the term which is usually translated as 'tribe' or 'clan.' The *uji* were large groups of families related to a main line of descent 'ruled' by a family head, who was regarded as being descended from the founder of the line and whom the members of the *uji* worshipped as a god. The *uji* chief, there-

fore, was both priest and king, combining both hereditary and religious authority in his person. Beneath these aristocratic *uji* were the *be*, the workers, grouped not by hereditary but by place of residence and occupation. Most of the *be* were farmers, but others were potters, fishermen and the like.

In a process that was to be repeated in the future by competing samurai families, the *uji* formed coalitions with neighbors, absorbed weaker ones, extended their landholdings by developing virgin lands, and defeated rivals in battle. Out of these battles the *uji* that was to achieve dominance over the others was the one that claimed descent from the ultimate in sacred founders, the sun goddess, Amaterasu. According to Japanese mythology Amaterasu was the first-born of the gods who created Japan and thus inherited the earth. The connection with the Imperial descent is made via her great-great-grandson, the first earthly emperor, Jimmu.

Such a claim of descent thus put the dominant 'Sun-line' *uji* in a virtually unassailable religious position beside the political one they had achieved by force. By about 200 AD the descent of the Imperial family from the sun goddess was enshrined in the religion of Shinto, the 'Way of the Gods.' Central to Shinto is the notion of *Kami*, which can best be translated as holiness. Certain places, such as the tops of mountains, possess *kami*, making them the places where the gods may be worshipped. From the point of view of the history of the samurai the important thing is that the emperor too, had *kami*. This is not to say that the emperor was worshipped as a god, but that the Imperial line had an unquestionable religious position that made it sacred. Consequently, throughout the period of samurai dominance, control of the emperor is exercised by making him more important in the religious sense while less in the political, thus making his daily function one of continuing ritual and ceremony. The whole basis of the samurai government, the shogunate, was that the duty of ruling the country was delegated to the shogun, while the possessor of *kami* performed spiritual duties.

The word shogun, for the military dictator at the head of the samurai, is now almost as familiar a word as samurai itself, and is in fact of considerably older vintage. It is during the time of the consolidation of power by the Imperial sun line, that the word is first used to describe the four generals sent by the tenth emperor, Sujin, to quell rebellions in about 200 AD. This was the pattern to be followed as the early emperors constantly expanded their authority by military expeditions. The shogun's commission to go forth and make war was always

Above: *A* haniwa. *These pottery figures, placed around the tombs of the early emperors, give us a good idea of the appearance of the forerunners of the samurai. This example is a replica cast from an original.*

a temporary one. The shogun set out on his task, and when the job was completed the commission ceased.

Thus the power of the emperors grew, reaching a peak during the fifth century AD, and by the sixth century we can see the outlines of a recognizable governing structure, with the emperor as head, and the other *uji* chiefs as his officials. As the power of the sun line increased, so did that of the other *uji*. Even at the peak of the emperors' power they merely presided over a coalition of aristocratic *uji* houses, some of whom gave military assistance to the sun line while others provided opposition to it. There was thus a continual background of military activity involving the Imperial house itself or the troops of their two main military *uji*, the otomo and the mononobe, the hereditary palace guards, to maintain the status quo.

The military exploits of the Japanese military elite at this time were considerable. For a century Japan was involved in Korea, allying herself with one of the three Korean kingdoms that were competing for control of the peninsula. The mere fact that the Japanese were able to continue military operations for so long, involving the use and equipping of a large army which

Right: *Prince Yamato and the grass-mowing sword. According to legend the heroic son of Emperor Keiko was surrounded by enemies who set fire to the long grass. Prince Yamato escaped by cutting his way through with his sword.*

Left and below: *From ancient times the wealth of a samurai was expressed in terms of the rice yield of fields such as these. The struggle for land is the key to understanding much of samurai history.*

was transported by a fleet of ships, shows that the samurai had distinguished antecedents. The Japanese warriors were driven from Korea in 562, but continued efforts to regain a foothold until the unification of Korea in 668. At home there were rebellions by certain *uji*, and also aboriginal tribes to subdue in Kyushu and the north of Honshu, but the greatest achievement of the early emperors was that in the face of opposition from unruly *uji* they were actually able to go beyond military suppression to a state of civil control that put the military side of Japanese life firmly into the background, from where it was to emerge centuries later as the samurai.

The impetus for the suppression of militarism came from China, and one of the decisive factors was the introduction to Japan of the religion of Buddhism. To the emperors of the sun line, Buddhism was at first seen as a threat, as much of their prestige was based on the religious grounds of Shinto. The resulting disagreement about whether Buddhism should be accepted led to civil war, won in 587 by the pro-Buddhist Soga *uji*. For the next 70 years the Soga dominated Japanese life, and in 592 arranged the assassination of the ruling emperor, who was replaced by an empress and a regent, Prince Shotoku. Fortunately for the continuation of the sun line, Prince Shotoku valued the interests of the ruling family, and it was during his reign that Buddhism came to be seen not as a threat but as an opportunity for Japan to share in the glorious culture of T'ang China, which would enable the sun line rulers to become real 'emperors' after the pattern to be seen on the mainland. This Shotoku achieved,

Right: *A statue of Buddha. One of the most decisive factors in the suppression of militarism was the introduction of Buddhism in the sixth century AD.*

Left: *The East Pagoda of the Yakushui-ji Temple, Nara. It is often referred to as the pagoda of frozen music because of its beauty.*

Left: *The Daibutsu-den of the Todai-ji. This hall, built to house the Great Buddha, is the largest wooden building in the world.*

but other far-reaching reforms which he planned had to wait until after his death and another coup d'état. Thus in 646 the Taika reforms were proclaimed. They were put into operation by Fujiwara Kamatari, the first of a long line of Fujiwara statesmen who were to leave their mark on Japanese history. Essentially the aim was to break the powers of the rival *uji*, largely by depriving them of their land, and replace the system of government by *uji* coalition with a civil bureaucracy under the emperor, based on the Chinese model, with the warrior activities firmly curtailed.

In terms of devaluing the military side of *uji* life the reforms were successful, but as a method of avoiding power politics they were not. They merely enabled the *uji* elite to abandon military opposition for the political rivalry of court life. The *uji* leaders were not stripped of wealth. Instead many moved to Nara (the first true capital city of Japan) to form a new aristocracy where political rank and influence were identified with closeness to the Imperial line. Their independent military existence had been left behind, and replaced by new prestige and security as *kuge*, or court nobles.

The city of Nara was a great monument of the new aristocratic age. Another was the Taiho Codes, a set of laws put into effect in 702. One of the most important provisions concerned the ownership of land. The original concept of the state on the Chinese model envisaged that all land should belong to the emperor, who would then distribute it among his subjects. The rice land was therefore systematically surveyed, and the population registered by households. Cultivators were assigned equal grants of land according to an agreed system, whereby a male over six years old received two *tan* (about half an acre) and a female two-thirds this amount. Those who received land would pay certain taxes for the privilege: in rice, in textile produce, and in the form of corvée for public works and military service. The latter proposal was particularly aimed at putting the previous tribal military elite firmly into the past. It would create a national conscript army for the emperor, owing allegiance to none but him, which was ready to be mobilized and disbanded as the need arose. Theoretically a third of the adult males in a province were placed on the conscription list, and were to be summoned in rotation. A man was liable from the age of 20–59, and during this time was expected to serve for one year in Nara and to spend three years fighting aboriginals on the frontier of civilization. The conscript's household was required to supply the warrior with armor, weapons and provisions, which was quite a burden for a poor family. The proposals were unfortunately weakened right

from the start by concessions to the wealthy to buy themselves out, resulting in an army consisting of undisciplined bands of unwilling warriors under *uji* aristocrat leaders, and eventually the whole scheme had to be abandoned.

The land reforms were nearly as great a failure as conscription. If land was to be redistributed by the emperor it had to come from somewhere or someone, and the magnates in the provinces, particularly in the east, who had not succumbed to the lure of Nara, were too powerful to be deprived of their lands by the emperor and his court. So they and their dependants became the secondary and lower levels of the aristocracy by allowing the emperor to appoint them as provincial governors with responsibilities for tax collecting. Such offices naturally attracted a high salary, which was paid in the form of land grants way over what the Taiho Code would have originally given. Such grants, with additions for rank and

Left: *The Horin-ji Temple and its environs in the Nara Prefecture.*
Below: *Nearby is the Horyu-ji Temple. This beautiful temple was founded in 607 AD by Prince Shotoku, and has survived almost unscathed through the years of civil wars.*

Above: *The most important weapon for the early samurai was the bow. In this illustration from a woodblock-printed book a samurai in court costume prepares to slay a rather splendid-looking dragon.*

meritorious service, tended to become hereditary private possessions. This growth of private rice lands, or *shoen*, soon extended much further down the social scale than the aristocracy. This was partly a result of the gradual abandonment of the land redistribution scheme, which effectively ceased after 840, and partly a result of the energy of farmers in opening up new tracts of land from reclamation projects. Reclamation was in fact encouraged by the government, which permitted reclaimers to keep new fields for up to three generations of the family, after which they would have to be returned for redistribution, but even this requirement was dropped in 743.

It was also possible to secure various tax immunities on private land. The ultimate immunity was to have one's land exempt from inspection by the government land-tax inspectors. This privilege in particular converted originally allotted lands into private *shoen*, where the proprietor was his own lord and master, collected his own taxes and ordered the domain himself. To some extent this was allowed for under the Taiho Code, but not to the extent to which the *shoen* system grew. Some *shoen* were enlarged by purchase, others by illegal absorbing of public allotment lands, but most by the practice of *kishin*, or commendation, whereby a tax-paying landowner would nominally donate

his land to a tax-exempt *shoen* proprietor, which could be a provincial aristocrat or even a temple. These *shoen*, however, were not a continuous territory, like the domains of the provincial samurai lords in the sixteenth century, but widely scattered holdings. A good example is the territory of Fujiwara Yorinaga Yorinaga, who in 1150 held 20 *shoen* which were distributed through 19 provinces.

Under different circumstances the *shoen* system might have been a great support to the Imperial government, as an efficient use of devolved power in remote and often unpleasant areas of the nation which were subject to attacks by bandits and aboriginal expeditions. However, as the *shoen* system grew, so the central government gradually lost its power to enforce law and order, and in the absence of central policing the proprietors of *shoen* had to look to their own devices to protect and increase their territories. As the *shoen* were the products of private agreements, so similar agreements were made for the defense of the territories between the *shoen* owner and the smaller landowers who had commended their lands and received protection. The smaller landowners promised to be loyal followers. They called themselves 'those who serve' – the 'samurai.' Once more Japan had a military elite.

This return from the shadows of a pre-Nara military style was not exclusively the result of the *shoen* system. The failure of the national conscript system had made it necessary for the government to think again about the means whereby its authority could be maintained in outlying areas. Thus the provincial families, the new samurai, were called upon to supply military manpower. During the ninth century is the first evidence of provincial governors appointed from the capital requesting permission to arm themselves and their staffs. Under the shogun system the governor was appointed from the capital, proceeded to the province, and as long as the system was working well, served his term of office and returned. However, as provincial appointments tended to be hereditary, so did the military commission, and increasingly the ability to exercise authority rested on military strength. The civil bureaucracy set up by the Taiho Code and previous reforms was thus necessarily changed into a military one, with the samurai leaders becoming officials who had a military as well as an administrative function. This was only to become a problem when the new ties of loyalty that military association bred began to cut across existing civil structures.

An important factor in the formation of samurai bands in the provinces was the aristocratic background of many of the leaders. The

Fujiwara *uji* had grown to dominate the Imperial court by intermarriage and close government service. The Fujiwara monopoly became so tight that it was customary for non-Fujiwara courtiers, often princes of quite high rank, and even some minor Fujiwara members to leave Kyoto for the provinces to seek their fortunes. Two families in particular, the Taira and the Minamoto, owed their founding to such processes. Noble connections, coupled with military skills, meant they were much in demand for marriage alliances and commendation of lands.

A samurai band was organized like an extended family, with a nucleus of real kinsmen. Kinship terms were used to define relationships between members even though they were not true blood relatives. Consequently it is not too inaccurate to speak of the Taira and Minamoto 'clans,' and this is the term used. The closest group to the clan leader, who was also the *shoen* owner, was his immediate family, *ichimon*. Branch families were called *ie no ko*, literally boys of the house, and nonkin samurai were *kenin*, or housemen. It is this latter relationship that particularly distinguishes the samurai re-

lationships from a bureacratic organization. The *kenin* received protection from the leader, to whom they owed loyalty in return for the rights to a certain portion of the clan *shoen* lands. This was a feudal relationship and, although feudalism is a term borrowed from Europe, the organization of the samurai clans is to all intents and purposes identical to the lord/vassal relationship characteristic of feudalism. At this stage in samurai history however, feudalism was incomplete, because in the majority of cases the feudal relationship stopped at the clan leader, who owed his position to the bureaucratic-type appointment by a central government, whose civil authority he recognized. Samurai society was later made completely feudal by incorporating all these separate samurai hierarchies under a central military dictator, the shogun, who confirmed his followers in their holdings in return for loyal seryice, thus fusing the civil, military and judicial elements of rule into one authority. In contrast these early samurai were small feudal groups of armed warriors living on the fringe of an expanding agricultural economy, much the same as the farmers and ranchers who pushed back the frontiers of the United States.

Below: *This detail from the Kasuga Gongen Scroll shows a warrior in a suit of armor with a basketwork quiver at his side, from which arrows were removed by lifting out of the base and pulling downward.*

18

Above: Yabusame *was a popular sport as well as providing excellent training in the skills of mounted archery. The contestants fired at small targets as they galloped along. It is still practiced today in Kamakura.*

Thus during the Nara period, and the early Heian (from the moving of the capital to Heian-kyo, or Kyoto, in 794) the services of the military elite were required by two divisions: within the growing *shoen*, where allegiance was to the aristocratic proprietor; and for the service of the emperor, which meant in some cases pitting samurai in this group against samurai in the former. Whereas aristocratic lineage may have been a great help in attracting followers, success in battle was absolutely vital, and a number of disturbances during the tenth and eleventh centuries provided opportunities for samurai leaders to prove their clan's worth. It is from the records of such expeditions, which no doubt are considerably glorified, that we get the earliest accounts of samurai values and behavior referred to at the beginning of this chapter. The first of these, which produced probably the first written account of samurai, was the rebellion of Taira Masakado in 935.

Masakado was a descendant of Emperor Kammu who served under the Fujiwara and coveted the important office of Kebiishi, a high appointment concerned with the arrest and punishment of criminals and whose notifications had the same value as imperial ordinances. When the title was refused him, Masakado revolted and began a guerrilla war in eastern Japan by attacking his uncle, Taira Kunika, and putting him to death. In 936 Yoshikane,

Kunika's brother, attacked Masakado but was repulsed to Kyoto. Masakado occupied Shimosa, Shimotsuke and Kozuke provinces, proclaiming himself Heishin-o, 'New Emperor from the Taira clan.' In 940 an expeditionary force led by Fujiwara Hidesato and Taira Sadamori set out to attack him. They defeated Masakado in the initial encounter, and pursued him for 13 days. In the final battle Masakado was wounded by an arrow and fell from his horse, whereupon Hidesato killed him and sent his head back to Kyoto. As the *Konjaku Monogatari* puts it:

'. . . when the new emperor joined battle he galloped forward on his swift charger, but divine retribution was at hand, for his horse would run no further, his hand had lost its cunning, and finally, struck by an arrow, he died. . . . (The enemy) rejoiced at this and commanded a fierce samurai to cut off his head.' It is said that Masakado later appeared to a man in a dream and proclaimed: 'When I was alive I did wrong, and never performed one good act. It is impossible for one person to bear this suffering for the fate I have made for myself.'

Taira Sadamori's defeat of his relative helped the clan achieve a fame for itself as successful samurai. Samurai achievements are not the only things related in the stories, they also give us many pointers to samurai life. One fact that comes over is that the traditional relationship between the samurai and his sword, where the sword was looked upon as 'the soul of the samurai,' was still some time into the future. The basic weapons of the tenth-century samurai were the bow and arrow, and the samurai referred to their calling as 'the Way of the Bow and Arrow,' or 'the Way of Horse and Bow.' At this time the samurai was a mounted archer, whose bow was kept as ready as the Western gunfighter's six-shooter. It was even used in duels, being fired from the saddle in much the same way as in *yabusame*, a sport performed to this day, where mounted archers gallop along and shoot arrows at small targets on the way.

This is implied by a story in *Konjaku Monogatari* of a duel between two samurai, who bring their war bands to a prearranged spot for a trial of strength. The skirmish begins with both sides shooting at each other from behind large wooden shields, which they gradually inch forward, until just as they are about to shoot at close range one of the samurai leaders suggests to the other that a better test of their skills would be individual combat. They draw up their horses some distance away, and release their first arrows as they begin to charge. Their second arrows are fired in true *yabusame* style as they pass at a gallop, and cause minor wounds. Each dodges the other's third arrow, fired from rest, after which they agree that honor has been more than adequately satisfied. The account tells us that both lived as close comrades thereafter, because it was only a challenge, and challenges between comrades did not necessarily imply that they had to kill each other.

A more striking account of the importance attached to the bow concerns Tachibana Norimitsu, who was attacked by robbers as he left the Imperial palace one night, armed with only a sword. He vanquished the robbers, but it is recorded that he noted with some relief that the robbers were armed 'only with swords, and not with bows.' Although it is obvious that three brigands armed with bows would have considerable advantage over a single swordsman at any period in Japanese history, the whole story is in complete contrast to the notion of the brave samurai swordsman that is the popular image from later times.

The story of the duel also illustrates a theme which recurs time and again throughout samurai history. This is the notion of honor, a concept central to understanding the samurai at any time in their history. In the archery duel mentioned above each demonstrates his skill, and honor is satisfied. Had the duel been fought for a more serious reason than rivalry among comrades the outcome would have been very different. The most serious case of the need to

Left: *Although during this early period the bow was regarded as the prestige weapon, when it came to hand-to-hand fighting the sword was essential. However, it did not acquire its special mystique until much later.*

satisfy honor is when one's father has been killed. One of the tales in *Konjaku Monogatari* is of a vendetta by a samurai against the man who has killed his father. Although the murderer is well guarded the samurai manages to slip into the courtyard where he is resting and slits his throat. It is the earliest account of a vendetta in Japanese history, antedating the classic story of the 47 *ronin* (masterless samurai) by eight centuries. The account ends with the words: 'To achieve vengeance on the murderer of one's father, even though the murderer may himself be a fine samurai, is something precious and of which the gods approve.' Many years later such sentiments were to be expressed more simply as 'a man must not live under the same sky as one who has injured his lord or his father,' and even in these early days the loyalty demanded by the lord/vassal relationship was regarded as equivalent to that of a man toward his natural father.

The concept of the honor of the clan is also invoked in one tale where a samurai is ordered to shoot a fox, and is reluctant to try because failure will bring disgrace upon his clan. When the prince presses him to try, he shoots and hits the fox, but attributes his success to his guardian deity, who guided the arrow so that his ancestors would not be disgraced.

Finally, although some samurai in *Konjaku Monogatari* fight to the death, there is no ritual act of suicide to preserve honor. Nor is there much elaboration of any warriors' code, beyond that of the call of honor. The greatest duties of the samurai, like their greatest glories, were yet to come.

CHAPTER 2

The Classical Warriors

22

Previous page: *The Battle of Dan-no-Ura, 1185. This print by Kuniyoshi depicts the exploits of Taira Noritsune, who attempted to capture the Minamoto leader, Yoshitsune.*

Below: *This section of armor is laced together in* kebiki *style, which is typical for the tenth to fourteenth centuries. Each scale of the armor is individually made and then fastened together with leather thongs.*

While stories such as *Konjaku Monogatari* give an excellent idea of the values which the early samurai held most dear, it is necessary to turn to later accounts to find out what they looked like. A number of painted scrolls, called *emakimono*, remain and, together with the few remaining suits of armor from the period, show clearly the appearance of the first samurai.

The most striking thing about their costume is the *yoroi*, the particular style of armor worn at this time. It is probably the most gaudy and uncomfortable-looking protective armor ever devised, yet its ungainly shape derived from practical considerations. The samurai were mounted archers and, although their stocky Mongol ponies possessed great endurance, they lacked the muscular strength of European knights' chargers. Consequently the samurai needed a suit of armor that combined strength with lightness, as speed was his main defense. The result was a particular variation of the lamellar style of armor that is found throughout Asia. Lamellar armor is made up from a series of small plates fastened securely together, in contrast to the well-known European plate armor, where each section of the armor is a complete sheet of metal. The lamellae in a *yoroi* were small scales of iron bound tightly together to make a horizontal strip which was lacquered, usually black. A series of such strips

were then laced together, each one overlapping slightly the one above, to make the full armor plate. The other predominant color of the armor came from the vertical cords, which were usually of silk or leather, dyed in brilliant colors, and arranged to make an attractive pattern.

The whole of the suit of armor was made in this way, giving the characteristic box-like appearance. Three sides of the 'box,' the back, front and left side, were made as one piece, while all the other parts were tied on with cords. Heavy shoulder plates called sode were worn on the upper arms. They fastened behind the back to prevent them from flying up and leaving the arms unprotected.

Armor for the arms consisted of a long cloth bag to which metal plates were sewn, but wearing one on the right arm made it difficult to draw the bow, so it was commonly dispensed with. The helmet was a heavy metal bowl made from a series of iron plates riveted together, and fitted with an enormous neckguard of lamellar plates, which hung down on to the shoulders. Taken as a whole the *yoroi* was relatively light and protected the most vulnerable parts of a mounted archer, but it was not very suitable for fighting on foot, for which reason its design was later abandoned.

The style that was to replace the *yoroi* was in fact already being worn by the rough foot soldiers

Below: *This well-mounted dummy depicts a samurai general seated on his camp stool as if in command on a battlefield. He holds his* saihai, *the tasselled baton of command, and wears a flamboyant helmet.*

Above: *The model for this photograph has been dressed in an accurate reconstruction of the armor of a common footsoldier of the Gempei War period. Note the protection for the face and the primitive version of the* naginata, *the pole arm he is wielding.*

Right: *In samurai warfare the only unquestioned proof of duty done was the presentation of the enemy's severed head. These trophies of war are illustrated in a woodblock-printed edition of the epic* Heike Monogatari.

Below: *Minamoto Yoshiie at war. In this section from the Gosannen War Scroll the hero Minamoto Yoshiie observes birds rising from a forest, warning him of an ambush.*

who followed the samurai, and outnumbered them by about 20 to one. The foot soldier wore a simpler 'wrap-around' armor, a *do-maru*, which was much more flexible though offered less protection. There were, however, numerous gradations between the two styles, as indeed there were between the ranks, a clear definition between samurai and common soldier being a later development.

The account of the duel between two mounted samurai related in the previous chapter is an excellent account of the ideal of the formal samurai battle. A battle should begin by an exchange of arrows, including specially made arrows with large perforated wooden heads that whistled as they flew through the air. This

should be followed by a series of individual combats between champions which, in the case of serious warfare, would be fought to the bitter end. In fighting such duels great care would be taken to select a worthy opponent, and so that an opponent would appreciate that the samurai making the challenge was also suitably noble and dignified it became customary to proclaim one's ancestry when giving the challenge. Great deeds of samurai forebears were recounted, such as the following example from the epic *Heike Monogatari*, which refers to the Battle of Uji in 1180. The samurai proclaiming the challenge is descended from Fujiwara Hidesato, the vanquisher of the rebel Taira Masakado in 940, and as the protagonist regards himself as fighting the enemies of the emperor it is only appropriate that such an illustrious descent should be shouted at the top of one's voice:

'Then Ashikaga Matataro . . . stood up in his stirrups and shouted loudly: "I am Ashikaga Matataro Takatsuna, aged 17, son of Ashikaga no Taro Toshitsuna of Shimotsuke, descended in the tenth generation from Tawara Toda Hidesato (that is, Fujiwara Hidesato), the renowned warrior who gained great fame and reward for destroying Masakado, the enemy of the emperor, and though it may be at the risk of divine anger that one without rank or office should draw a bow against a Prince of the Royal House, yet as I owe a deep gratitude to the Taira for many favors, here I stand to meet any on the side of Gensammi Nyudo who dares to face me."'

Gensammi Nyudo was the title of Minamoto Yorimasa, who had raised the rebellion against the Taira in company with an Imperial 'pretender,' Prince Mochihito, hence Ashikaga's reluctance to fight anyone associated with the Imperial house.

Note the mention of reward in the account of his ancestor's exploits. Loyalty to the point of death demanded a reward, particularly when the commission was made on behalf of the government, and would be expected in the form of grants of land to increase the warrior's *shoen* holdings when the samurai returned bearing proof that the undertaking had been successfully completed. Throughout samurai history the only competely acceptable proof of success was the presentation of the severed head of the rebel he had been sent out to chastise, as in the case of Taira Masakado's revolt. The failure to reward loyal service could provoke serious resentment. In 1086 Minamoto Yoshiie returned to Kyoto after the successful completion of a campaign against the rebel Kiyowara, known as the Later Three Years' War, the government refused to reward him. This was particularly galling as Yoshiie had not been given an official shogun commission before the war began, but had decided to carry out the campaign from his own resources. He was so disgusted at the government's action that he flung the heads of the rebels into a ditch, and rewarded his samurai from his own lands. It was a serious error for the government to make, for in refusing to recognize that the campaign had been

fought on their behalf they were giving official sanction to what had effectively been a private war between the Minamoto and the Kiyowara. As the growth of *shoen* estates indicated that such incidents would occur again, to give tacit approval to private conflicts between powerful samurai families was courting disaster.

This is in fact what did happen during the eleventh and twelfth centuries. Fighting between samurai clans was usually conducted for private reasons, and occasionally legitimized by an Imperial commission and some title, such as 'shogun.' By the beginning of the twelfth century there were two predominant samurai power groups in Japan, the Minamoto clan, established in the wild eastern provinces, and the Taira, based in central Japan and the region of the Inland Sea. Both clans were now indispensable to the Fujiwara-dominated government as quellers of rebel samurai, which both the Taira and Minamoto put down with great glee as rivals to their own position. It was also becoming obvious that sooner or later a member of one of these samurai clans would become powerful enough to take a hand in the internal politics of court and emperor, and upset the courtier/Fujiwara power structure for ever.

The stimulus for such intervention came from an unexpected quarter. Since the first use of the *kishin* system, commendation of lands, for avoiding taxes and seeking protection, one beneficiary of donated holdings had been the great monasteries and religious centers, whom early tax decrees had made exempt. As the

Above: *A footsoldier suffers a head wound from an arrow during a battle between Taira samurai and warrior monks, depicted in the Kasuga Gongen Scroll.*

Right: *The armies of warrior monks were among the most formidable forces in action during the eleventh and twelfth centuries. Note the armor worn under their clerical robes, their shaven heads and the* naginata, *or glaive.*

Below: *Taira Kiyomori, the man who brought the Taira clan to the height of their power, sees in his snow-covered garden a vision of the skulls of the men he has slain to reach his exalted position.*

centuries passed, certain foundations, such as the Enryaku-ji on Mount Hiei near Kyoto, and the Kofuku-ji at Nara, acquired enormous wealth, making the *shoen* in clerical hands some of the largest in the country. The change of capital from Nara to Kyoto had set in motion great rivalry between the two Buddhist centers. These were not religious disputes as we under-

stand them, but were almost invariably about land or prestige. Faced by the growing power of samurai clans, and remembering that all *shoen* holdings, including temples, were always scattered widely, it was natural for the more belligerent temples to train their inmates in the arts of war, and in many cases to recruit 'samurai-monks,' known as *sohei*, who were superficially ordained and used to swell the ecclesiastical armies.

Had the monastic disputes remained as inter-temple squabbles, small-sized campaigns, which invariably ended with the rival temple being set on fire, they may have given the government little concern. However, unlike the samurai clans, the monks were not averse to making their joint religious and military presence felt in the capital itself when pursuing a quarrel. Violent demonstrations by thousands of *sohei* and the proclamation of curses from the wronged monks greatly disturbed the equanimity of the Fujiwara, to whom rebellions were something reported by distant governors which happened in even more distant provinces. Instead, the courtiers were

forced to witness violence literally on their own doorstep from the *sohei* in their long robes and cowls over suits of armor, wielding their terrible *naginata*, a heavy glaive with a long curved blade.

The first samurai to exploit this situation was Taira Kiyomori (1118–81) the leader of the dominant Taira faction. He was the son of Tadamori, a great queller of pirates, who particularly attracted attention after a curious incident when he was on guard duty in the Imperial Palace. The emperor heard a strange noise and asked Tadamori to investigate. He discovered that the sound had been made by an old lamplighter, whom he promptly arrested. The emperor was so grateful to Tadamori for putting his mind at rest that he presented him with his favorite concubine, who gave birth to Kiyomori nine months later, so the young man had some pretensions to Imperial blood. His moment came in 1164 when the monks of the Gion shrine were causing trouble. With classic samurai disregard for religious scruples, Kiyomori fired an arrow at the *mikoshi*, a huge portable shrine, which the monks were carrying. Such dramatic treatment of the government's most embarrassing problem earned Kiyomori great respect and rank, and ultimately the Taira, led by Kiyomori, replaced the Fujiwara as the dominant clan.

The rise of the Taira was in no respect a bloody coup. It was a revolution that took place from the inside, the takeover being legitimate throughout. Like the Fujiwara before him, Kiyomori relied on acquiring high positions in the central government, by service, influence, and strategic intermarriage with the Imperial family. Kiyomori himself rose to the position of grand minister, while nearly 50 of his clansmen became courtiers of middle or higher rank. In 1180 his infant grandson became the Emperor Antoku. The Taira wealth depended, like the Fujiwara wealth, on widespread holdings of *shoen*, but where it differed decisively from the Fujiwara was that the Taira was a samurai clan, and all the legal court intrigue and intermarriage was backed up by the force of the 'Way of Horse and Bow.'

Such force was first used in 1156 in the Hogen Incident, so-called after the year name in which it took place. As in so many other cases in samurai history, it was caused by a succession dispute in the Imperial family. It was an argument that only force could settle, and the samurai families close to the court divided into two factions, not along clan lines, however, but on the basis of personal commitment. Thus we find Taira and Minamoto samurai fighting on both sides in the first clash of arms between the two clans.

The battle, if the account preserved in the

Hogen Monogatari is accurate, followed all the niceties of accepted samurai behavior, including the giving of challenges, duels between noble opponents, and some of the most celebrated archery feats in the history of the samurai. These were due to the skill of Minamoto Tametomo, a herculean samurai, the brother of Minamoto Yoshitomo, who had joined the opposing side. After an argument about who should be the first into the attack, an often to be repeated samurai obsession, Tametomo took his place at the western gate of the Shirakawaden, an old Imperial residence, to await the attack of Kiyomori.

The assault began with a challenge from three samurai surnamed Furuichi, one of whom, Furuichi Kagetsuna, proclaimed:

'I once captured Ono Shichiro the chief of the brigands on Mount Suzuka in Ise province, and have thus received the emperor's commands to become the vice-commander in chief of his army. My name is Kagetsuna. Watch my arrow and see whether or not it strikes you!'

It missed. It was now up to Tametomo, whose bow was supposed to be eight and a half feet long, to fire an arrow in return. He had already proclaimed his own past deeds. Tametomo replied:

'You are not a strong enough enemy for me, but your words are so courteous that I shall give you an arrow. Take it! It will be a great mark of honor for you in this world, and also something to remember me by in the next.'

Tametomo fired, not at Kagetsuna, but at one of his companions.

'The arrow pierced the breastplate of Ito Roku, who was first in the enemy's van, and

Above: *The arrest of the old lamplighter. The Taira clan began their ascendancy following this strange incident. Taira Tadamori (1096–1153), the father of Kiyomori, apprehended an intruder who had alarmed the emperor. The supposed monster turned out to be nothing more than an old lamplighter, but the incident served to advance the clan considerably.*

Above: *An illustration from the Kasuga Gongen Scroll showing the use of the* naginata. *A dismounted samurai runs over to attack a warrior monk. Both are armed with* naginata.

Opposite: *Samurai of the Later Three Years' War. In this illustration, taken from a nineteenth-century copy of one of the earliest painted scrolls depicting samurai, we see many features typical of the fighting man of the period. Note the large helmet, the archery gloves, the armor worn on the left sleeve only and the reel carrying a spare bow string.*

passing through him, turned the sleeve of Ito Go's armor inside out and hung there. Ito Roku at once fell dead from his horse.'

This example of Tametomo's skill inclined most of the enemy samurai to attack a different sector of the Shirakawa-den, and Kiyomori was about to lead them away, when a certain samurai called Yamada Koreyuki, nicknamed the 'Wild Boar,' saw the chance of glory:

'Then are you afraid of a single arrow? And are you going to retreat from a position that you have already attacked? Suppose it is Tametomo's arrow, it won't pierce my armor. I have been to war under five separate emperors, and have fought in 15 battles. I have often been hit in the arm by many arrows but these arrows have never pierced my armor. Look at me, all of you! I, at any rate, can let myself be hit by one of Tametomo's arrows and live to tell the tale.'

One of the common soldiers followed him. Koreyuki wore a suit of armor made of black leather, and his helmet, made with five layers of plates, was pushed back on his head. He carried 18 arrows with colored feathers, and his bow, wrapped with rattan, was lacquered from tip to tip. He rode a fawn-colored horse with a black saddle. Bringing his horse to a stand in front of the gateway, he said:

'I am not such a great man as men go, but I am an inhabitant of Iga province, a follower of Aki no Kami, and 28 years old. My name is Yamada Kosaburo Koreyuki. I am the grandson of Yamada no Shoji Yukisuye who was well known among the nobility for being the first to go into battle under Bizen no Kami at the attack on Tsushima no Kami Yoshihito (21 January 1107). My grandfather also captured innumerable mountain robbers and highwaymen. I too have been many times in battle and made a name for

myself. I should like to have a sight of this young samurai Tametomo, whose name I have heard.'

Tametomo said to those about him, 'Of course this fellow is ready to shoot one arrow. When he starts to let the second fly, I shall shoot him down. I shall show the enemy the power of my bow by hitting him at a spot where the arrow will go right through him.' Tametomo rode a horse the color of white reeds with a saddle bound in metal. He galloped out and announced himself, 'I am Chinzei Hachiro Tametomo.'

Koreyuki had an arrow ready and shot it with a loud twang of the bowstring. The arrow, weaving through the air, cut and pierced the skirt of Tametomo's armor, but did not touch his flesh. The first arrow having thus missed, Koreyuki tried to shoot a second, but Tametomo shot before him and his arrow whistled through the air. It pierced the pommel of Koreyuki's saddle, and cutting through the skirt of his armor and his own body too, went through the cantle and stuck out three inches beyond. For a moment he seemed to be held in his saddle by the arrow, but suddenly he fell head first to the ground. The arrow head remained in the saddle, and the horse ran out into the river bed. Some samurai quickly ran to Koreyuki, and putting him on their shoulders, carried him back to their camp. All the samurai saw what had happened, and none would attack the gate again.

Such heroics were ineffectual against the most deadly of samurai weapons – fire. There had been no rain for some time, and a strong wind was blowing. The buildings ignited like tinder, and soon the whole Skirakawa-den was ablaze. As the defenders fled the flames they were picked off by archers, and the leaders, including Tametomo, were captured. Most were later executed, but Tametomo was exiled, the precaution being taken of cutting the sinews of his arm so that he could not wield a bow again. In fact during his exile his arms healed, and his last act was to sink a boatload of Taira samurai with one arrow. He then retired and committed suicide by cutting open his abdomen to release his spirit, the first recorded instance of hara-kiri (*seppuku*), the practice that was to become a feature of the notion of samurai honor.

The Hogen Incident, though brief, marked the entrance of the samurai into the internal politics of emperor and government. The real winner was Taira Kiyomori, who had the satisfaction of having served the emperor and weakened his greatest possible rivals, the Minamoto. In fact one of the prominent Minamoto had greatly helped the process by supporting Kiyomori. This was Yoshitomo, and the deaths of his father and brother on the opposing side stung him into following the dictum that 'a man

Above: *The burning of the Sanjo Palace from the* Heiji Monogatari Emaki. *A dramatic moment during the Heiji Rebellion in 1160 was the assault by the Minamoto samurai on the palace of the ex-emperor Go-Shirakawa.*

Below: *A scene from another section of the Heiji War Scroll, showing samurai attacking a noble's ox carriage.*

could not live under the same heaven as the murderer of his father.' So in 1160 Minamoto led the Heiji Rebellion, again called after the year name. It was the first time that Taira had opposed Minamoto along clan lines, and it was as much of a disaster for the Minamoto as the Hogen Incident. It began well, with a brilliant attack by the Minamoto on the Sanjo Palace, an incident depicted in one of the best-known scroll paintings, the *Heiji Monogatari emaki*. However, the Taira hit back, and followed up a com-

paratively easy victory by a series of executions that decimated the Minamoto clan, leaving a few young boys and an aging courtier, Minamoto Yorimasa. For the next 20 years the Taira ruled Japan, secure in their court rank, their productive *shoen* lands and, above all, in their victorious samurai.

Had Kiyomori been a little more ruthless he could well have ensured his family's hegemony, and made their position as unshakable as the Fujiwara's had appeared. Kiyomori's model of a samurai government ruling by means of and through the existing institutions lasted only until 1185, and the children that Kiyomori had spared were to lead the newly formed Minamoto clan in the most celebrated of all encounters between samurai, the Gempei War.

The Gempei War was fought between 1180–85, and takes its name from the first two syllables of the Chinese reading of the characters of the Minamoto (Genji) and Taira (Heike). It resulted in a new hegemony by the Minamoto, and more importantly, a new institution of government, ruled by a military dictator, the shogun, that was to last for the next 800 years.

The war began with a rising in 1180 by Minamoto Yorimasa, the aged courtier who survived the Heiji Rebellion. The emperor in 1180 was Antoku, Kiyomori's grandson, but there were so many potential princes that

Yorimasa had no trouble in persuading Prince Mochihito to raise the flag of rebellion against the Taira. It was an ill-planned and badly co-ordinated affair, and soon the Minamoto band, allied with a contingent of warrior monks from Mii-dera, near Kyoto, was withdrawing south to join up with another monk army from Nara. Had they delayed the rebellion it might have been possible to coordinate their effort with a general rising in the Minamoto heartlands to the east, but when the rebellion was hardly a day old the Minamoto were once again on the defensive, facing a huge Taira army across the river Uji.

As an added defense the Minamoto and their monk allies had torn up a section of planking of the Uji bridge, which the mounted Taira samurai discovered as they tried to gallop across it in the early-morning mist. Both sides began to release arrows across the river as the mist cleared, and many individual combats took place on the broken beams of the bridge. A warrior monk called Tsutsui Jomyo Meishu proclaimed his name and achievements:

'And loosing off 20 arrows like lightning flashes he slew 12 of the Taira samurai and wounded 11 more. One arrow yet remained in his quiver, but flinging away his bow, he stripped off his quiver and threw that after it, cast off his footgear, and

springing barefoot on to the beams of the bridge he strode across. All were afraid to cross over, but he walked the broken bridge as one who walks along the street Ichijo or Nijo of the capital. With his *naginata* he mows down five of

Below: *The race between Sasaki Takatsuna (on left) and Kajiwara Kagesue to be the first to ford the Uji river in 1184.*

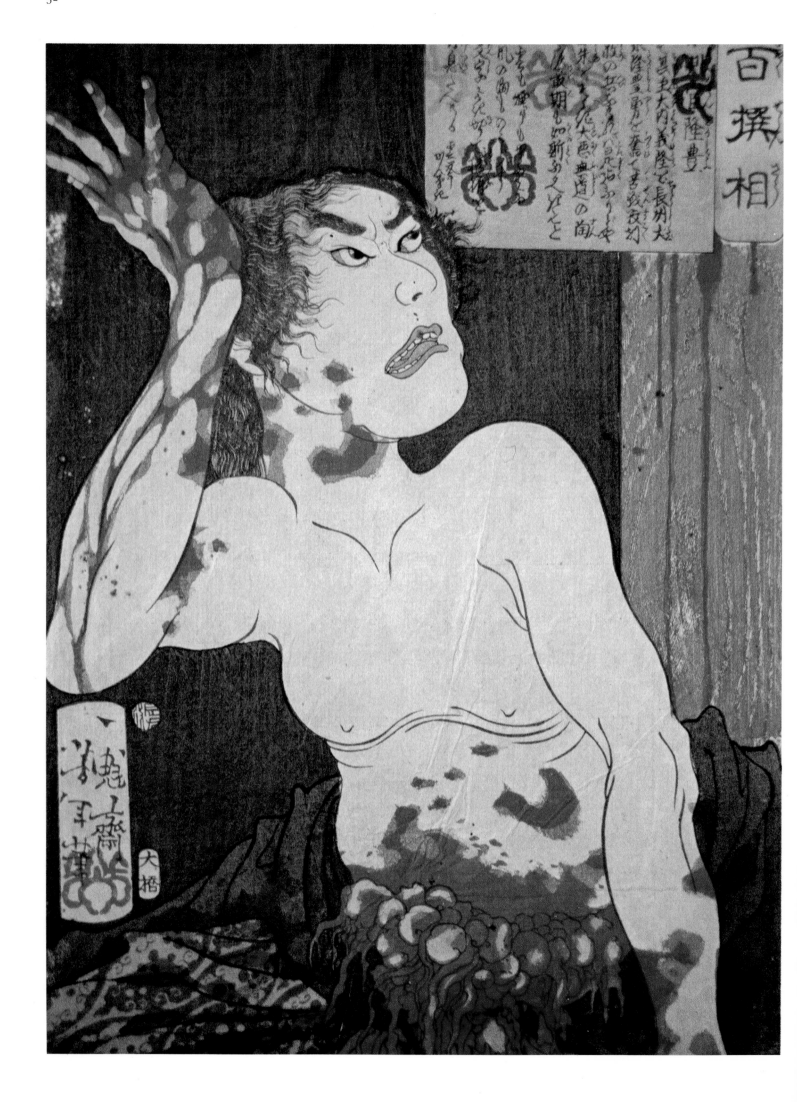

the enemy, but with the sixth the blade snaps asunder in the midst and flinging it away he draws his long sword wielding it in the zigzag style, the interlacing, cross, reverse dragonfly, waterwheel and eight-sides-at-once style of fencing, and cutting down eight men. But as he brought down the ninth with an exceedingly mighty blow on the helmet, the blade snapped at the hilt and fell splash into the water beneath. Then seizing his dagger, which was the only weapon he had left, he plied it as one in a death fury.'

When Jomyo finally retired he counted 63 arrows sticking out of his armor, of which only five had pierced through.

Shortly afterward the Taira forded the river and defeated the Minamoto once again, but the sons of Minamoto Yorimasa managed to hold the Taira off for long enough for their father to perform what has come to be regarded as the classic act of hara-kiri by a defeated samurai on a battlefield. According to *Heike Monogatari*, numerous unnamed samurai 'cut themselves open' and jumped into the river, but Yorimasa did it in style. He first composed a farewell poem, which he wrote on the back of his war fan, then cut two long slits in his abdomen, a slow and extremely painful way of dying. So painful was hara-kiri that in later years it became modified so that a friendly second would cut off the head of the man performing it at the moment he cut himself open. Hara-kiri also came to be regarded as a way of keeping one's honor, if not one's life, following some disgraceful incident, and for samurai became an alternative to public execution. Hara-kiri was always much more than merely a punishment. In many cases it was used as a very effective protest, or a way of proving loyalty when one had been falsely accused. An Englishman, Richard Wickham, writing from Kyoto in 1616, reported the fate of a governor of

Nagasaki, who, being out of favor with the shogun, had become a monk. 'I mean he hathe shaved his hair, and I do not doubt that he will be giving his guts a shaving before the year is out.' This is a somewhat crude but undeniably vivid description of hara-kiri.

The Minamoto had suffered another tragic defeat in the Kyoto area. But as the Gempei War continued the focus of activity shifted to the east, the homelands of the Minamoto and, with Minamoto Yoritomo as clan chief, the balance of power also began to move in their favor. A blow to the Taira was the death of Kiyomori in 1181. His last words are supposed to have been 'Place upon my tomb the head of Yoritomo.'

Yoritomo's military encounter with the Taira began almost as inauspiciously as had the exploits of his relatives. It was only when Yoritomo decided to settle in Kamakura, and entrust the military side of the war to his younger brother Yoshitsune that the Minamoto began to rise to a position of strength. Yoritomo was a consummate politician. From the Kamakura he built up a feudal network of relationships between himself as overlord and his *kenin* (vassals), whom he rewarded generously. Throughout the Gempei War he remained in the east, controlling the conduct of the war, and arranging such a thorough political system that Kamakura acquired the characteristics of an alternative administrative center.

However, while Yoritomo's political plans were to prove decisive in the history of the samurai, the glory of the Gempei War belongs entirely to his brother Yoshitsune, whose exploits against the Taira were to inspire more plays, poems, prints and scrolls than any other samurai in the whole of Japanese history. The legends begin with his early life, when as a mere youth he fought with and defeated the mighty warrior-monk Benkei on the Gojo bridge in Kyoto. Benkei afterward became his

Above and above left: Two representations of the same event, the victory of the boy Yoshitsune over the monk Benkei, who thereupon became his devoted follower.

Far left: A print from the series 'Kwaidai Hyaku Senso' by Yoshitoshi, depicting the aftermath of hara-kiri, a savage form of suicide.

Below: Minamoto Yoritomo, the first shogun of Japan and the victor of the Gempei War. Yoritomo was a cold and calculating politician who had the sense to leave the business of fighting to his relatives.

faithful follower. Yoshitsune is said to have learned his swordfighting skills from the *tengu*, wood goblins, half man and half bird, who lived in the forests near Kyoto. During the Gempei War Yoshitsune first served Yoritomo by defeating his cousin Yoshinaka, who had started a private war of his own against the Taira and was proving so successful that he represented a threat to the Minamoto balance of power. With Yoshinaka disposed of, Yoshitsune could concentrate on the defeat of the Taira. Fortunately for Yoshitsune, his late cousin had been extremely successful in his private war, and the Taira court, together with crown jewels and the infant emperor, had abandoned Kyoto for a base on the coast of the Inland Sea near present-day Kobe.

The Taira fortress, which probably resembled a western stockade, was called Ichi-no-tani. It was built in a clever position for a seafaring clan (the Taira had always been great pirate quellers) as it opened on to the sea, where the Taira ships lat at anchor, and was protected at the back by

Left: *The death of Atsumori. One of the most tragic tales of the Gempei War tells how, at the Battle of Ichi-no-tani in 1184, the youth Taira Atsumori was killed by Kumagai Naozane. This picture is from an eighteenth-century woodblock edition of the* Heike Monogatari.

Below: *The Minamoto army on the march. With the monk Benkei at their head, and under the command of Yoshitsune (on horseback), the determined-looking Minamoto set off along the seashore.*

very steep cliffs. Sending his other brother Noriyori to make a frontal assault on Ichi-no-tani, Yoshitsune led a picked band of samurai in a perilous descent of a cliff path at the rear that locals regarded as being too steep even for monkeys. It is a scene often depicted in art, the samurai on their horses slipping and sliding into the undefended rear of the fort, and charging through toward the ships. A series of desperate encounters followed, as Minamoto samurai faced Taira samurai in single combat on the beach, producing some of the most poignant accounts of samurai fighting ever written. The most touching is that of the death of the young Taira Atsumori at the hands of Kumagai Naozane:

'Quickly hurling him to the ground he sprang upon him and tore off his helmet to cut off his head, when he beheld the face of a youth of 16 or 17, delicately powdered with blackened teeth, just about the age of his own son, and with features of great beauty. "Who are you?" he enquired; "Tell me your name, for I would spare your life."'

The youth told him, and Kumagai was inclined to let him go, but all around swarmed the Minamoto samurai, any of whom would have been glad of such a prize head. So Kumagai killed the young courtier-warrior, and when he was wrapping up the head, discovered a flute in the young man's belt. None of the rough Minamoto samurai was sufficiently cultured to play the flute. From this time Kumagai abandoned the profession of samurai and became a

Above: *The ghosts of the dead Taira appear to Minamoto Yoshitsune as he flees from the wrath of his brother. Yoritomo eventually pursued Yoshitsune to his death in 1189.*

Above: *In this print by Kuniyoshi, Kumagai Naozane, the slayer of Taira Atsumori, is shown as the villain in the* kabuki *play about the incident.*

Below: *In the final moments of the battle of Dan-no-Ura the Imperial Grandmother, Kiyomori's widow, prepares to jump into the sea with the child emperor Antoku.*

monk, living a peaceful life.

Yoshitsune pursued the Taira from Ichi-no-tani to their base at Yashima on Shikoku island. Here he inflicted a heavy defeat upon them, but once again the main prize, the child-emperor, was taken away to safety. The Taira then withdrew to another base they had established in the straits of Shimonoseki between Honshu, the mainland of Japan, and Kyushu. The final battle of the Gempei War, the Battle of Dan-no-ura, took place here in April 1185. Few battles in samurai history were as decisive as Dan-no-ura. It was a seaborn encounter between the Taira and the Minamoto, which the former, with their naval expertise, might have been expected to win. An unexpected defection from their side of one samurai, who disclosed in which ship the Emperor was kept, and the change in the current at midday, ensured a complete

victory for the Minamoto. The Taira were totally annihilated, including the infant emperor, who was drowned by his grandmother lest he fall into the hands of the Minamoto. It is said that the sea was dyed red with blood.

Yoshitsune's victories meant that there was now no opposition to his brother Yoritomo entering Kyoto, setting up his own family in the court and ruling as Kiyomori had done, but Yoritomo's aims were different. While accepting every power and rank that Kyoto could grant him, and confiscating all the Taira *shoen* estates, Yoritomo remained resolutely in Kamakura where he found himself in possession of a unique organization that was capable of assuming all the functions of government. This organization was the samurai feudal system which clans like the Minamoto had used for many years. Yoritomo was to apply it to the whole nation. His most decisive step was to have himself proclaimed shogun in 1192. The shogun commission to go forth and make war on the emperor's enemies before always had been a temporary one, but the commission that Yoritomo received in 1192 was to be finally handed back to a Japanese emperor in 1868. During the early years of the shogunate, the samurai government in Kamakura and the civilian courtier government under the emperor in Kyoto existed in a state of balance, but it was abundantly clear that the Gempei War was to have lasting effects on Japanese life. In its legends and mythology, in its ideals of behavior and in its form of government, in all three the samurai had triumphed.

Armor: Mark of the Samurai

The basis of Japanese military dress during the age of the samurai was the suit of armor. Many specimens have been preserved, giving a very clear idea of what samurai must have looked like on a field of battle. However most of the suits of armor are fairly modern, and were not specifically intended for wearing in battle. These ornate creations from the Tokugawa days were rare at the time they were made, and an important daimyo might commission such a fine piece of work for presentation to the Shogun or some other dignitary.

It is perhaps just as well that the owners of such suits of armor had no need actually to fight in them because the decoration seriously weakens the metal and the more ornate the fitments and gilding, the weaker the armor.

For the majority of samurai during the Age of War, and even into the Tokugawa period, the notion of a suit of armor just did not exist. His pocket, or that of his commanding officer, would dictate what could be bought, and many pieces were 'recycled' after a battle. In fact, selling suits of armor stripped from the bodies of dead samurai was almost a way of life for some peasant farmers.

To trace the evolution of the suit of armor it is necessary to begin with the very few preserved specimens of twelfth-century armor, all of which are kept in Japan. These show the characteristic shape of the 'yoroi' style, eventually to be superseded by more streamlined varieties, which by the seventeenth century look remarkably similar to European armor, apart from the use of lacquer for rustproofing and the facemask. This style, associated with the latter days of the Age of War, is the supreme example of samurai battle dress. It may have been succeeded by less functional styles, but later writers on the subject always considered such armor the best style to buy, offering the samurai maximum protection and allowing easy movement.

Below: The various parts making up a suit of armor.

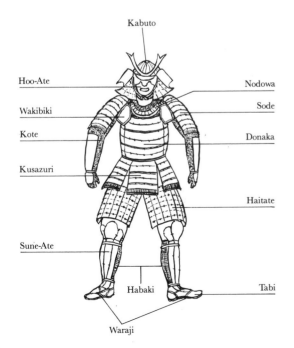

Kabuto

Hoo-Ate

Nodowa

Wakibiki

Sode

Kote

Donaka

Kusazuri

Haitate

Sune-Ate

Habaki

Tabi

Waraji

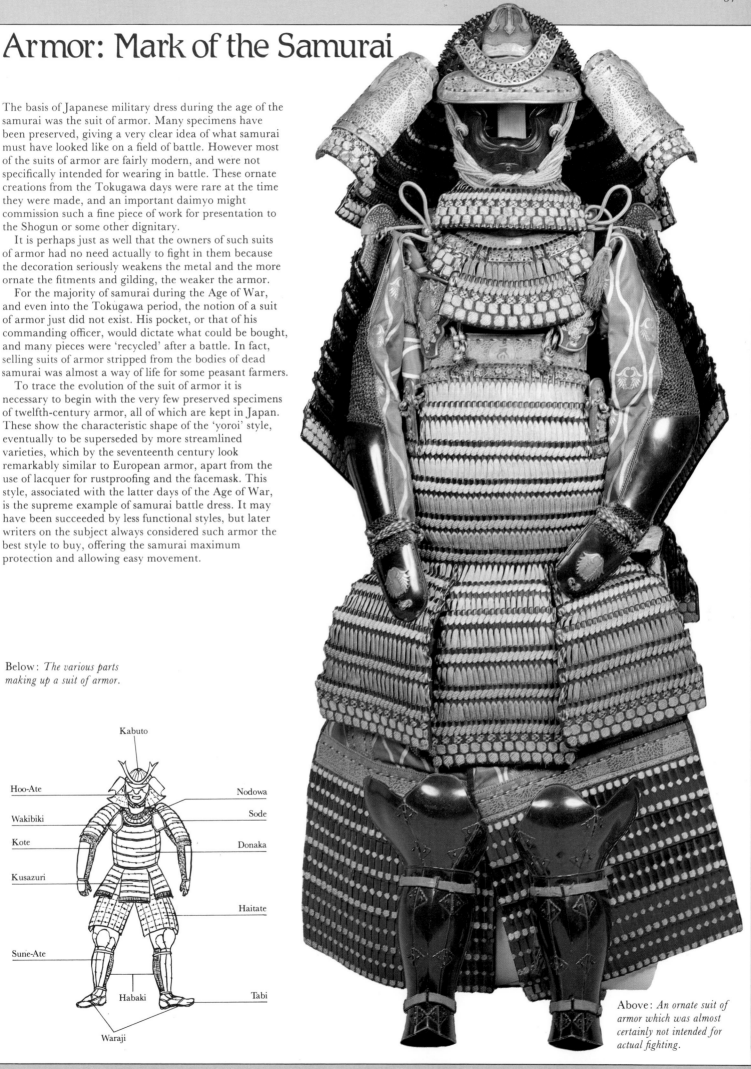

Above: An ornate suit of armor which was almost certainly not intended for actual fighting.

38

Left: *A rather damaged example of a very practical style of armor dating from the Momoyama Period. The* do *(body armor) is made from solid plates, proof against firearms.*

Above and top: *An unusual folding helmet. When the catch is released the concentric plates fold flat for storage.*

Below: *A section of armor plate.*

Above: Haidate *(thigh guards),* which fastened behind the leg.

Above left: *A tatami gusoku (mat armor) which would fold into a small bundle.*

Left: Sode *(shoulder guard). This particular example has a slight curve.*

Above left: *The body armor shown on the opposite page opened out and laid flat to show its construction. Note the bracket to hold a* sashimono, *but the absence of other items of decoration.*

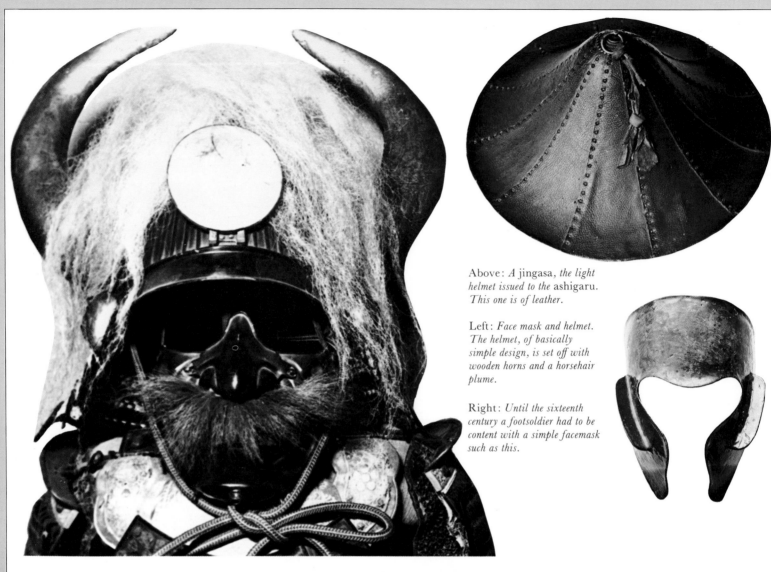

Above: *A jingasa, the light helmet issued to the* ashigaru. *This one is of leather.*

Left: *Face mask and helmet. The helmet, of basically simple design, is set off with wooden horns and a horsehair plume.*

Right: *Until the sixteenth century a footsoldier had to be content with a simple facemask such as this.*

Right: *An example of a multiplate helmet. Note the numerous rivet heads.*

Below: *A pair of iron stirrups, inlaid with silver.*

Below: *A samurai putting on armor. This samurai, in the service of Takeda Shingen, is fastening the toggle on his right shoulder plate, prior to putting on his helmet.*

The Sons of Hachiman

In uniting a number of samurai clans under the command of a newly united Minamoto clan, and using this alliance to defeat a samurai clan identified with the central government, Minamoto Yoritomo had demonstrated that an alternative to this central government existed. The alternative was Kamakura, and throughout the Kamakura Period (1185–1333) that is what it remained, an alternative rather than a replacement. It was a century and a half characterized by a political and cultural balance between Kyoto, the city of the emperor and *kuge* (nobles) and the cultural center of the nation, and Kamakura, the seat of the shogunate, the apex of the feudal hierarchy in the center of the samurai homelands. The institution of the shogun represented this balance perfectly. The justification for its existence was the formal and legal delegation of power from the emperor, a sensible division of labor.

Kamakura therefore grew from being a small fishing village to a settlement of some size and the home for numerous high-ranking Minamoto vassals who formed the shogunal bureaucracy. The shogunate itself, or *bakufu*, was a far simpler organization than the Imperial government in Kyoto. One of its most important organs was the *samurai-dokoro*, 'the Office of Samurai,' which Yoritomo had set up at the

start of his campaigns against the Taira. The duties of the *samurai-dokoro* were effectively those of a military and police headquarters, with the policing function coming to the fore once the defeat of the Taira had been accomplished. It supervised strategic requirements, organized the recruitment and deployment of military personnel, and generally managed affairs connected with the *kenin*. Apart from the *samurai-dokoro*, two other offices of administration sufficed for the whole of the shogunate's existence. These were the *mandokoro* (general administration) and the *monchujo* (the office of enquiry, dealing with legal matters).

As the shogun's loyal followers, bound by oath and tried in battle, some *kenin* were entrusted with administration away from Kamakura, such as governorship of provinces and control of *shoen* estates. All were samurai, and all performed civil functions as part of the feudal hierarchy. The previous *shoen* managers, who had been *taira* (court appointees) were now placed by order of Kamakura, and were accountable to the shogun, not to the court. These officials were known as *jito*. They had the responsibility of seeing that an already existing land administration was functioning properly, and that taxes were correctly assessed and collected. They were richly rewarded, usually with part of the tax

番
弓

Above: *A wooden statuette depicting a seated nobleman of the Kamakura Period.*

which they had collected.

Over each province, or combinations of smaller provinces, Yoritomo placed a *shugo* (military governor) who fulfilled a more military function than the *jito*, in effect the shogun's strongman in the provinces. They would work alongside any remaining civil governor, and control the military side of the Minamoto supremacy. It was such *shugo* who would later become the provincial barons, or daimyo, who are a prominent feature of samurai history, but in the Kamakura Period this initial appointment of *shugo* did nothing but guarantee stability, as they were the shogun's most loyal samurai.

Loyalty held the shogunate together. In one respect it was a form of loyalty going back to the old *uji* of the Yamato state, who worshipped a deified ancestor as the clan god. In the case of the Minamoto the clan god was Hachiman, the name under which the Emperor Ojin (201–312) was honored as a deity. His main shrine was the Tsurugaoka in Kamakura, making the administrative center an important base for vital clan-centered religious feeling. Under the guidance of Hachiman, to whom Yoritomo ascribed all his victories, the newer and more tenuous form of family feeling that arose from becoming a *kenin* would receive enormous support.

The number of *kenin* grew over the years. Many were allies whom Yoritomo had invited to receive the status, others were there by recommendation of high-ranking *shugo*. Even former enemies were accepted as *kenin*, including many

of Taira origin. In such cases the contractual tie was strengthened as much as possible by matrimonial alliance, but even so it was in complete contrast to the accepted samurai tradition of not living under the same sky with the destroyer of one's father. Throughout the Kamakura period the status of *kenin* was something to be prized, a rank that could be withdrawn as a punishment for bad behavior. The rank of samurai was also strictly defined, though the division between warrior and farmer, so characteristic of the later Tokugawa period, was not recognized. In the Kamakura period samurai was the upper rank of fighting men, and a warrior who was the follower of a *kenin* could not become a samurai without the official permission of the shogun, even if he had performed valuable military service. In the chronicle *Azuma Kagami* it is related that one of the Minamoto's most prominent *kenin* wishes to promote one of his foot soldiers to the rank of samurai, but is refused permission by the shogun, on the grounds that if the man is made a samurai he will forget his origin and try to become a *kenin*. This is the crucial point. The numbers of *kenin* were growing so large that it was becoming almost a formality for a samurai to become a *kenin* of the Minamoto. Consequently the shogun had to restrict entry into the samurai class, which was easier to control than the *kenin* class, where the shogun had to deal with men who were already of high rank.

The *Azuma Kagami* was completed in about 1270 and is largely compiled of nobles' records and the official records of the Kamakura government. It therefore gives a good account of contemporary samurai behavior and its portrayal of samurai heroics and loyalties hardly differs from the accounts quoted earlier. The samurai's pride in his ancestors, his willingness to lay down his life for his lord, and his bravery are all recorded. Of more interest is another work compiled a few years earlier, the *Kakun*, or family instructions, of Hojo Shigetoki. It was written for the guidance of his son, Hojo Nagatoki, who was appointed shogun's deputy in Kyoto in 1247 at the age of 18. It is the first specific written example of anything resembling a warrior's code, but differs fundamentally from the later bushido in that Hojo Nagatoki is being groomed for leadership, rather than to be a follower. He is to be based in Kyoto and represent the samurai in the presence of courtiers. Consequently much of the instruction concerns etiquette and good manners, and the problems of personnel management that Nagatoki is likely to meet when he takes command of a group of high-spirited young samurai from the east who have been appointed to the grandeur of Kyoto. Such young samurai were styled *wakato*, in

effect officer trainees. They were of the same social class as Nagatoki, and thus would require very different handling by him from the treatment given to common footsoldiers.

Questions of courage and loyalty on the battle-field find no place in the instructions, not because they are regarded as unnecessary, but simply because in a true son of Hachiman such qualities are taken for granted. The warrior's duty is summed up in a few general principles. He should believe in the gods and buddhas, and be untiring in his practice of the martial arts. He must be aware of the effect of *karma* (fate), in particular the effect his actions will have on future generations. The supreme emphasis is on *giri* (duty), a theme which we shall meet throughout the history of the samurai and the development of samurai ethics. Duty and 'a good heart,' says the young man's father, 'are like two wheels of a carriage, and of these it is duty that is the making of a samurai.'

The legacy that Yoritomo left to his successors was unwritten, and it is tragic that a man who could set up and maintain the Kamakura system was unable to guarantee the survival of his house. He was succeeded by two worthless sons, and the control of the shogunate fell into the hands of the Hojo, a family closely related to the Minamoto through Yoritomo's widow, and the compilers of the *Kakun*. The coup occurred in 1203, but with the curious Japanese regard for existing institutions, particularly those with Imperial connections, the shogunate was maintained under a succession of Hojo regents. It was under Hojo leadership that the samurai faced their fiercest test, the attempted Mongol invasions of 1274 and 1281.

Kublai Khan's colossal attempts to invade Japan are not only fascinating from a military point of view, but also reveal the balance between Kamakura and Kyoto in governing the country. Japan was merely one of a number of countries which the Mongols wished to subdue during their vast campaigns begun by Kublai's grandfather, Genghis Khan. It is sufficient to record here that by the time the invasion of Japan was planned Mongol soldiers had been in action in countries as far apart as Poland, Palestine, Persia and Korea, and the wild horsemen who were to take on the samurai had already defeated the Teutonic knights of Germany.

Japan's great advantage was her natural barrier, the sea. This meant that the Mongols, who had won their reputation by great man-euverability, surprise attacks and feigned retreats, would have to be shipped across miles of ocean before they could come to grips with the enemy. The Mongolian conquest of Korea had laid an extensive fleet at the khan's disposal,

which set sail in November 1274 with 25,000 Mongol troops and numerous Koreans, impressed into transport duties. They landed at Hakata, in Northern Kyushu island, and the subsequent battle provided a number of lessons for the samurai. The most important lesson concerned tactics. The Mongol invasions were a century later than the Gempei War, and the samurai who faced the alien foe had been brought up on the tales of heroism of those days. Since then there had been no major war, so every samurai waiting on the beach desired nothing more than a prized Mongol head to take back to his commander. Unfortunately the example of their ancestors was to prove woefully inadequate when applied to fighting men of an entirely different culture and language. In particular, the ideal of challenging a worthy opponent, and reciting one's pedigree, was completely irrelevant, and was replaced by bitter hand-to-hand fighting whenever the samurai could get close enough through the hail of Mongol arrows and the occasional fire-bomb thrown by catapult.

The first invasion came to an end after a storm destroyed much of their fleet, but the Mongols returned in 1281 with a vastly increased army. The first wave was beaten off by fierce fighting on the beaches, and by a number of raids by boatloads of samurai on the Mongol transports, but when the main body of the invasion force joined the attack there was the very real prospect of the samurai being overrun by sheer weight of numbers. Here the balance of function between Kyoto and Kamakura came fully into its own. While the Sons of Hachiman fought, the Sons of the Sun Goddess prayed, and an Imperial envoy was sent to the Great Shrine of Ise to petition the goddess to destroy the invader. Few prayers can ever have been answered in so dramatic a fashion. That evening the sky began to darken and a strong wind rose

Above: *The Tsurugaoka Shrine at Kamakura. This shrine is dedicated to Hachiman, the God of War, and the tutelary deity of the Minamoto clan. It was thus especially honored, situated as it was in the Minamoto heartland.*

over the sea where the Mongol fleet lay at anchor. The waves grew and the Mongol ships began to rock violently as the wind developed into a fierce tornado. It utterly destroyed the invasion fleet, and was dubbed the *kami-kaze* (divine wind) by the samurai whose task had been so speedily reduced to one of mopping up survivors.

From the military point of view it was a glorious victory, but as no territory had been acquired, the government was in a quandary over how to distribute rewards. Owing to the religious nature of the Mongol defeat, Kyoto and the great temples were also in line for a grant of lands. The Hojo regency was thus forced to reward brave exploits by grants from its own resources. The samurai were very insistent in pressing their demands. One warrior called Takezaki Suenaga went so far as to commission a scroll painting of his exploits to back up his claim. The scroll, the *Mongol Invasion Scroll*, is one of the most important paintings of the period for depicting samurai dress and equipment. Apart from paying rewards, coastal defenses were maintained as late as 1312, and this added considerably to the Hojo's financial problems.

The *kami-kaze* was not the sole religious manifestation to attract the samurai's attention, for the thirteenth century also witnessed something of a religious revival among the Sons of Hachiman. The most important influence on the samurai was Zen. Zen, the meditative sect of Buddhism, encouraged personal enlightenment and rejected the scholasticism of the older Buddhist sects. The samurai who followed Zen was expected to undergo a rigorous physical and spiritual discipline, not unlike the military demands of his calling, which would lead to sudden enlightenment. This enlightenment would enable the samurai to be somehow separated from the world, without care or

Above: *Samurai wait behind the defensive wall for the attack from the Mongols.*

Opposite page: *Inamuragasaki of Kamakura. In 1333 Nitta Yoshisada led an army to attack Kamakura, but found it strongly defended along the narrow passes which surrounded it. He therefore approached by the sea coast, and at Inamuragasaki ascended a cliff and flung his sword into the sea as an offering to the Sun Goddess, at which the waters parted before his army.*

Above: *Go-Daigo, the unfortunate emperor whose anachronistic attempt to overthrow the Shogunate and reestablish the primacy of the emperor merely led to the replacement of one dynasty of shoguns by another.*

worry. It was thus perfectly suited to the samurai tradition. Its emphasis on cool detachment from the world fitted the behavior on a battlefield as much as in a Zen monastery. Other sects, such as Nichiren, Jodo and Shinshu, also owed their popularity to the Kamakura Period, but none had such a hold on the samurai.

Buddhist ideas were also reflected in art. The *Heike Monogatari*, the classic of the *gunkimono*, is in some respects a long Buddhist parable using the Gempei War as a vehicle to moralize. The Taira are seen as doomed because of their evil deeds, in particular the destruction of temples in their campaigns against the warrior monks. Taira Kiyomori is painted as an utter villain, the victim of his own wicked *karma*. Among his evil deeds are his attempts to prevent the sun from setting by beckoning to it with his fan because he desired to complete the building of a temple in a certain day. However, there is immense sympathy for the eclipse of the Taira, and the extinguishing of the beauty of their court life by the rough Minamoto from the east.

The subsequent replacement of the Minamoto *shogunate* by the Hojo meant the removal of the figurehead to which the *kenin* loyalties, the 'glue' of the system, had been directed. By the end of the thirteenth century many *kenin*, particularly those who were disappointed by the rewards they had received in return for service against the Mongols, became increasingly dependent upon the *shugo*, to whom they transferred their allegiance in return for economic support and protection, the other half of feudalism which the Hojo were now able to give. The *shoen* managers, the *jito*, were also

starting to take larger and larger shares of the dues they collected, and increased in wealth and influence. By the 1330s resentment against the Hojo began to come into the open, but was set in motion from an entirely different source. *Kenin* of long standing were ready to be courted for rebellion, and the unifying force proved to be, of all things, the emperor, in an anachronistic attempt to restore the long-lost prestige and power of the throne. The emperor was Go-Daigo. His coup began with an unsuccessful revolt in 1331, after which he was captured and exiled. He managed to escape in 1332 and found that he had become the nucleus of a full-scale revolt against the Hojo, and a powerful symbol for expressing the discontent that many samurai clans felt against the regency. The Ashikaga clan, led by Ashikaga Takauji, captured Kyoto and Nitta Yoshisada led an expedition against Kamakura. In a legend the fall of Kamakura and the destruction of the Hojo are given great symbolic value as the triumphs of the emperor. The legend recounts how Nitta Yoshisada, when advancing on the city, was prevented from entering by its natural defenses. He tried to go round by the seaward side but the tide was in. He ascended a high rock and cast his sword into the sea as a prayer to the Sun Goddess to aid her Imperial descendant's cause. The tide rolled back, and the Imperial forces entered Kamakura.

From 1334–36 Go-Daigo held Kyoto and set in motion his plans for a full restoration of Imperial government. This was to include full control by the emperor over the samurai, who were to be pushed back into the shadows. As a first step he appointed his son, Prince Morinaga, shogun and replaced the *shugo* with specially selected civil courtiers. It was not an arrangement welcomed by many of the samurai clans who had supported him. They were also less than pleased with the rewards which their service had gained. In 1335 Ashikaga Takauji, the leader who had captured Kyoto, turned against Go-Daigo and set up a new shogunate of his own. As the title of shogun could only be granted by an emperor, Ashikaga Takauji chased Go-Daigo out of Kyoto and set up another member of the Imperial family in his place, who proclaimed Takauji as the first Ashikaga Shogun.

Go-Daigo did not, however, give up the struggle and for the next 60 years there were two emperors, one ruling in Kyoto, the Northern Court, and the other based in the mountains of Yoshino, the Southern Court. The civil war that lasted throughout this period is known as the Nambokucho War. It was fought between the Ashikaga and their allies and a number of clans who stubbornly supported Go-Daigo's line,

among which the most fervent were the Kusunoki. Kusunoki Masashige was killed in 1333, and is one of the most glorious figures in samurai history. He is revered for his perfect performance of all the standard samurai heroics, such as following his duty where it led, which was ultimately the Battle of Minatogawa which Masashige knew he could not win. He committed an heroic hara-kiri, and left a young son who continued his father's fight for many years. Kusunoki Masashige is held to be a paragon of loyalty to the emperor, and the example he set was to be quoted repeatedly in the nineteenth century when a similar revolt to Go-Daigo's was being contemplated. In fact one of the earliest acts of the new Meiji emperor in the 1860s was to erect a statue of Masashige on the site of his last battle. The glorification reached its peak in the 1930s when he was extolled as an example by the nationalist propagandists. It is well known that the suicide pilots of World War II took their title of kamikaze from the divine wind which shattered the Mongol fleet, but it is less well known that Kusunoki Masashige served as the human example of their endeavors. The desperate suicide attacks on Okinawa were called *kikusui* in reference to Masashige's chrysanthemum crest.

The long wars of Kusunoki and the Ashikaga produced several changes in the nature of samurai warfare. Kusunoki Masashige often had to defend positions in wooded, mountainous countryside where the horse was useful only as a means of approaching the seat of conflict. The bulky *yoroi* armor was inconvenient for long periods of fighting on foot in difficult terrain, so the samurai began to see the advantages of the foot soldier's simpler *do-maru*, which wrapped round the body. An increase in hand-to-hand fighting also meant that the sword at last came into its own, and there was a corresponding change in the design of the helmet neckguard, which was lifted up high to allow the warrior to wield his weapon with ease. A new variation on the Japanese sword was a longer version called the *no-dachi*, rather like a long-bladed *naginata* with an extended handle rather than a spear shaft. Other innovations included the introduc-

Above: The use of the yari *(spear) and* naginata *(glaive) in combat.*

Left: Wakiya Yoshisuke, the brother of Nitta Yoshisada and a lifelong supporter of the legitimate line of emperors based in Yoshino. Yoshisuke shows clearly the cutting power of the Japanese sword.

Below: *A conch-shell trumpet. They were commonly used for signalling on a battlefield. Note the mouthpiece and the carrying cords.*

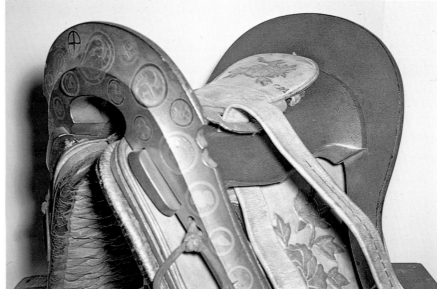

tion of armor for the thighs and knees and the use of straw sandals rather than heavy boots.

Go-Daigo's rebellion was the last attempt by a member of the Imperial family to overthrow the shogunate. Its failure was so total that a repetition was unthinkable, and the decision of Ashikaga Takauji to make Kyoto his shogun capital meant that all future emperors would be very closely watched. The luckless rebellion had thus replaced one shogunate by another, and in his efforts to reestablish a unified system of government Go-Daigo had brought together the civil and military functions which had been separate and balanced. Consequently, when the rebellion failed, the military government was more military than ever. Go-Daigo also succeeded in weakening the Imperial wealth, for the very best reasons. When he was established as emperor he turned many of the Imperial family's holding over to the public treasury which he was to administer but with his flight from Kyoto these lands remained permanently confiscated, making many a future emperor dependent upon the charity of powerful families – an important factor in later history.

Above: *A great deal of craftsmanship has gone into producing the elaborate designs of mon (family and clan badges) on this ornate saddle, which is of typical construction.*

Opposite: *The Battle of Minatogawa 1333. The drum is beaten and the bell rung as Kusunoki Masashige prepares to sell his life dearly for the emperor. Note the design of the chrysanthemum on the curtains.*

The Shogun of the Golden Pavilion

Right: A samurai viewing cherry blossom. There was no more poignant symbol of the life of the samurai than the fragile cherry blossom, which is beautiful for such a short time, then is gone. It is a theme repeated time and again in Japanese art.

Below: Map showing the geographical distribution of shugo *lands at the time of the Ashikaga Shogunate. In many areas, however, power was largely nominal, and the lack of* shugo *control played a decisive part in the future breakup of the Shoguns' authority.*

The rise of Ashikaga Takauji to the position of Shogun marks the beginning of a new period of Japanese history, known either as the Ashikaga period or, more commonly, the Muromachi period because the headquarters of the Shogunate were located in the Muromachi district of Kyoto.

The Ashikaga supplied 15 shoguns to rule Japan between 1338–1573, the same number as the most successful dynasty, the Tokugawa, between 1603–1868. The family was of Minamoto descent, the prior requisite for using the term Shogun and as a ruling dynasty has suffered much from the deprecations of an earlier generation of historians, who tended to show the Muromachi period as a succession of governmental disasters. In this view the early achievements of Takauji were all lost by the addiction to pleasure of his later successors. They spent their time performing the tea ceremony instead of governing so that with the Onin War in 1467, which destroyed Kyoto, the whole country dissolved in chaos. Even their cultural achievements were lost, until the 'Age of War' was brought to an end by the great unifiers, Nobunaga and Hideyoshi. Recent historians however, paint a very different picture and see in the Muromachi period a number of trends in the history and culture of the samurai which are commonly thought to have only begun two centuries later. On studying the Muromachi period it becomes obvious that the Ashikaga shoguns had to contend with so many problems of government that one is led to view more kindly their attempts to cope. One great obstacle to the exercise of power was the fact that the Ashikaga's strength was not based on an overwhelmingly large owership of land. Even during the fifteenth century there were no more than 35 Ashikaga *shoen* estates scattered about the country, none of which amounted to more than a fraction of the total cultivated territory in any one province. It is interesting to compare this to the later Tokugawa shoguns, whose founder, Tokugawa Ieyasu, controlled a quarter of the rice lands in Japan, most of the mines and nearly all the important cities. Neither did the Ashikaga have an out-and-out military superiority, which was to be another of the Tokugawa's great assets. They relied on alliances as the only military force under an Ashikaga shogun's direct control was his military guard (*hokoshu*), which never numbered

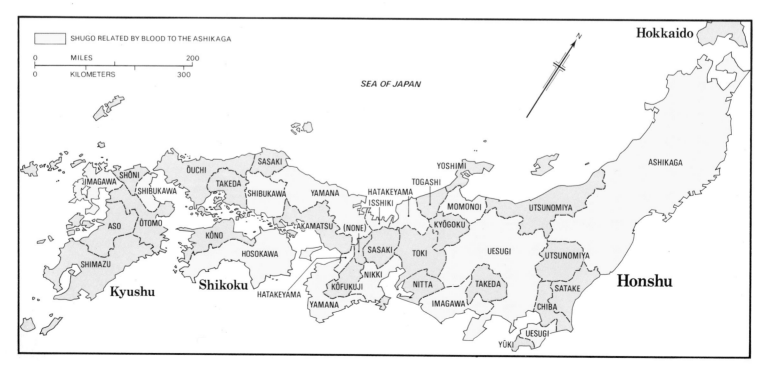

SHUGO RELATED BY BLOOD TO THE ASHIKAGA

more than about 350 men. Whereas the Tokugawa were able to build up an elaborate system of family and feudal relationships backed up by military and financial power, the Ashikaga family and feudal relationships *were* that power. It was a precarious situation.

The most important of these relationships were those between the shogun and the *shugo*. The *shugo* were the military governors of provinces established by the Kamakura shogunate to provide the military and police function at a local level, and to back up the civil administrative functions of the tax-collecting *jito*. The Nambokucho Wars had effectively phased out the *jito*, leaving the samurai *shugo* as the purely military organ of local administration. The appointment of *shugo* was in the gift of the shogun, and it was clearly stated in the basic Ashikaga Code, the *Kemmu-shiki-moku*, published in 1336, that *shugo* should be appointed on the basis of their ability to govern, not as a reward for military exploits or alliances. However, because of the need to strengthen the clan's position by extending relationships with powerful groups, the shoguns frequently went against their own rules and appointed *shugo* as a means of winning strong families on to their side. This often took the form of simply appointing a member of the strongest samurai family in a particular province as *shugo*, regardless of his ability to govern or whether he had unqualified power in the province with which to govern. The dilemma facing the Ashikaga was therefore maintaining a balance between strengthening the *shugo* so that they could play their part to the full in the ruling of the country, while at the same time controlling their unofficial activities, the most common of which was stealing each other's lands.

It was fortunate for the early shoguns that the rise of the *shugo* was accompanied by an equal rise in Ashikaga fortunes as the Nambokucho War came to a successful conclusion in 1392. By this time the shogun could claim a relatively secure authority over a coalition of *shugo* houses who governed the country in the name of the shogun. There were 20 *shugo* in all in 1370, about half of whom were related by blood to the Ashikaga. Others, like the Shimazu in Southern Kyushu island, were recognized as *shugo* of the lands their ancestors had held for many years.

Among the powers given to the *shugo* were measures that enabled them to control samurai who held smaller plots of land in the provinces over which they had nominal overall control, because, in the same way that the shogun only controlled a fraction of the national lands, so the *shugo* only held a minute portion of the province allocated to them.

The shogun therefore permitted the *shugo* to supervise all transfers of land within his province and to grant lands as a reward for military service, as well as the straightforward task of collecting taxes. There was also a very convenient tax dodge known as *hanzei*, or 'half rights.' It meant that a *shugo* could hold back, 'for military purposes,' half of the tax due from lands under his jurisdiction owned by absentee landlords, such as courtiers or temples. This had been introduced by Ashikaga Takauji as a wartime measure but was now being used to extend the *shugo*'s influence into nonmilitary areas. Their military control was strong, as they had the rights to recruit within their domains. Thus the shogun's army was merely a set of separate contingents led by the *shugo*. The *shugo*, therefore, were gradually transforming themselves from bureaucratic governors into what historians have

Above: Spear fighting in the mountains. The Wars of the Nambokucho Period, which Ashikaga Yoshimitsu was to bring to a successful close, were largely fought in and around wooded and mountainous areas, where fierce hand-to-hand fighting, rather than carefully planned actions on horseback, was the common form of combat.

termed *shugo-daimyo*. Daimyo eventually came to mean an independent landowning samurai warlord, who, at the height of daimyo power, came to rule a province as if it were his own private kingdom, with no reference to any central authority, whether shogun or emperor. In the late fourteenth century the *shugo-daimyo* needed the support of the shogun as much as the Shogun needed them.

The steps which the shogun undertook to control his *shugo* are uncannily like the actions of the later Tokugawa shogunate, who were faced with a similar, though much more serious, problem. The *shugo* of the 10 eastern provinces were made accountable to the shogun headquarters in Kamakura, where they were required to live. (Kamakura was still maintained as a subsidiary seat of government even though the capital had been moved back to Kyoto.) The *shugo* of Kyushu island were made accountable to one of their number who was appointed as shogun's deputy. The remaining *shugo* covering the central area of Japan were kept under direct surveillance of the shogun by being required to live in Kyoto while their administrative tasks were performed in their provinces by *shugo* deputies.

In contrast to the similar 'alternate attendance' system of the Tokugawa, the rules of residence of the Ashikaga were never framed as written law, but in practice they were rigorously adhered to. To return to one's province without permission was regarded as an act of treason; the system made the *shugo* into hostages of the shogun. While they were in residence the shogun took full advantage of the large numbers of relatives, samurai and servants which the *shugo* had with them. When Shogun Yoshinori (ruled 1428–41) began the reconstruction of the shogun's palace the Hosokawa family supplied 3000 men to the labor force, and the Akamatsu a further 2800. Others supplied materials, including a large quantity of rocks for his garden. There were many compensations to living in Kyoto. It meant that the *shugo* were at the center of decision making, notably by the shogun's *shugo* council, which on several occasions restrained the shogun from unwise policies, such as in 1434 when Yoshinori's plan to attack the warrior monks of Mount Hiei was thwarted. It also meant that *shugo* were able to enjoy the considerable commercial and cultural life of the capital.

The original decision by Ashikaga Takauji to move the shogun capital from Kamakura to Kyoto was made on both political and economic grounds, and was arrived at only after much consideration. It was a recognition that the western half of the country was the center of trade, largely because it was nearer to China, in contrast to the 'rice bowl' of eastern Japan. It also meant the fusion of two aristocracies; the civil, as represented by the courtiers of the imperial house, and the samurai of Kamakura. The close proximity of *kuge* (courtier) and *buke* (military) was given physical expression by building of a new imperial palace across the road from the new shogun palace, (known as the *Hana no gosho*, or 'Palace of Flowers,' from the splendor of its gardens). It is significant that it was also twice the size of the Imperial palace. It was completed in 1381 by Ashikaga Yoshimitsu, the third shogun.

Ashikaga Yoshimitsu succeeded his father as shogun at the age of nine, and thus lived under the guardianship of a regent from the Hosokawa. As he grew to manhood he became a vigorous samurai leader in war, and it was largely owing to his efforts that the balance between shogun and *shugo* was maintained so well. In 1379 at the head of an allied *shugo* army, he put down a revolt by the Shiba, Kyogoku and Toki families, and in 1390 defeated another Toki rebellion. In 1391 he contested Yamana, *shugo* of 11 provinces, and cut his authority down to two. In 1392 he finally settled the question of the rival courts.

It is as a cultural leader that Yoshimitsu is best known as he was the first real samurai patron of the arts. In 1394, at the ripe old age of 36, he retired from the post of shogun in favor of his son Yoshimochi and entered the religious life. He retained for himself the office of chancellor of the realm, and kept an eye on affairs of government from the palace he had built for himself to the north of Kyoto. The palace, called Kitayama after the hills nearby, gave its name to the culture Yoshimitsu associated with it. Of the various buildings of Kitayama the most famous is the Kinkakuji, the 'Golden Pavilion.' Although destroyed by fire in 1950 it has since been reconstructed, even to the covering of gold leaf applied to its exterior. It perfectly represents the man who built it: a man of riches, of a complex personality with respect for religion, and of enormous self-confidence and taste. The location of the palace, beside a pond, is a convention of 'pure land' Buddhism. Its lower two floors are in the traditional shinden style of court architecture, while the upper floor resembles a Zen temple.

Kitayama received its noblest guest in 1408, when Yoshimitsu entertained Emperor Go-Komatsu and occupied a seat opposite to and on the same level as his majesty. The festivities lasted 20 days, and marked Yoshimitsu's zenith, for he died shortly afterward. He had established a new principle in samurai life. Not only were they the equals of the emperor and his court in government and military power, they were also

second to none in esthetic appreciation. Under this remarkable shogun the samurai became a true warrior aristocrat.

The other great achievement of Yoshimitsu's rule was the increase in foreign trade, especially with Ming China. Japanese pirates had been trading unofficially for some time. The Chinese called the pirates *wako*, literally 'dwarf robbers,' and their activities resemble the exploits of English sea dogs raiding the Spanish Main and occasionally indulging in a little peaceful trading when it suited them. The Japanese raids began soon after the defeat of the Mongol invasions, and the origin of many pirate groups in Kyushu and around the Inland Sea suggests that they were the same Japanese who had conducted the little ships' raids on the Mongol armada. They increased in scope and intensity during the early Ming period (from 1368). Between 1350–75 there was an average of five raids a year along the Chinese and Korean coasts. For the next decade the average rose to 40 a year, and what had started out as sporadic raids by a few ships had grown into organized expeditions by well-armed samurai. Some of the larger raids are recorded as having been conducted by as many as 3000 men carried in 400 ships. Eventually, the interior of China became subject to attacks by *wako* mounted on horses.

It is very likely that Chinese and Koreans joined the *wako* raids as local guides, and may also have conducted raids themselves, disguised as Japanese. The main objective of plunder by the *wako* was rice. They would attack either the warehouses where it was kept or the ships on which it was carried. The completion of a grand canal in China was stimulated by these raids, so that rice could be safely transported from the southern provinces to Peking, as the *wako* intercepted most of what was taken by sea.

Above: *This print by the eighteenth-century artist Shimposai depicts a samurai in travelling dress accompanied by his servant. The samurai's trousers are pulled up round his knees to make walking easier. He wears a large brimmed hat, pulled down around his face.*

Early efforts to control the pirates proved ineffective in both countries. Korea was still
recovering from the Mongol occupation, and
the early Ashikaga shoguns were too pre-
occupied with the Nambokucho War. Requests
from the Ming emperor to control the *wako*
were sent in 1369 and 1370, but it was not until
Yoshimitsu had achieved stability that a mean-
ingful intercourse between the two countries
could be attained. In 1401 a mission was sent
to China and presented the Chinese emperor
with numerous gifts, including Japanese swords,
and returned to their homeland 40 Chinese
captured by the *wako*. The mission returned the
following year bearing a document which
referred to Yoshimitsu as the 'King of Japan.'
This odd title, which implies incorrectly that the
Chinese were ignorant of the existence of the
emperor, was a standard Chinese diplomatic
procedure. According to the Chinese world view
the many races of mankind were united under
the virtuous rule of the 'Son of Heaven,' the
title given to the Chinese emperor. Foreign
rulers were expected to request formal relations
with the son of heaven by presenting their local
products in the form of tribute, after which the
emperor would invest the ruler with an appropriate title such as 'King.' In return for the
tribute the emperor would hand over quantities
of Chinese articles, so that the transactions had
all the essential characteristics of trade.

Only once in Japanese history had a Japanese
ruler accepted such investiture. This had been
in the sixth century, when the title had been
given to the emperor of Japan. Now Yoshimitsu
was to take the unprecedented step of acceptance
by a shogun of investiture, with all the tributary
relationship it entailed. Such subservience to
China aroused fierce opposition in the capital,

Above: *This excellently
preserved example of a
samurai's house is the
Yokobue-An near Yokohama.
Note the simple thatched roof,
and the unpainted wood.*

Opposite page: *The famous
Golden Pavilion, built by
Ashikaga Yoshimitsu in 1397
as part of his palace of
Kitayama. It is at once
magnificent and luxurious, yet
subtly avoids the least
suggestion of vulgarity. After
recent reconstruction it remains
the perfect monument to the
man and his age, and is one of
the most popular sights of
Japan today.*

especially from the court nobility but Yoshimitsu saw clearly the enormous potential for legitimate trade which it would provide.

The potential was soon realized. The Ming government sent three successive delegations to Japan, in 1405, 1406 and 1407. The first brought a message of praise from the son of heaven for the Japanese suppression of *wako* activity. In 1405, for example, the Japanese handed 20 *wako* over to the Chinese authorities. The Ming allowed the Japanese escort to decide the manner of execution of the pirates. They were grilled to death over a slow fire, a prolonged and very painful end, which showed clearly the shogun's determination to control their activities.

Meanwhile trade continued to grow, from 'tribute' trade to genuine commercial undertakings by the shogunate, and later by major *shugo-daimyo*, under the protection of the tally system. Outgoing Japanese vessels carried tallies which confirmed that they were official vessels and not pirates. All this came about because Yoshimitsu had taken the strange step of subservience to China.

Yet increased trade may not have been Yoshimitsu's only motive. As one who was a military leader and a cultural leader Yoshimitsu was a complete ruler. He had a close relationship with the emperor. In fact, his relations with the imperial court were even more intimate than is implied by merely entertaining. In 1407, when the widow of the former emperor died, Yoshimitsu had his own wife appointed as empress dowager, a remarkable achievement. It is as if Yoshimitsu was attempting to embrace, if not quite take over, the Imperial house and that his investiture by the Chinese emperor as monarch of Japan was a means of legitimizing the eventual fusion of the positions of emperor and shogun. Had this ever been achieved the history of Japan would have been very different, but circumstances were against the Ashikaga shoguns. Yoshimitsu had raised the prestige of the shogun so high that it could only decline. Yoshinori, the sixth shogun (ruled 1428–41) looked like coming close to converting the shogunate into something like a feudal monarchy in the pattern foreseen by Yoshimitsu, but he was assassinated in 1441 by one of his own followers. The status of shogun reverted to that of a hegemony over an uneasy coalition of powerful *shugo-daimyo*.

The shogun's influence was reduced to maintaining the balance of power but the house of Ashikaga still retained sufficient power to produce yet another era of high cultural achievement. This occurred during the reign of Yoshimasa, the eighth shogun, especially from his retirement in 1473 to his death in 1490.

This was a period marred by the terrible civil war of Onin. Yoshimasa has been much criticized for withdrawing from the world to his esthetic pursuits, but in face of the uncontrollable power of the *shugo-daimyo* there was really little else he could do. The Higashiyama culture, named after the hills to the northeast of Kyoto where he built his palace, was about the only positive achievement of the Onin period.

Yoshimasa was Yoshimitsu's grandson, and like his illustrious grandfather has left us an architectural monument to the man and his times. Yoshimitsu had built the Golden Pavilion, so Yoshimasa built the Ginkakuji, the silver pavilion. It is a perfect mirror of the age. It was built on the ruins of a temple destroyed during the Onin War. It is recorded that when his son and heir Yoshihisa advised his father against withdrawing from the world Yoshimasa replied that as the daimyo did what they liked and did

Above: *A view of a Zen-inspired garden at the Ryoan-ji Temple in Kyoto.*

Right: *The well-known yet still tantalizing garden of the Ryoan-ji. It was first laid out in 1473, and remains one of the best examples of the influence of Zen Buddhist-inspired ideas in Japanese art.*

not obey orders there could be no government. The Higashiyama villa was therefore to be a place of repose. Whereas the Golden Pavilion is always brilliant because the sun is on it throughout the whole day, the Silver Pavilion seems to be always in shadows as the sun is hidden behind the eastern hills. Its darkness and quietness of style is made the more somber by the fact that no funds were available to cover the building in silver, so it has remained black to this day.

It is to Yoshimasa that we owe the raising of the tea ceremony from a small esthetic gathering of friends to an art form of the utmost exquisiteness. Nothing was better suited to the samurai who wished to detach himself from the noisy world of his warrior calling. In the tea ceremony could be found the appreciation of form, as shown by the tea bowl, and the beauty of restraint. The simple decoration of the tea house and tea garden was symbolic, and overall the ceremony portrayed harmony, where poetry, art and the world of nature were perfectly combined in an intense ritual.

The influence behind the tea ceremony, indeed behind much of the Higashiyama style, was the deeply introspective quality of Zen Buddhism, which sought the inner meaning in both nature and art. A work of art produced in the spirit of Zen left something unsaid, something which the viewer could add, as shown by one of the other great cultural achievements of Higashiyama, the perfection of the *suiboku* style of painting. *Suiboku* was monochrome work using black ink on a brush, which emphasized skilled brushwork in place of a balance of color. The master of this style was Sesshu (1420–1506).

The same principles also led to what might be called the monochrome garden. The Daisen-in, built in 1509, is one of the best known examples, and is itself a three-dimensional re-creation of a monochrome screen painting within the building of the Daisen-in. By a subtle arrangement of rocks, raked gravelly sand, and the minimum of plant life, the Daisen-in invites the viewer to see the sand as a roaring torrent of a river symbolizing the soul's terrestrial journey, a suitable theme for contemplation by those whose profession carried them on like a fast-flowing stream. If the Daisen-in leads one to a conclusion, the famous garden of the Ryoanji gives no clue as to its inner meaning. This stunningly simple area of rocks and sand is the ultimate in the detached contemplation which Yoshimasa sought in Higashiyama. It can be seen as islands in a sea, or the tops of mountains above the clouds. It was laid out in 1473 and has tantalized visitors ever since.

One art form closely associated with the Ashikaga shoguns was the *noh* drama. *Noh* is the classical Japanese theater, a stately form of entertainment much patronized by the samurai, who would see acted the valiant and tragic lives of their own ancestors. *Noh* took its subjects almost exclusively from samurai legend, in particular the heroes of the Gempei War. One *noh* play told of the death of the young Taira Atsumori at the Battle of Ichinotani in 1184 and the grief of the samurai who had killed him. There were stories of ghosts, such as the haunting of Benkei and Yoshitsune by the spirits of dead Taira warriors, of the warrior woman Tomoe, and of self-sacrificing retainers. The result was a very stylized music drama, similar to Greek tragedy. Some theaters still show *noh* plays and all the actors wear masks and there is a chanting chorus which appears at several stages in the play. In contrast to Greek drama the costumes of *noh* are of exceptional splendor and color, yet on a bare stage, and acting with a precision of form, all gaudiness is avoided, and the *noh* takes its place perfectly in an esthetic setting where the ideals of Zen are paramount.

An unexpected addition to the *noh* is the inclusion of short farces, known as *kyogen*, between plays. They are designed to lighten the

Below: A feature of most Japanese gardens is a stone basin with a ladle for drinking or rinsing the hands. This particular example is at the Ryoan-ji in Kyoto, with a design in the shape of a coin. The motto is a rebus, each character making use of the square character in the center. When this is added it reads 'I just know enough.'

Left: *A samurai wearing armor typical of the early Muromachi Period. He carries a* nodachi, *the extra-long sword.*

Left: *A blade of* katana *form by the great swordsmith Masamune (1264–1343).*

Above: *A connoisseur of swords. No matter how deadly, a sword was always a work of art.*

serious atmosphere which *noh* provides. Many *kyogen* are miniature masterpieces, satirizing the patrons of *noh* themselves.

One aspect of trade with Ming China is of particular interest in the history of the samurai. Even by the early fifteenth century the Japanese had achieved an international reputation for the quality of their arms and armor, which had been among the first tribute goods sent by Yoshimitsu. Once regular and private trade became established large quantities of Japanese swords were exported. The initial demand is believed to have been occasioned by the need for good-quality weapons to repulse the *wako* on their own terms, but during the Muromachi period the number sent abroad increased dramatically. At one point the Japanese brought 30,000 swords for sale, which led to a major disagreement over the price which they were fetching in China.

The important point in the history of the samurai is the fact that the Japanese sword is commonly regarded as a very precious and symbolic weapon, the soul of the samurai. The long, ritual-like process by which a fine sword was forged has been often described, but here is the clearest evidence that such efforts must have been reserved for a minimum of special orders, and that the overwhelming number of swords must have been manufactured on a 'production line.' Apprentices must have performed the minor operations and the master only the skilled ones, holding the blade for the tempering and so on. Such a view is supported by the fact that as the civil wars grew in number and intensity the need for swords grew too, so that there was no time for a sword maker to pass on his secrets to his chosen apprentices, and by 1600 the old secrets of sword making had been lost forever.

A similarly laconic view of the value of very fine swords is found in the House Laws of the Asakura *daimyo, circa* 1480:

'Do not excessively covet swords and daggers made by famous masters. Even if you can own a sword or dagger worth 10,000 pieces it can be overcome by 100 spears each worth 100 pieces. Therefore, use the 10,000 pieces to obtain 100 spears, and arm 100 men with them. Thus you can defend yourself in war.'

Asakura Toshikage is perhaps being a little unfair to the individual samurai, as the lengthy and expensive processes of sword making were all designed to produce a sword that would cut well and not break in battle. Whatever esthetic considerations the shogun of the Golden Pavilion and his successors may have applied to a tea bowl or an ink painting, when it came to a sword such points must always be secondary to its function. The semimystical Japanese sword was first and foremost a weapon for killing other samurai, and even in the court of Yoshimitsu war was never far away.

Sieges: Storm and Stealth

If the accounts that have been preserved are to be believed, there was nothing the samurai enjoyed more than a large-scale set-piece battle, with waving flags, drums and skillful encounters between horsemen. However on many occasions the enemy could not be coaxed out of his castle, and a siege had to be undertaken.

Carrying out a successful siege required a virtue found little in the samurai armory – patience. To sit down outside a wall and wait until one's opponent starved to death was a not particularly glorious undertaking, so it is not surprising that nearly every recorded siege was accompanied by several attempts at direct assault, though one suspects that in many cases this was more to relieve boredom among the investing troops than for any other reason.

Some generals, such as Hideyoshi, almost made a profession of siegecraft. The long campaign Hideyoshi conducted on Nobunaga's behalf during the early 1580s was little more than a succession of weary sieges. As the years went by Hideyoshi's ingenuity grew, until he had built up a formidable catalogue of siege techniques ranging from bribery to flooding (Takamatsu castle surrendered after Hideyoshi had diverted a river into it) and mining (Kameyama in 1583; the commander of the castle literally felt it fall about his ears).

The siege of Odawara in 1590 was a very gentlemanly affair, and in fact a temporary town grew up round it where the attacking samurai lived. Various siege engines were designed and used, such as catapults, and moveable palisades. The latter consisted of bundles of bamboo tied together on a wheeled framework, which soldiers would push near to the walls so that snipers could aim at close range. During the Korean War Kato Kiyomasa carried out several sieges against Chinese castles, and in one encounter filled the moat with bundles of rice grass so that the samurai could cross.

The acquisition of cannon from European ships was a more than useful addition to the implements of siegecraft. The Japanese never really developed the skills of metal casting on a scale to make strong cannon barrels, so any ship that arrived stood a good chance of having its entire armaments confiscated. Many large cannon were used during the epic siege of Osaka castle in 1614, and one employed by the besieging force succeeded in lobbing an 18-pound shot into the keep. The siege of Osaka was, however, completed largely by trickery, involving a spurious peace treaty.

In 1638 the defenders of Shimabara fell to an assault by Tokugawa troops, but it was not until 1877 that the efficiency of castles was demonstrated when Kumamoto held out to the Satsuma insurgents – proof indeed of good design.

Overleaf, and below in detail: *An excellent impression of the act of besieging a Japanese castle is given by these two sections from the painted screen depicting the Battle of Shizugatake, preserved in Osaka Castle Museum. Shizugatake was one of series of frontier fortresses built by Hideyoshi. Its commander, Nakagawa Kiyohide, was killed during the assault by Sakuma Morimasa, but the castle garrison held out until relieved by Hideyoshi. In the detail below footsoldiers on the battlements fire through loopholes, while two intrepid samurai attempt to scale the rock on which the castle is built. A party from the garrison sallies out to the attack through the gateway.*

CHAPTER 5

The Age of the Country at War

Previous page: *The army of Takeda Shingen before Kawanakajima. One of the most successful of the Sengoku-daimyo was Takeda Shingen, who possessed large resources of samurai and had the skill to use them to their best effect. Many of his campaigns were directed against his neighbor and rival Uesugi Kenshin, with whom he fought many battles, notably on the plains of Kawanakajima.*

Below: *This sketch by Hokusai shows the use of the signalling conch and the* taiko *(big drum). Both are performed by* ashigaru.

The pivotal event in the Muromachi period was the Onin War, which began in 1467 and continued for nine years. Before the war the Ashikaga shogun had managed to maintain the balance between shogun and *shugo* which Yoshimitsu had established, but the Onin War was an event over which the shogunate was unable to exercise any control. As it was largely fought in and around Kyoto an examination of the state of the capital city is necessary.

Kyoto during the Ashikaga period was a lively and vigorous place and because the central *shugo-daimyo* were required to reside there it provided a commercial and cultural focus for the whole country. Whereas the Kitayama culture of Yoshimitsu had been almost exclusively aristocratic, the culture associated with Yoshimasa, which after the building of the Silver Pavilion was called Higashiyama, was founded on the economic power of a growing mercantile elite, particularly the *doso* (warehouse keepers), who also served as money-changers. All the paintings and pottery from China that delighted Yoshimasa and his coterie first passed through the hands of these merchants. This exposure to refined taste, allied to their increasing wealth, made possible the birth of a genuine urban culture that was strong enough to maintain the Ashikaga artistic traditions even when the Ashikaga themselves were overwhelmed by warfare. In fact, many of Yoshimasa's closest artistic acquaintances were not aristocratic samurai but men of comparatively

low birth, who had acquired a sensitivity to such disciplines as flower arranging and the tea ceremony, even though their approach tended to be utilitarian.

Early fifteenth-century Kyoto was also characterized by a communal spirit that reached much further down the social order. This spirit was expressed in the formation of *machi* associations, a *machi* being a number of neighboring city blocks. The people living in the same *machi* acted as the members of a communal body for crime prevention, mutual protection and above all fire precautions, a very frequent danger in a city largely built of wood. Toward the middle of the century they acquired another function, that of protecting the citizens against attacks from rural rioters.

Riots and similar disturbances in Kyoto were the result of the formation of rural leagues known as *ikki*. The *ikki* served as the vehicle for grievances by peasants and small samurai landowners in the provinces, who had been left to their own devices by absentee *shugo*. The main force of their attacks was directed against the moneylenders and pawnbrokers, who were reaping immense profits from the countryside, but all who lived in the same *machi* suffered. Hence the urban poor of Kyoto could not ally themselves with the rural *ikki*. Moreover the *doso* were an indispensable source of finance to the smallest shopkeeper or artisan, so the townsmen joined as one against the *ikki* incursions.

The first raid on Kyoto took place in 1428 but the fiercest of all occurred in 1441, after the murder of Shogun Yoshinori. With the shogunate temporarily disoriented, the warehouse keepers were without protection and within a month even members of the shogun's guard were looting warehouses. A few weeks later thousands of *ikki* members attacked the city, looting and burning to such an extent that when the chief shogun administrator gave orders to quell the riots he found no *shugo-daimyo* willing to enforce them. Only the issuing of a debt-cancelling edict, the first granted by the Ashikaga, staved off the complete destruction of the city's warehouses.

The success of the 1441 riot established a pattern and the *ikki* returned four times in the next 20 years. During the 1457 disturbances the *machi* associations hired mercenary samurai to defend them but they were beaten by the *ikki*. The *ikki* then took on a shogun army and defeated them too. However, from the point of view of the ordinary citizen the experience of withstanding *ikki* attacks was to stand the Kyoto population in good stead, and enabled them to survive the destructive war of Onin and to rebuild their capital afterward.

One of the indirect causes of the Onin War

was the shogun's policy of requiring the *shugo-daimyo* to reside in Kyoto. As they were without direct contact with the provinces they were supposed to be ruling, court intrigue took the place of open rivalry, with rival *shugo-daimyo* fighting far away, almost by proxy. The conflict that was to develop into the Onin War arose out of succession disputes in two families, the Hatakeyama and the Shiba. The rivalry between opposing contenders was seized upon by two of the most powerful *shugo-daimyo* families, the Hosokawa and the Yamana. The situation may well have been resolved amicably had not Shogun Yoshimasa expressed a desire to abdicate in the face of what he saw as uncontrollable forces. Yoshimasa wanted his brother to succeed, while Yoshimasa's wife assumed that the post of shogun should go to their baby son. Sensing the opportunity for a trial of strength, the Yamana declared for the infant while the Hosokawa pledged support for the brother. Two strong *shugo* families were now opposed to each other over a matter concerning the central government within Kyoto.

As both sides had large armies already with them in Kyoto and their mansions were the seats of *shugo* power it looked certain that if war should start a part of it at least would be fought in the city streets. As extra samurai poured in and neighboring *shugo* declared their allegiances the ordinary townsfolk began to flee. The fighting began in May 1467 with an attack by Hosokawa samurai on the mansion of the Isshiki, across the road from the shogun's 'Palace of Flowers.' The battle continued for a few days, and set a pattern for the style of fighting that was to characterize the war. Groups of samurai fought from house to house through the narrow streets of northern Kyoto and in their wake came the looters and arsonists, until soon the whole *machi* containing the Isshiki mansion had been burned to the ground. The fighting spread, and within a few months a front line had been established between the two factions, who glared at each other across a no man's land of blackened timbers. As a stalemate developed the fighting spread to the provinces until several *shugo* armies were busily fighting each other, while the shogunate could do little but look on.

During the next few years the majority of *shugo-daimyo* families literally fought each other into extinction, or found themselves powerless and stranded by the decline of the shogunate whose eclipse as a hegemony they had helped to bring about. To understand what replaced them it is necessary to recap a little on the nature of the power which the *shugo-daimyo* had actually possessed. While they were individually the most powerful military figures in Japan, they

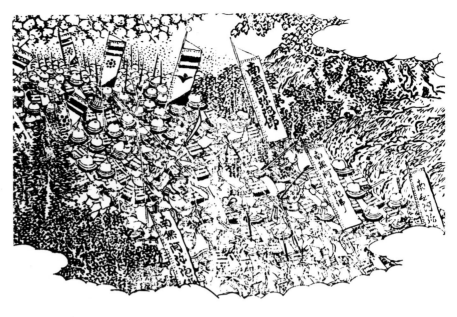

Above and left: *Flags of the* Ikko-ikki. *Of some consequence during the wars of the sixteenth century were the monastic-based forces, backed up by samurai and peasant support, exemplified by the* Ikko-ikki. *Oda Nobunaga conducted a long campaign against the* Ikko-ikki's *fortified 'cathedral' of Ishiyama Hongan-ji, built where Osaka Castle now stands. Their religious inspiration is shown clearly by these banners. Those illustrated above bear the slogan* Namu Amida Busatsu, *an invocation of Buddha, while the flag on the left bears the design of a* sotoba *in gold on red. The five elements of the* sotoba *represent sky, wind, fire, water and earth. Alternatively the lower three elements may be seen as the praying hands (triangle) of man (the circle) on earth (rectangle) gazing toward heaven. This flag is believed to have been carried by the contingent from the* Zempuku-ji *of Edo during the siege of Ishiyama Hongan-ji.*

were nevertheless far from all-powerful in the provinces in which the shogun had placed them. To take two examples: the Kyogoku were *shugo* of northern Omi, but only held land rights to six small areas in the province, the rest being scattered throughout distant provinces. The authority of the Ko was even more tenuous. They were *shugo* of Yamashiro province, but actually owned no land there at all. In terms of landowning, the basis of all wealth, the *shugo* was just another *kokujin* (man of the province). His *shoen* lands made up a patchwork of rice fields ranging from the meager, the typical *ikki* member, to the substantial, the *ji-samurai* who became the *ikki* leaders. Any authority the *shugo-daimyo* might possess was based on the

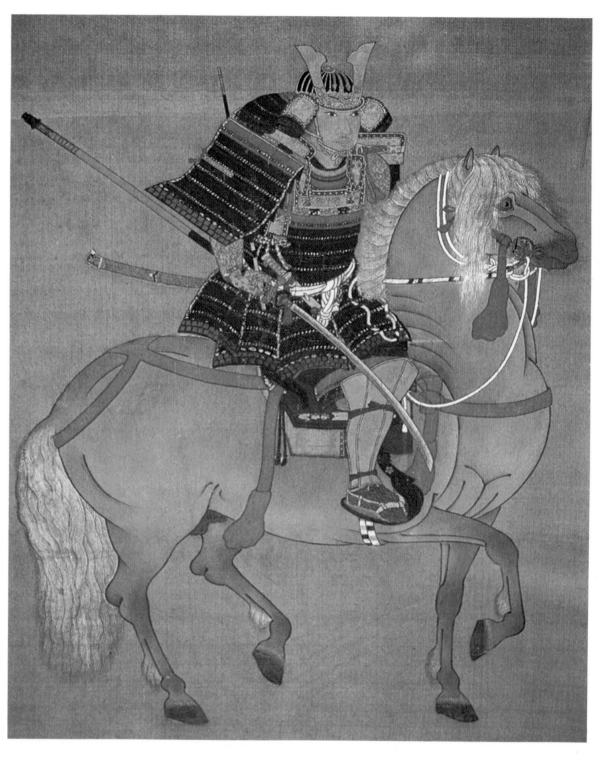

allegiance of such men, in exactly the same way as the authority of the shogun depended on the *shugo*.

Consequently the self-immolation of the *shugo-daimyo* left a vacuum in the provinces which the smaller landowners rushed to fill. It is this struggle for power among regional lords that dominates the rest of the Muromachi period. The struggles were so numerous that the period from 1467–1568 is often given the alternative title of the *Sengoku-jidai*, a name that referred originally to the 'Period of Warring States' in ancient China, and adopted for Japan although it was not a time of war between states as such. The best translation is 'The Age of the Country at War,' or simply, 'The Age of War.'

By the middle of the sixteenth century the *shugo-daimyo* had disappeared as a result of such war, either by fighting each other or by being swamped by rival landowners. The new regional rulers who emerged are known as *sengoku-daimyo*, 'The daimyo of the Age of War.' The large majority were *kokujin*, some of whom had held inferior positions in local administration. Others were followers of *shugo*. A very few were *shugo* who had made the transition to *sengoku-daimyo*, and all of these, such as Shimazu of Satsuma, and Imagawa in the Kanto, were located in peripheral areas. The essential difference between the *shugo* and *sengoku-daimyo* was that the former depended for their authority on their appointment by a shogun. The *sengoku-daimyo* depended on nothing other than sheer military force. In other words the new daimyo were completely independent samurai warlords with considerable power.

The power held by such men consisted of their samurai, their farmers, in many cases the two being one and the same, their castles, and the lands they held. Such lands bore no relationship to previous domains, or even to the boundaries of provinces. Their domains took shape from within, being limited only by the area which could reasonably be defended. They were thus much smaller at first than previous *shugo* holdings but were much more securely held. They tended to follow the lines of mountains and other strategic features as the domain increased in size by conquest or by absorption, in either case maintaining the domain as a contiguous territory. Daimyo territories that were split up were very rare because they were difficult to defend. In what was Bizen province there is archeological evidence of the fierce competition between *kokujin* to become daimyo for in this one small province there are the remains of over 200 small hilltop fortifications dating from the Age of War. The daimyo domains also differed in several other aspects. There were no absentee landlords, there was no contact with Kyoto and there was a very different relationship between a daimyo and his followers.

Whichever way a daimyo acquired territory, and with it followers, the relationship that was created was a feudal one of lord and vassal, just like the early samurai. This meant that in seeking protection, or acknowledging a daimyo's superiority, the new arrival would pledge an oath of allegiance to his overlord. A hierarchical relationship was thus formed that was considerably stronger and more stable than the precarious tie between the absentee *shugo* and the *kokujin*.

In return for the swearing of allegiance the daimyo would enfieff his vassal. This meant either confirming the vassal's holding of the lands he had brought with him, under the over-

Left: *An* ashigaru *armed with an harquebus. A painting by the author, based on the Osaka Castle screen.*

lordship of the daimyo, or in the case of a new acquisition of land by conquest, granting them in fief to the follower. The lord/vassal relationship was often adopted in the case of village headmen, who controlled very small units of land and to whom vassalage was a guarantee of protection. As vassals they provided military service in times of war, and as cultivators in the villages in which they lived they maintained order and collected taxes. As administration was difficult at all levels in war, so the daimyo came to depend more and more on the abilities of the farming communities to manage their own affairs.

The daimyo domains were therefore 'petty principalities,' yet their small kingdoms were governed better than had been possible under previous systems, in contrast to the view that after the Onin War the country dissolved in chaos. This is shown by surviving examples of 'House Codes' produced by *sengoku-daimyo*. One of the most comprehensive sets belongs to the Chosokabe of Tosa province, Shikoku island.

Left: *Almost as decisive as the use of firearms was the disciplining of the low-class soldiers, the* ashigaru. *This contingent bear a red mark on their black armor which identifies them as belonging to the Honda.*

Above and right: *Two ways of putting on armor in a hurry.*

Opposite page, above: *A print by Sadahide showing the retainers of Takeda Shingen putting on their armor. Each figure depicts a different stage in the process.*

Opposite page, below: *A warrior armed with a* nagamaki. *Note the thigh guards, and the wooden shield, typically used to protect the harquebus corps and archers.*

Below: *An illustration from a treatise on the wearing of armor showing one of several ways of fastening the helmet cords securely using the face mask.*

it the duty of the samurai to serve his lord with loyalty, even so far as to sacrifice his own life. Whatever might be contained in the house codes, the house stood or fell by this one principle. In the later years of peace ideals such as duty, loyalty and self-sacrifice were to be enshrined as the 'warrior's code,' bushido. In the Age of War, as in the former days of Kamakura, they were the basic requirements of service, without which no daimyo could survive.

During the Age of War, therefore, we see numerous daimyo competing to establish and maintain their territories, almost like a gigantic game with human counters, a game very like the Japanese game of *go*, which had long been a popular samurai pastime. *Go* begins with an empty board, on to which the players in turn put their pieces. Once placed, the counters do not change position, but bit by bit the territory

The Chosokabe were one of half a dozen families left to compete for supremacy in the area after their former *shugo*, Hosokawa, had left. In a pattern to be repeated all over Japan, the Chosokabe fought, made alliances, broke promises and fought again, all the while hoping that they would not be attacked in the rear while fighting the adversary of the moment. The code they produced consists of a hundred articles, and covers every conceivable facet of domain life. There are rules concerning Buddhist priests, '. . . any who return to lay life without permission of the daimyo are to be put to death. . . .' There are rules for the conduct of law suits, '. . . . they should first be taken up with the unit commander, and thereafter submitted to the daimyo . . . any interference by wives in legal matters is strictly forbidden. . . .' There are detailed regulations concerning laboring, and a specific clause clarifying the position of a samurai who wishes to surrender his fief. This came about as a result of attempts to move the samurai to castle towns, which will be described more fully later. Many of the poorer Chosokabe samurai could not afford to leave their land, and petitioned to be allowed to abandon their status as samurai and return to being farmers.

There are also rules governing morality, the treatment of servants, the irrigation of land, wages for artisans, width of main roads, the sale of horses and numerous other matters. The most important rule of all was never written down in any house code. This was the regulation implied by the acceptance of vassalage status, the oldest of the samurai ideals. It simply made

increases as enemy pieces are surrounded and
absorbed, until at the end of the game the
winner has the entire board under his control.
It would be nearly a century before that stage
was reached in the real life game and one daimyo
controlled the whole of Japan.

In a situation where political and economic
gains were to be made and lost by military force
it was essential that a daimyo strive to be at the
forefront of military innovation. One of the
main trends of warfare during the Muromachi
period had been the use of peasant troops or
ashigaru, which means 'light feet.' They had first
come to be used during the Nambokucho War,
because as wars increased in size and scope
daimyo needed every man they could get for
their armies. As many hands were also needed
for agricultural work it was the mark of a skilled
daimyo that he could have a large army of
ashigaru, who had received a certain amount of
military training, but not thereby denude his
fields of farm workers. One of the most successful
in this respect was a famous daimyo called
Takeda Shingen (1521–73), who was the first
daimyo to properly discipline his *ashigaru* and
turn them into an effective fighting force that
would not desert once the battle was over, or
worse, before it had begun. It was a measure of
Shingen's success that he managed to inculcate
in his *ashigaru* some of the loyalty that was
expected from his samurai, most of whom were
his enfeiffed vassals, and thus under a bond
completely different from the *ashigaru*.

In fact the bond between *ashigaru*, or any
farmer, and daimyo, was at this time a very
delicate one. If a farmer was not well treated he
could cross a domain border and till the fields of
a rival. Most house codes had regulations for
dealing with absconding peasants but in the
volatile situation of the Age of War the lower

of armor received almost as much attention as the design of swords. As one authority wrote:

'When he goes forth to war the samurai is ready for the onslaught of arrows and bullets, prepared to leap into fire and boiling water. His death-defying bearing may be due to his loyal spirit and his natural bravery, but if his armor be not strong he can avail but little.'

The armorer, therefore, had a special duty:

'The samurai . . . ordered good armor from expert makers and spared no expense. Wearing it at once and going to battle, if he fell victim to arrows or gunshot wounds . . . even his own family could not feel more poignant grief than the armorer himself. . . .'

The most difficult task for an armor maker was to make it proof against both harquebus shots and arrows. The only way to test if a metal plate was proof was to fire a bullet at it, hence some of the most prized suits of armor worn in the Age of War sported large dents. The same need also influenced the overall design of armor, and made it look much more like European plate armor than the traditional lamellar style. The lamellar was composed of many more plates and had a correspondingly greater number of cords fastening it together, which tended to freeze together in winter and become sodden with

Above: A section from the 'Namban Screen.' This painted screen shows foreigners in Japan during the sixteenth century. In the foreground are Jesuits and two Franciscans, while in the rear a priest celebrates mass in what may well be a converted Buddhist temple.

Right: A view in springtime of the countryside of Kai, where Takeda Shingen held sway.

Opposite page: Uesugi Kenshin, Shingen's great rival. Kenshin was a monk, and wore the monkish cowl when in armor. He is shown here defeating Shingen's army, the Takeda badge being depicted clearly on the overturned shield.

class soldier had everything going for him. In fact the samurai who was eventually to bring all of Japan under his rule started off as an *ashigaru*.

The *ashigaru* therefore added a new dimension to the samurai battle, and engagements changed from being a collection of individual encounters to a disciplined movement of large bodies of troops. Technical innovations were also eagerly grasped and put to use, the most important being the introduction of firearms by European traders. Within months of the first guns being brought to Japan they were being copied and mass produced for the daimyo armies. The design was that of an harquebus, a lightweight musket, fired by dropping a lighted match on to the touch hole. As it was not very accurate its effectiveness was increased by large-scale volley firing. It had the advantage of being comparatively easy to learn to use so the harquebus gradually replaced the bow, which required strong muscles and years of practice, as the main missile weapon of the ashigaru.

The battles of the Age of War must have been very colorful affairs, largely because of the *sashimono*, a little banner worn on the back of the armor bearing the *mon*, or badge, of the samurai to whom the wearer was in service. The design

本勘助入道道鬼

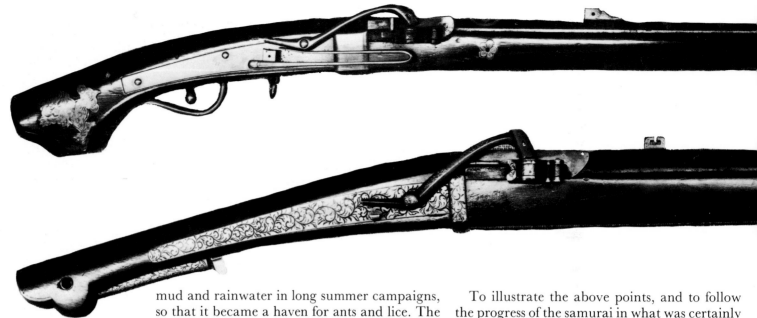

Right: *A wooden statue of Imagawa Yoshimoto (1519–60). As one of the few daimyo to make the transition from* shugo-daimyo *to* sengoku-daimyo *it is unfortunate that he is known today chiefly for being the loser at the Battle of Okehazama in 1560.*

mud and rainwater in long summer campaigns, so that it became a haven for ants and lice. The new styles of the Age of War therefore tended to look simpler with far cleaner lines than previous models, except for the helmet, where flamboyant decorations of feathers and horns brightened up what was essentially a functional battle dress.

To illustrate the above points, and to follow the progress of the samurai in what was certainly their heyday, it helps to examine the histories of three families of *sengoku-daimyo*: the Oda, the Imagawa and the Tokugawa. Their relations with one another show perfectly the bonds of lord and vassal, the ideals of samurai loyalty, and the tremendous intensity of samurai warfare.

The three families were neighbors along the Tokaido, the Eastern Sea Road that follows the coast of the Pacific Ocean. The Oda were based in Owari, the Imagawa in Suruga and Totomi, with the less significant Tokugawa squeezed in between, in Mikawa. The Tokugawa were then called the Matsudaira, and the main character in this description, Tokugawa Ieyasu, changed his name four times during his long lifetime and it was changed after he died. For the sake of convenience he will be referred to as Ieyasu throughout, which is the name by which he has gone down into history.

The Tokugawa were a reasonably successful example of the process of making a *sengoku-daimyo* and by the beginning of the sixteenth century were in possession of over a third of Mikawa province. However, their fortunes suffered when the grandfather of Ieyasu was killed by one of his own samurai in a confusing incident involving suspected treason. His son Hirotada was only 10 years old and was eventually taken by a retainer to the protection of their powerful neighbors, the Imagawa.

The Imagawa were almost unique in being one of the few *shugo-daimyo* families who had successfully made the transition to *sengoku-daimyo*. Imagawa Yoshimoto (1519–1560) was a relative of the incumbent Ashikaga shogun and was married to the daughter of a court noble. Consequently the life in Sumpu, the Imagawa castle town, echoed the Higashiyama culture which his ancestors had enjoyed. In the fashion of the times Sumpu was made into a 'little Kyoto,' with the beauty spots named after famous scenes near the capital. Imagawa and his 'court' held flower-viewing parties, performed the tea ceremony and enjoyed paintings and poetry. With an income of 100,000 *koku*

Right: *A fully armed samurai of the Age of War. He carries a long-bladed spear and wears on his back the characteristic* sashimono, *which served to identify a samurai's followers on the battlefield. He is seated on the box in which his armor would have been carried to the field. The sword is worn* tachi *style (with the cutting edge downward) which is the only practical way when wearing a suit of armor.*

hostage. It was a painful decision for his father to make as Ieyasu was his heir and his samurai felt it was a blow to their prestige, but there was little he could do except agree.

However, Ieyasu never reached the Imagawa for on the way his retinue was attacked by samurai of the Oda and the six-year-old Tokugawa heir was bundled on to a boat and taken round the coast of Oda territory. Oda Nobuhide wrote to Tokugawa Hirotada, saying that if he did not want his son to be killed he had better surrender Okazaki castle. Hirotada replied at once that it would make no difference whether Ieyasu was killed or not because he had sent his son in all good faith to Imagawa, and that it was certainly not his fault that he had not made it. Imagawa, he added, clearly understood the position and the alliance between Imagawa and Tokugawa was as strong as ever. In fact, it was likely to be a lot stronger when Imagawa saw that he was willing to sacrifice his own son for the good of the Imagawa.

Imagawa could no doubt afford it but what he could not afford was to lose battles. However, he was well served in warfare by an uncle who combined the professions of samurai and Zen monk with great skill.

On the other side of the Tokugawa lands was the petty kingdom of the Oda and as Tokugawa Hirotada grew to manhood he witnessed the conflict between the esthetes of Imagawa and the less wealthy, but far more belligerent, Oda. Four months before the great Tokugawa Ieyasu was born the Battle of Azukizaka took place, where the daimyo Oda Nobuhide repulsed an attack on his province by Imagawa, aided by the Tokugawa. The conflict, alliance and treachery between the three rivals continued throughout Ieyasu's infancy and came to a head in 1548. Oda Nobuhide had incited one of his samurai leaders to attack the Tokugawa castle of Okazaki. Ieyasu's father, Hirotada, tricked the potential attacker into receiving an envoy, who turned out to be a very efficient assassin. Enraged at his plans being foiled, Oda Nobuhide gathered as large an army as he could muster and set off to raze Okazaki to the ground and the cunning Tokugawa with it. The Oda army was a force which the Tokugawa could not hope to withstand, so Hirotada asked the Imagawa for help. Imagawa was willing enough to assist because apart from the chance to take on the Oda it was a good opportunity to bring the Tokugawa more closely into his service. Since the days when they had protected the youthful Hirotada, the Tokugawa had gained a considerable amount of independence from the Imagawa so although they agreed to support the Tokugawa they asked for the boy Ieyasu as a

Above: *One of the most colorful aspects of samurai warfare during the sixteenth and early seventeenth centuries were the* sashimono *(flags), worn on the back of the suit of armor. Top row: 1–4, used by the Ii clan during the siege of Osaka 1615; 5 Tokugawa unit. Center Row: 1, Toyotomi; 2, Oda; 3, Yamauchi; 4 and 5 unidentified. Bottom row: 1, Honda; 2, Ankokuji; 3, Sakai 4, Mizuno; 5, Kuroda.*

Opposite: *The armor of Oda Nobunaga (1534–1582). It is of* do-maru *style, with dark-blue silk lacing. The thigh guards are unusual, being composed of metal hexagons sewn on to a cloth backing. The large shoulder plates balance the wide sweep of the helmet's neck guard, and a notable feature is the large helmet badge bearing Nobunaga's* mon *(badge) in gold.*

The nobility of the sentiment so impressed Oda Nobuhide that he did Ieyasu no harm, but kept him safe while he got on with the serious business of trying to defeat the Tokugawa and Imagawa in war. The methods varied from pitched battles to the knife in the dark until in 1549 both Tokugawa Hirotada and Oda Nobuhide died, both from natural causes. As the heir to the Tokugawa was still held hostage the Imagawa led the Tokugawa troops against the two sons of Oda, the eldest was Nobuhiro and the younger was the famous Nobunaga. The campaign against the elder brother was most successful and in 1550 the Imagawa had him penned up in his castle. The Imagawa were determined to get back the hostage they had been promised four years before and offered to exchange Nobuhiro for Ieyasu. Oda Nobunaga agreed and Ieyasu was finally taken to the Imagawa capital.

Here Ieyasu stayed, enjoying the gracious surroundings of Imagawa's 'little Kyoto,' where he performed his *gembuku*, the ceremony of entering manhood. From 1555 the fortunes of the Imagawa began to decline as Yoshimoto's samurai-monk uncle died and the elegant courtier now had to do his own fighting. It was soon realized that Ieyasu was to prove an able general so he was given his first command of an army in 1558, at the age of 17.

Previously Ieyasu had paid a visit to his castle of Okazaki, which he had not seen since the age of six. It was a visit which shows clearly the lord/vassal relationship which characterized the Age of War. The purpose of the visit was for Ieyasu to pay respects to the tomb of his father and also, as the heir, receive the homage of the senior Tokugawa samurai, who were pleased to see him. The years had dealt harshly with the Tokugawa samurai. All the revenues from their lands had been taken by the Imagawa and the poorest of the Tokugawa fief holders had been forced to work as farmers. It is related that one such samurai was working in the fields when he saw Ieyasu arriving whereupon he smeared his face with mud so that his young lord would not recognize him in such a poor condition. However Ieyasu did recognize him so the samurai thrust his sword into the piece of rope that held his coat together, washed his face and paid his respects. Ieyasu was greatly moved, for he knew that his samurai had been forced to put up with such conditions in case Ieyasu was harmed by his captors. Moreover, the Tokugawa had had to bear the main brunt of the fighting against the Oda so that Imagawa Yoshimoto's own men might be spared, and the Tokugawa be even more weakened. They had suffered great losses but their loyalty held them together in a common purpose and forged them into some of

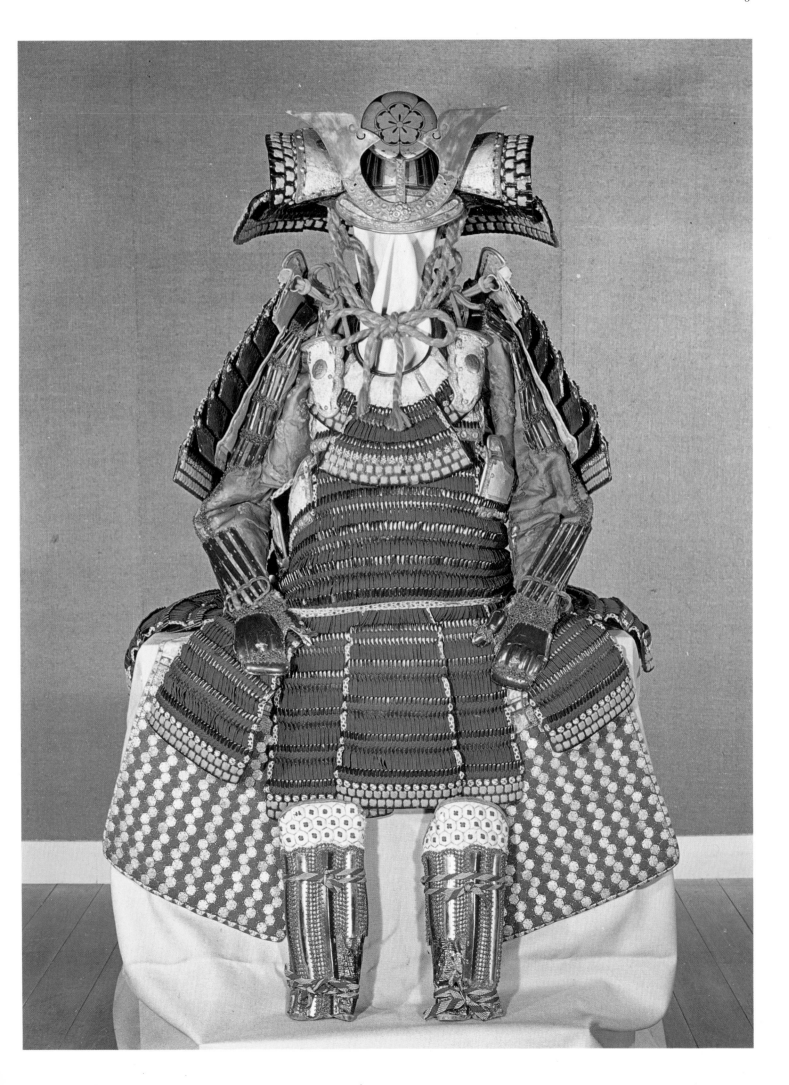

84

Above: *The flag of the
Monto monks. The Monto
sect were among the fiercest
opponents encountered by
Tokugawa Ieyasu. Their
fighting spirit was summed
up by the slogan on their flags:
'He who advances is sure of
heaven, but he who retreats of
eternal damnation.'*

Right: *A well-sculptured
dummy dressed in typical
'battle dress' of the Age of
War. The cords which
secured the sleeves tightly to
the arms are clearly shown, as
is the staff for a* sashimono.

the more formidable samurai to be found in
Japan.

Now that Ieyasu was to lead them, their
loyalty and enthusiasm were greatly increased.
The first action Ieyasu saw was against a castle
in Mikawa called Terabe whose commander
had deserted to the Oda side. The leader of the
Oda was now the younger brother Nobunaga,
who had driven the elder brother out of the
province in an act of ruthlessness that was to
characterize his life. Ieyasu personally led the
attack on Terabe and burned the outer defenses.
The main castle was strongly defended and
Ieyasu realized that if his men captured it they
would be laying themselves open to a counterattack by one of the neighboring fortresses, so he
contented himself with setting fire to the main
castle and withdrawing. He also had the satisfaction of anticipating that Nobunaga would
send a force to take the Tokugawa in the rear.
Ieyasu was ready for them and beat them off.
As a reward for his success Imagawa Yoshimoto
presented Ieyasu with a fine sword and added
to it the inexpensive reward which vassaldom
entitled him to give. This was a grant of land,
Ieyasu's own, naturally, not Yoshimoto's.

Ieyasu's success at arms led the Tokugawa
samurai to press Yoshimoto to let him return
and reside in Okazaki. The Tokugawa were,
after all, bound by a considerable oath of loyalty
to the Imagawa. But Yoshimoto wished to keep
Ieyasu close to his influence because he was
planning far greater things than a continuing
war with Oda.

Imagawa Yoshimoto's aim was nothing less
than an advance on Kyoto. He secured his rear
by a combination of alliances but between him
and Kyoto was Oda Nobunaga's Owari. This
long and unresolved conflict would have to be
settled if any grand design was to be accomplished. Tokugawa Ieyasu was to take charge
of operations on the Mikawa/Owari frontier,
supporting the Imagawa-held fortresses and
acquiring any others that were to hand. He
began with a small-scale operation to provision
Otaka, a frontier fort that the Imagawa owed
to the treachery of its commander, who had
come to their side from Nobunaga. Otaka was
strategically very important, as Nobunaga had
built it at one end of a chain of five forts which
guarded his frontier. Ieyasu's approach was
careful and methodical. His men first attacked
the two forts at the far end of the line from
Otaka, making as much noise as they could.
The garrisons of the next two forts along sallied
out to help, leaving Otaka unguarded so that
Ieyasu was able to guide the pack horses into
Otaka with no opposition.

In July 1560 Imagawa Yoshimoto finally set
off to crush Nobunaga with about 25,000

samurai and *ashigaru*. The first obstacle was the
chain of forts. The Imagawa men took one,
Washizu, while Tokugawa Ieyasu was to attack
Marune. Once again Ieyasu showed his military
skill. He first made a sharp attack which was
repulsed with some loss. The commander of
Marune then opened the gates and charged out
at the withdrawing Tokugawa samurai, exactly
as Ieyasu had planned. He had lined up his
harquebusiers and archers to meet them. They
stopped the sally and also killed the commander
with a bullet. Immediately the Tokugawa
samurai counterattacked in force and burst in
through the gates before the garrison had time to
close them.

The capture of two forts was enough to open a
road into Nobunaga's province. The samurai
the Imagawa had assembled far outnumbered
Nobunaga's 2000, but with odds of 12 to one
against Nobunaga set out to meet them.

Ieyasu was resting in the fortress of Otaka.
Had he been with Yoshimoto it is possible that
the great disaster that was about to strike the
house of Imagawa could have been avoided. As
it was, Nobunaga's scouts brought him the news
that Yoshimoto's main body were resting in a
little valley near the village of Okehazama.
They were so elated that they were feasting and
drinking to further triumphs, with very little
guard on the camp. It was Nobunaga's opportunity to settle 60 years of daimyo rivalry.
He rigged up a dummy army of banners and
flags, then took as many samurai as he dared
risk in a forced march to behind the hills where
Yoshimoto was camping. It was territory which
Nobunaga knew from boyhood. The day was

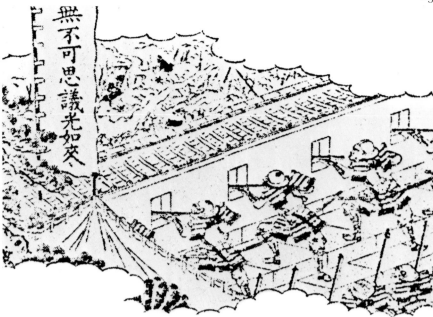

stiflingly hot and as Nobunaga's men drew near a violent thunderstorm began and concealed their final movements. As the rain ceased the Oda samurai poured into the gorge. Within a few minutes Imagawa Yoshimoto was dead and his army scattered.

Ieyasu was thus stranded in Otaka. He ascertained that Yoshimoto was actually dead and then withdrew to Okazaki, but prudently camped outside it, for although it was his own castle it had been largely garrisoned by Imagawa men. They soon withdrew to Sumpu, leaving Ieyasu, then 19, master of his own castle and samurai; a free man for the first time in his life.

He was, of course, free only to the extent that the defeat of the Imagawa, which the Tokugawa had avoided, had reversed the military positions of the two families. Yoshimoto had an heir, Ujizane, a very ineffectual man who preferred his samurai to know the good points of a tea bowl than the good points of military command, and Ieyasu was bound to him by his oath of allegiance. Ujizane also had a number of hostages in Sumpu. Ieyasu realized that the Imagawa's days were numbered whether he remained allied to them or not. As the Tokugawa were still not strong enough to operate on their own, the overtures Ieyasu was receiving from Nobunaga made very good sense. He also had to consider the threat from the northeast, the domain of Takeda Shingen, whose glee on the downfall of the Imagawa knew no bounds. So, in the face of fierce opposition from some of his senior advisers, Ieyasu decided to risk the lives of the hostages, leave Ujizane to his fate, and ally himself with Oda Nobunaga. Some hostages were indeed killed, but the alliance between the Oda and the Tokugawa was to prove one of the staunchest and most successful in the whole of the Age of War. It was a strange reversal of loyalties. Ieyasu was now allied to the son of the man who had kidnapped him at the age of six and threatened to kill him. Nobunaga himself had exchanged Ieyasu for the life of his brother, whom he later banished. That was Japan in the Age of War.

Above: The siege of the Ishiyama Hongan-ji. The monk soldiers of the Ikko-ikki were among the first large-scale users of firearms following their introduction by the Portuguese, and this woodcut indicates the firepower they possessed. A rank of soldiers with muskets at the ready stand prepared to take their comrades' places at the loopholes. The banner bears a Buddhist slogan. It was men such as these who held out against top-quality samurai for many years.

Left: This unusual helmet was owned by Tokugawa Ieyasu. It is known as the 'ichi-no-tani' style, from the battle of the same name in 1184. During the battle Yoshitsune led his army down a precipitous mountain path, and the helmet has the shape of a cliff edge.

CHAPTER 6

The Professionals

Previous page: *Detail from a painted screen depicting craftsmen. This particular section shows swordsmiths. The figure at the low bench is examining sword fittings and arrowheads. Note the completed blades stacked in the* tokonoma *(small alcove) in the far corner.*

The process of competition and conquest illustrated by the Oda, Tokugawa and Imagawa is but one instance of a process that was going on throughout Japan in the Age of War whereby the new local powers first consolidated the territories they had acquired, and then began to fight among themselves. The Oda took this process a stage further, the struggle for local hegemony grew into a struggle for national hegemony. Many of the most powerful *sengoku-daimyo* saw this as a possibility. Some, such as Takeda Shingen, clearly demonstrated that they had the administrative skills needed to rule a country and the military skills to achieve it. They were prevented from doing so by the presence of other great daimyo, or coalition of daimyo, who had the same idea. Any thrust toward Kyoto would create an opportunity for a local rival to seize the daimyo's own territory behind his back.

Thus for a considerable period of time any attempt at national control had to put aside for the business of increasing local control. From the 1530–60s most areas of Japan saw large-scale warfare similar to that between the Oda and the Imagawa, resulting in another metamorphosis of the daimyo. Few of the original *sengoku-daimyo* were to survive the fighting to come out on top as the large-scale warlords with greater capaci-

ties for military leadership and civil organization. Those who did have been termed the *shokuho-daimyo*. The *shokuho-daimyo* were the daimyo who were to survive into the Tokugawa period and retain their status, after much reorganization of fiefs and wealth, until 1869. An example is the Shimazu of Satsuma, who managed to make the transition from *shugo-daimyo* to *sengoku-daimyo*, and from thence to the summit of their power, which was to conquer the whole of Kyushu island as *shokuho-daimyo*.

The basis for the success of the *shokuho-daimyo* was their military prowess, so that it is not surprising to find that they depended far more upon a military-type organization of their samurai than the previous lord/vassal relationship. Nobunaga is probably the best example of this, but as his early career has already been described the example of Bizen Province will illustrate the process.

By the 1540s Bizen was split up between the Urakami and Matsuda *sengoku-daimyo*. The Urakami territory consisted of 172 separate fiefs held by 59 major vassals, each of whom had individually pledged allegiance to the Urakami. A further bond between the Urakami and its vassals was the time of kinship, as many vassals had married into the family over the years. The Matsuda had a similar arrangement, so that the vassals of Urakami and Matsuda occupied the 200 castles in Bizen whose remains exist to this day.

Ukita Hideie was one of these vassals. In 1545 he was given the command of a small fortress under the Urakami, a small fief of land nearby and 30 men. It is the relationship between Ukita and these men which is so different from that existing between the Urakami and Ukita. The men were not his vassals. He was in command of them as a military leader of professional soldiers. As they were not his vassals they did not own land, instead Ukita supported them from the proceeds of his land. The samurai were thus dependent upon him not only in the military sense of leadership, but also economically. Naturally enough, as Ukita's power and lands grew by conquest on the Urakami's behalf he had to appoint some of his senior samurai as keepers of outlying castles. This required some degree of lord/vassal relationship, but Ukita made sure that the risks of his domain splitting up were kept to a minimum by rotating commands frequently and periodically recalling his major vassals to his own castle. Also he made sure that the largest part of his army was always under his direct control and based on his castle. Such careful considerations ensured that by 1573 the fiefs he had received from the Urakami totalled one-tenth of the whole of Bizen, and he had a fighting strength of between 10–15,000 samurai

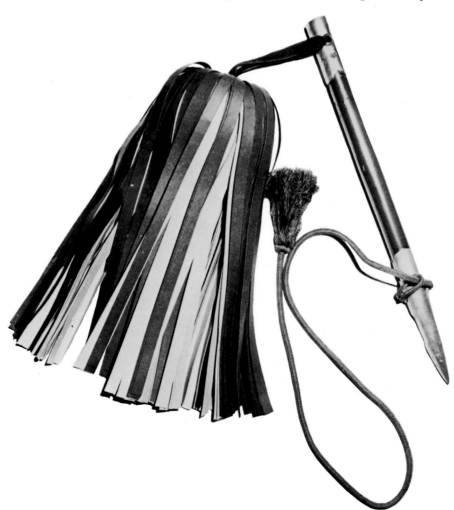

Below: *A* saihai *(commander's baton) was carried by high-ranking generals in the field. The tassels were made of oiled paper.*

and *ashigaru*; a substantial force.

This is similar to the relationship between the Ukita and Tokugawa Ieyasu. The Imagawa had taken control of the Tokugawa at a time of the Imagawa's weakness, and maintained it by keeping Ieyasu as hostage. Even when Ieyasu was allowed command of samurai on Imagawa's behalf he was kept on a long lead and was only free when Imagawa Yoshimoto was killed. The Urakami similarly depended on their vassals to fight battles on their behalf but allowed them a dangerous degree of freedom. In fact their vassals were sufficiently independent to make alliances with other daimyo outside the province. Ukita grew strong by such alliances, until, after destroying the other Urakami vassals for disciplinary reasons, he defeated the Matsuda, the main Urakami rivals. Then, seizing the opportunity provided by a succession dispute in the family, Ukita turned against the Urakami and took control of the whole Bizen province.

Ukita Hideie was then a *shokuho-daimyo*. He controlled the whole province from his castle town of Okayama and personally held lands valued at 400,000 *koku*. Land was the basis of wealth, so shortly after inheriting the province Ukita had it systematically surveyed. This ensured that 'hidden' fields could be properly taxed, and the boundaries between fiefs clarified. However, an entire province could not be defended from one castle so Ukita defended his borders by a number of subsidiary castles, each held by a samurai who was granted lands of 10,000 *koku*. To minimize the risk involved Ukita adopted the same system he had used when he was a minor vassal of the Urakami – he required them to reside in Okayama. As residence in the capital had been one reason for the Ashikaga downfall, Ukita made sure that the samurai left in charge of castles had an army-type relationship with their followers, with a minimum of family, kinship or locality ties. Also, as before, he kept the largest army to himself, and personally controlled a quarter of the lands. He could then afford to pay samurai to fight, to buy loyalty from them. The samurai had become professionals.

It was a logical development because only truly professional samurai maintained by their daimyo could be expected to give proper attention to the large campaigns that would now have to be fought. Whereas Takeda Shingen had been able to balance the military and agricultural use of his *ashigaru* and of some of his samurai too, domains were now large enough to permit a strict division of labor between the two operations. At the same time, as a domain grew, it was only by separating the samurai from the land that a daimyo could hope to maintain proper military and civil control over them. The

achievement of Nobunaga, and of smaller scale daimyo such as Ukita Hideie, was to produce a professional corps of samurai who did nothing but fight, while the farmers did nothing but till the land. The castle town was the major physical embodiment of this. In place of the mountain fortresses of the *sengoku-daimyo*, the new castles were built as the economic center of the domain. They were also very large so that, if necessary, a daimyo's entire army could be housed. Their massive stone walls encircled wide baileys to protect the garrison from harquebus and cannon fire. One surprising feature is the dramatic suddenness with which the process came about. In the 30 years between 1580–1610 Japan witnessed an amazingly active period of urban construction. Many of the castles which exist to this day, such as Himeji, Hikone, Kochi, Hiroshima, Okayama, Edo and Osaka, were built at this time by the *shokuho-daimyo*.

Those who had previously combined the professions of samurai and farmer were now forced to choose between them or, more fre-

Above: *The unfortunate wounded man prepares to receive the attentions of his comrades. Note the rice bags tied round the torso of the* ashigaru *on the right, and the harquebus on the ground inside a waterproof carrying case.*

Below: *An* ashigaru *brings water to his master's horse, using his helmet as a makeshift bucket. The horse's front legs are tied together with what appears to be a band of cloth.*

quently, told which they were going to be. Chosokabe Motochika (1539–99), the author of the 100-article house code, was one daimyo forced to face this problem. He had risen to power in Shikoku island on the shoulders of part-time samurai, for reasons of sheer economic necessity. It had moved Tokugawa Ieyasu to see his samurai forced to work in the fields for the Imagawa but for the poorer Chosokabe such work was fully accepted and carried no slur. These rustic samurai were known as *ichiryo gusoku*, because that is what they possessed, 'one fief and one suit of armor.' They were essentially rough-and-ready characters, whose armor came to pieces where the plates were laced together. The only thing they prized was courage in battle, and it is said of them that when they were working in the paddy fields they stuck their spears into the ridges between the irrigated sections and fastened their sandals to the shafts, so they could be ready to fight at a moment's notice. During the wars within Shikoku they had been pitted against their counterparts from neighboring provinces and their fighting spirit had carried all before them, but they met their match in the professionals from the mainland.

Once confirmed in his holdings Chosokabe began to build up a professional army of his own to match the samurai who had defeated him. It was a difficult process as the *ichiryo gusoku* clung tenaciously to their original land holdings, and were most reluctant to move to the splendid

Above: *Okayama Castle, or 'Castle of the Crow,' was originally the seat of Ukita Hideie, one of the most successful of the 'professionals.' With the establishment of the Tokugawa Shogunate it became the property of the Ikeda.*

Left: *A distant view of Okayama castle, showing the use made of the natural defenses afforded by the river.*

new castle of Kochi which Chosokabe had founded. Their main problem was financial, hence the clause in the 100-article code permitting the *ichiryo gusoku* to give up samurai status for that of farmer if they could not afford the move. By the end of the sixteenth century the professional warrior corps was far from completion. The growth of Kochi was much less than Chosokabe desired, and a large number of *ichiryo gusoku* remained, in contrast to the development of the samurai in other parts of Japan.

The background to the historical narrative which continues from Nobunaga's victory of Okehazama is therefore the growth of the samurai as professional soldiers, based on castle towns and organized totally on military lines. The lord/vassal oath now exists only as a means of absorbing large existing daimyo domains covering provinces until, with Nobunaga's successor, Toyotomi Hideyoshi, one daimyo achieves national hegemony. Hideyoshi controlled the whole of Japan just as Ukita Hideie had controlled Bizen.

Toyotomi Hideyoshi, the second of the 'Great Unifiers' of Japan, fought at the Battle of Okehazama, the short but decisive engagement by which Oda Nobunaga crushed the Imagawa and gained his most valuable ally. Hideyoshi's background was very different from either Nobunaga's or Ieyasu's. He was not a *sengoku-daimyo* nor an heir held hostage but the son of a peasant woodcutter, who had run away from the temple where he was being trained as a monk to enlist in an army as an *ashigaru*. He subsequently absconded from his first master and joined Nobunaga, again as an *ashigaru*, in 1558. Nobunaga had an eye for talent, and Hideyoshi rapidly rose through the ranks. In 1559 he married (legend has it that he was so poor that his wedding garments were made out of Nobunaga's old battle flags) and by the time of Okahazama had achieved a position of some responsibility.

Okehazama not only quelled the Imagawa, it also showed that Oda Nobunaga was a commander of the highest quality. He had already begun the process of the division of labor between samurai and farmer that was to characterize the age and, with the help of Tokugawa Ieyasu, he was in an excellent position to succeed where Imagawa had failed and march on Kyoto.

It may be asked why such a move was considered necessary, as the mere existence of *shokuho-daimyo* demonstrated that the shogunate had no power of its own, and surely none to convey to another. In fact, even though the shogun was powerless he was symbolically very significant, and a daimyo seeking large-scale hegemony by military conquest had to legitimize his position. Thus, in 1558 when the daimyo Uesugi Kenshin (1530–1578) was planning to seize the Kanto provinces (around present-day Tokyo) from the Hojo and Takeda, he first visited Kyoto to be invested with the title of

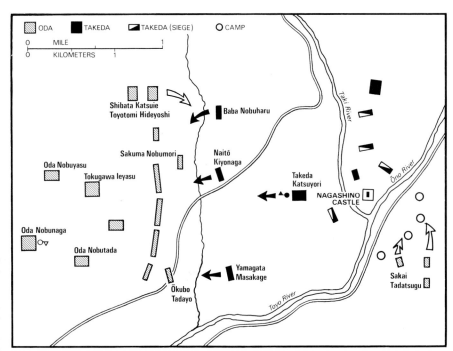

ODA   TAKEDA   TAKEDA (SIEGE)   CAMP

0   MILE   1
0   KILOMETERS   1

Shibata Katsuie
Toyotomi Hideyoshi

Baba Nobuharu

Taki River

Sakuma Nobumori

Naitō
Kiyonaga

Ōno River

Oda Nobuyasu

Tokugawa Ieyasu

Takeda
Katsuyori

NAGASHINO
CASTLE

Oda Nobunaga

Oda Nobutada

Yamagata
Masakage

Ōkubo
Tadayo

Toyo River

Sakai
Tadatsugu

Kanto kanrei, Governor General of the Kanto. This title dated from the *shugo* era and had long ceased to have any meaning. Similarly, when Ukita Hideie won Bizen he received a legal authority for his actions from the Mori, who had been *shugo* under the Ashikaga.

To achieve this legitimacy, and to use Kyoto as a central base for further conquests, Nobunaga had first to secure his rear. Here Tokugawa Ieyasu was his main guarantor. Nobunaga consolidated his defense by marrying his daughter to Takeda Shingen's son. In 1564 Hideyoshi defeated the Saito of Mino for Nobunaga, and the road to the capital was open. Once again a succession dispute in the Ashikaga provided the excuse for a warlord to take over and on 9 November 1568 Oda Nobunaga entered Kyoto in triumph, accompanied by Ashikaga Yoshiaki, shortly to become the fifteenth and last Ashikaga shogun.

The city which Nobunaga entered had been entirely rebuilt since the devastation of the Onin War. The spirit of cooperation that had kept the members of the *machi* together in the face of *ikki* attacks and civil-war street fighting had enabled them to restore the capital to its former eminence and to achieve a remarkable degree of self-government within the city. At its peak in the 1530s representatives of the townsmen were in effect fulfilling the functions of a city government in a coalition of class interests. The coalition even included impoverished nobles who had fled from the worst of the Onin fighting. Nobunaga's entry ended all this. He installed Ashikaga Yoshiaki as shogun and rebuilt the shogun and Imperial Palaces, but within five years his differences with Yoshiaki became pronounced. In 1573 Nobunaga submitted a list of 17 articles which contained the ways in which the shogun administration ought to be reformed. This wounded Yoshiaki's dignity and he approached Takeda Shingen to rid him of Nobunaga. Nobunaga was warned of the plot and, as Shingen was being constantly watched by the faithful Ieyasu, Nobunaga seized the shogun and imprisoned him in a distant castle. The Ashikaga shogunate thus came to an ignominious end.

As he was not descended from the Minamoto Nobunaga was unable to take the title of shogun for himself, but it is doubtful if such an omission greatly disturbed this ruthless warlord. As if inspired by his de facto position as ruler of Japan Nobunaga accelerated his campaigns. He defeated the Asai and the Asakura, two daimyo who had given him great trouble, began a major blockade of the Ishiyama Hongan-ji, the headquarters of the *Ikko-ikki* (an army of warrior monks) and reached the peak of his military career with the famous Battle of Nagashino in

1575, which may be regarded as the first major victory of 'the professionals.'

Takeda Shingen, one of the ablest *shokuho-*

Above: *A map showing the Siege and Battle of Nagashino, 1575, Oda Nobunaga's most celebrated victory. The final charge by the Takeda cavalry is shown.*

Left: *Torii Suneemon, who escaped from the besieged castle to warn Nobunaga, but was captured by the Takeda and crucified. A Takeda samurai had this banner painted of him. Suneemon is depicted in red, on a brown cross, on a white background.*

Above: *A samurai with a large-caliber musket known as a wall-gun. Some varieties fired wooden rocket-shaped projectiles.*

daimyo, died in 1573, to Nobunaga's immense relief, after being hit by a bullet during a siege of one of Ieyasu's castles. His son Katsuyori was brave enough but lacked his father's enormous talents. The showdown between the Takeda and the Oda came about as the result of a siege of Nagashino castle in Mikawa, Ieyasu's territory. In June 1575 Takeda Katsuyori moved into Mikawa and laid siege to Nagashino, which was set in a naturally strong position at the confluence of two rivers. The castle managed to hold out against the Takeda attacks but supplies of food and ammunition were rapidly running out, so a samurai called Torii Suneemon slipped out of the castle and managed to get a message to Ieyasu in Okazaki requesting help. Unfortunately for Torii he was captured by the Takeda, who crucified him by the bank of the river opposite the castle walls. His bravery, though, did not go unregarded by either side, and one of Takeda Katsuyori's samurai was so impressed that he had a war banner made showing Torii fastened to the cross.

The relief of Nagashino was an opportunity for Nobunaga to settle the Takeda once and for all. Accordingly he personally led 30,000 troops and was joined by Ieyasu with a further 8000. As Katsuyori only had 15,000 men altogether he would have been wise to withdraw to his own province, and this was the course of action which his senior samurai advised him to take, but the young daimyo was set on a battle. As the Takeda had been used to fighting in the flat plain of the Kanto they had developed their mounted troops to a point of perfection and a cavalry charge of Takeda samurai, their long spears swinging, had become a decisive weapon. This was the threat facing Nobunaga's professionals, and the manner in which he faced it made a turning point in Japanese military history.

He chose a strong position from which he could receive the charge and instead of advancing toward the castle to meet the Takeda he constructed a palisade across the broken ground to the foot of Mount Gambo, leaving a narrow stream between him and the enemy. Gaps were left in the palisade every 50 yards or so for counterattack. From his 10,000 harquebusiers he detached the 3000 best shots, and lined them up behind the palisade in three ranks. This was probably the first time that *ashigaru* had been given such a prominent place in any battle, demonstrating very clearly the discipline that Nobunaga had over his army. As the Takeda charged in the *ashigaru* brought the horsemen crashing down with volleys of harquebus fire. Most accounts of the battle credit Nobunaga with ordered firing according to rank, one group firing while the others reloaded. Such an arrangement would put Nobunaga's army a

Above: *Toyotomi Hideyoshi, one of the greatest samurai leaders in Japanese history.*

good hundred years ahead of any other army in the world, and it is by no means beyond the bounds of possibility that he did it.

Nagashino thus showed that Nobunaga was at the forefront of military technology. In a similar way the castle he built the following year also demonstrated the power of the man. Azuchi castle was designed, like Ukita's Okayama, to be a central command post for the territory. Azuchi differed from all other castles built up to that time in that it was designed to control the whole country, and was thus as much a palace as a fortress. It was built outside Kyoto, on a 600-feet high promontory jutting into Lake Biwa. On top of this was built a seven-storey keep, surrounded by monumental walls. In the same way that the Golden Pavilion symbolized the rule and character of Ashikaga Yoshimitsu, Azuchi stood for Nobunaga, and like the Higashiyama culture of the great shogun, the castle gave its name to another flowering of Japanese art, the Azuchi-Momoyama. It may seem strange that a daimyo as completely a soldier as Nobunaga could be an enthusiastic patron of the arts, but this was one expression of his personality. Momoyama taste was exotic and flamboyant, the perfect expression of the most complete ruler of Japan since Yoshimitsu. Nobunaga allocated his conquered domains. The daimyo who had yielded were enfieffed on swearing loyalty, and his trusted followers given the castles of the defeated warriors as a prize.

By 1577 Nobunaga was sufficiently secure in central Japan to undertake the major campaign of subduing the west, along the coast of the Inland Sea. The territories were chiefly held by Ukita Hideie and the very strong Mori family. The task was entrusted to Hideyoshi and the campaign proved long and costly, until in 1582 Hideyoshi had to request reinforcements from Nobunaga. Nobunaga prepared to set out in July and dispatched a large part of his army on ahead, leaving himself with a small force of about 300 samurai. While resting for the night at the Honniji temple in Kyoto he was attacked by one of his own generals, Akechi Mitsuhide, and slain in the burning temple.

Nobunaga had controlled about a third of Japan at the time of his death and there were only two daimyo in the whole of Japan who were possibly strong enough to inherit Nobunaga's domains – Hideyoshi and Ieyasu. Upon hearing the news of Nobunaga's murder Hideyoshi hastily agreed peace terms with the Mori and hurried back to Kyoto to become Nobunaga's avenger. This he achieved with great rapidity, vanquishing Akechi Mitsuhide

Below: *The author is indebted to Dr Sokichi Tokoro of Tokyo, for supplying the original illustration from which this photograph has been taken, as it has long been a mystery how cannons were mounted for use. This example is set in a pile of rice-straw bales stuffed with sand. The Japanese never really developed cannon, preferring to use those they obtained from the Europeans.*

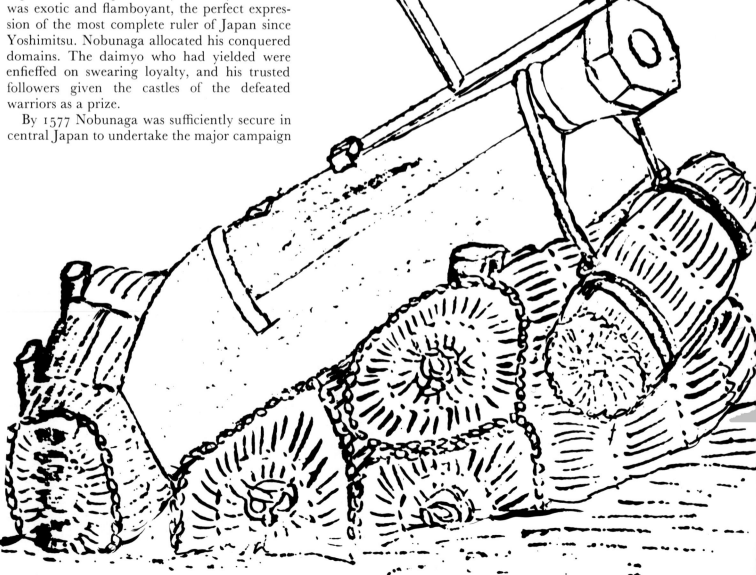

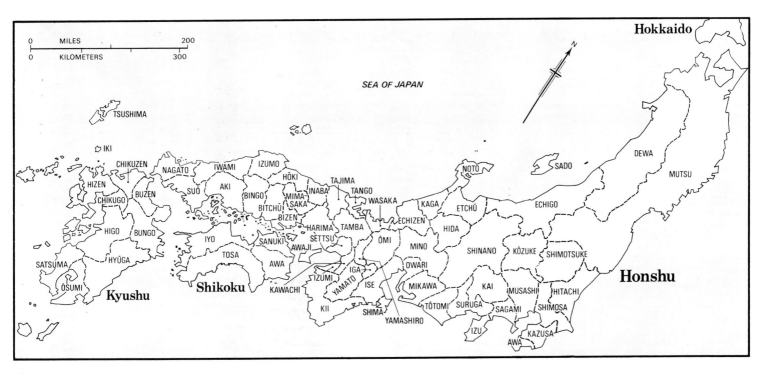

Above: *A map showing the premodern provinces of Japan circa 1580.*

at the Battle of Yamazaki just 13 days after Nobunaga's assassination. Hideyoshi then occupied a position of major importance in the council to determine Nobunaga's successor. The decision reached was that the heir should be Nobunaga's one-year-old grandson, a decision that effectively gave control straight to Hideyoshi.

He thus continued the process Nobunaga had started, but with one important difference. Hideyoshi's approach was characterized by his liberality to defeated enemies. The bond of lord and vassal was always a tenuous one, particularly when forced on a defeated enemy. The example of Akechi Mitsuhide was a prime example of how trust could be misplaced, and even the military general/soldier relationship had been breached in this case. Hideyoshi therefore sought to make gratitude the basis for loyalty if at all possible. All his future conquests had this aim in view, of winning genuine gratitude that would positively guarantee loyalty. He did everything possible to make obstinate enemies side with him. All the time the approach was backed up with force, the force of the best-organized samurai armies that Japan had yet seen. Hideyoshi added to Nobunaga's disciplined professionals an excellent eye for strategy. It was a wide-scale strategy that looked at the whole of the map of Japan at once, so that one by one the *shokuho-daimyo* would be persuaded, coerced or crushed into professing a vow of allegiance, making all Japan Hideyoshi's domain.

As early as 1583 Hideyoshi was looking toward unification, as indicated in a private letter to the daughter of Maeda Toshiie, though no doubt the information was intended for her father. He envisaged two processes that would compliment his purely military exploits. One was the redistribution of fiefs according to

loyalty and services rendered, as Ukita had done in Bizen, the second was the reduction in the number of castles. By 1584 it was clear that the only real opposition to Hideyoshi in central Japan was Tokugawa Ieyasu, who was now a *shokuho-daimyo* of five provinces. To his own Mikawa he had added Totomi and Suruga, the former lands of the Imagawa, and the defeat of the Takeda which he had completed after Nagashino had given him the territories of Kai and Shinano.

The two former comrades in arms thus gathered their forces for a major clash of arms. One factor was decisive in preventing it. Both leaders had fought at Nagashino and its lessons of well-defended, disciplined troops against traditional samurai dash had not been lost on either of them. As a result both armies took the defensive and built earthworks and palisades opposite each other near the village of Komaki. From these positions the two armies stared at each other like soldiers in a World War I trench system, neither daring to make a frontal attack against the firepower the other could bring to bear. It was a situation that could not last for long and eventually contingents from both armies left the Komaki positions, chased each other round the province for a few days and finally fought a grand-style pitched samurai battle at Nagakute. Hideyoshi's troops came off decidedly worse, though Hideyoshi himself was not with them. After a few months of stalemate, during which allies of both commanders fought in other parts of the country, an understanding was reached between Hideyoshi and Ieyasu, and the latter submitted and pledged his allegiance. He had every reason to. It was obvious even in 1584 that there would be trouble over Hideyoshi's successor once the great man died, and Ieyasu would be the natural one to pick up the pieces.

Between 1582–86 Hideyoshi built Osaka castle, an enormous sprawling fortress whose outer walls measured nine miles in circumference. With this as his base, and Ieyasu pledged to good behavior, he had enough confidence to continue the conquest of Japan. He first turned against the remaining armies of warrior monks, completing the subjugation which Nobunaga had begun. From this time on there would be no further armed confrontation between the Buddhist clergy and the ruling powers. In 1585 he conquered Shikoku island, then controlled by Chosokabe Motochika and his part-time *ichiryo gusoku*.

Two years later Hideyoshi began the largest campaign of his career to date – the conquest of the southern island of Kyushu. By 1587 the Shimazu of Satsuma had subjugated nearly the whole of Kyushu and were in arms against the combined forces of two daimyo, the Otomo and the Arima who had been asking Hideyoshi to help for several years. It was only when Otomo Sorin went personally to Osaka to beg Hideyoshi to intervene that he decided the time was ripe. He sent a message to Shimazu Yoshihisa ordering him to withdraw to Satsuma. The letter provoked an indignant reply, contrasting the Shimazu's long rule in Satsuma and their unique achievement of metamorphosis from *shugo* to *shokuho-daimyo* with Hideyoshi's very humble origins.

The invasion force consisted of three armies. Two armies crossed from Honshu to Kyushu across the narrow Shimonoseki Straits, the third was a contingent from Chosokabe Motochika in Shikoku, his submission to Hideyoshi being complete. The Kyushu campaign was a personal tragedy for Motochika for his son was killed by the Shimazu army. The grief-stricken Motochika prepared to commit suicide until he received a message from the victorious Shimazu, 'We regret exceedingly to have killed your son in yesterday's engagement. Meanwhile we realize how difficult it is to get to your boats over the quicksand. Wait patiently till the tide comes in. We wish you a safe return.'

The total army mustered by Hideyoshi came to about 200,000 men, a colossal number to transport, arm and feed. Slowly the forces advanced down Kyushu, pushing the Shimazu before them, but what had perhaps seemed an easy task turned out to be extremely difficult at times. The Shimazu knew the terrain and even at the last moment of the campaign, when the Shimazu were considering Hideyoshi's surrender terms, the issue was in doubt. Hideyoshi's huge army was bogged down by the rainy season and was forced to halt while the negotiations took place. Difficulties with supply and illness among the samurai all contributed to an unusually low morale, so Hideyoshi asked one of his daimyo, Takayama Ukon, to work out an escape route if the Shimazu did not surrender. As it happened the Shimazu had overestimated the size of Hideyoshi's army and capitulated only five days before the deadline Hideyoshi had set himself for withdrawal.

In 1589 Hideyoshi began the final military campaign of his unification program. The target was the Hojo, who ruled the rice bowl of the Kanto from their castle of Odawara behind the natural barrier of the Hakone Mountains. The Kanto was eastern Japan, the land of the brave samurai enshrined in all the chivalric epics. Hideyoshi therefore began preparations that were on as large a scale as the Kyushu campaign. Supplies, including 200,000 *koku* of rice, were to be conveyed by sea.

The Hojo leaders decided on a siege. Odawara castle was large and well stocked with guns, so the Hojo recalled most of their samurai from outlying castles back to this central strongpoint. This of course laid all the other Hojo castles open to easy conquest, and Hideyoshi's army quickly destroyed the entire Hojo power structure. Then they proceeded to sit down in front of Odawara until the Hojo were starved into submission. Perhaps Hideyoshi remembered the difficult times his army had in Kyushu because he decided right from the start that besieging Odawara was to be as pleasant an exercise as possible. He transferred part of his court to the temporary town which constituted the camp, and the samurai were entertained by prostitutes, musicians, dancers, actors, sumo wrestlers and merchants selling their wares. The samurai were also invited to bring their wives along and grew their own vegetables in little gardens. Beyond this noisy and happy scene lay a ring of walls and two moats encircling the besieged city, which made a striking contrast to the gaiety outside. Hideyoshi wrote to his wife that he had shut the Hojo up like a 'bird in a bird cage.'

It was a successful strategy and after Hideyoshi's patient waiting the Hojo surrendered. Not long afterward Hideyoshi received the homage of the Date of Uesugi, the daimyo of the northern part of Japan, and the unification was complete. Like Nobunaga, Hideyoshi was unable to take the title of shogun but used the rank of regent instead.

Hideyoshi's domestic policy was as thorough as his military campaigns. His aim was political stability, in particular ensuring the succession of his infant son Hideyori, who was born in 1593. Hideyoshi's other main political consideration was to ensure that where he had led, in the rise from peasant *ashigaru* to ruler of Japan, none should follow. The result was an act that defined more clearly than ever the different roles of the samurai and farmer. Nobunaga and his contemporaries had begun the trend of settling the samurai in the castle towns. Hideyoshi extended it by disarming the peasantry. The 'sword hunt' edict, as it is called, was proclaimed in 1588. Its objective was the collection of all weapons of every type from the nonsamurai classes. Needless to say, the edict was dressed up in pious invocations, pointing out how the possession of unnecessary weapons leads to unrest and war and interrupts agriculture. The farmers were told that, freed from the danger of these weapons, they would feel secure not only in this world but also in the next, for all the swords collected were to be melted down and used to make nails and bolts for the construction of a giant statue of Buddha. Thus phenomena such as *ikki* riots by armed bands were effectively brought to an end, and henceforth the wearing of two swords was the exclusive badge of the professional military class – the samurai.

Unfortunately, the later years of Hideyoshi saw a deep decline in his health and behavior. In 1592 he launched an army of samurai to attack Korea, and then, it was planned, China. The operation was in marked contrast to his earlier triumphs in Kyushu and the Kanto. The initial invasion was marred by disagreements and rivalries between the commanders, particularly on the question of who was to gain the merit of being first into battle. It was only the weakness of the Korean army compared to the Japanese professionals that allowed the invading

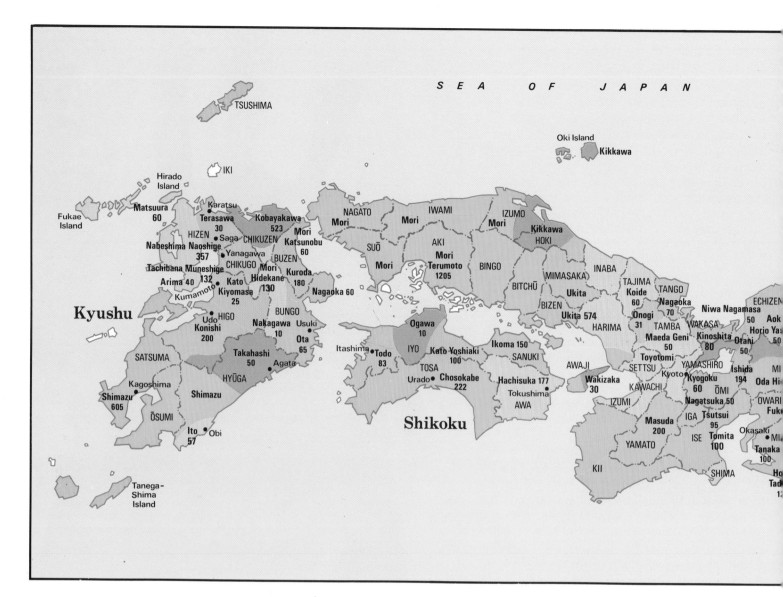

SEA OF JAPAN

TSUSHIMA

Oki Island
Kikkawa

Hirado
Island
IKI

Fukae
Island

Matsuura
60
Karatsu
Terasawa
30
Kobayakawa
523
Mori
HIZEN
Saga
CHIKUZEN
Katsunobu
60
Nabeshima Naoshige
357
Yanagawa
BUZEN
Tachibana Muneshige
CHIKUGO Mori
Kuroda
180
Arima 40 132
Kato
Hidekane
130
Nagaoka 60
Kumamoto
Kiyomasa
25

Kyushu
Udo HIGO
Konishi
200
BUNGO
Nakagawa Usuki
10
Ota
65

NAGATO
Mori
IWAMI
Mori
IZUMO
Mori
Kikkawa
HOKI

SUŌ
AKI
Mori
Terumoto
1205
BINGO
MIMASAKA
INABA
TAJIMA
Koide
60
TANGO
Nagaoka
70
Niwa Nagamasa
ECHIZEN

BITCHŪ
Ukita
Onogi
31
TAMBA
WAKASA
Aok
50
Horio Yas

BIZEN
Ukita 574
HARIMA
Maeda Geni
Kinoshita
80
Otani
50

Takahashi
50
Agata
Itashima
Todo
83
Ogawa
10
IYO
Kato Yoshiaki
100
Ikoma 150
SANUKI
Toyotomi
AWAJI
SETTSU
YAMASHIRO
Kyoto
Kyogoku
60
ÖMI
Ishida
194
MI
Oda Hi

HYŪGA
SATSUMA
Kagoshima
Shimazu
TOSA
Urado
Chosokabe
222
Hachisuka 177
Tokushima 50
AWA
Wakizaka
30
IZUMI
KAWACHI
Nagatsuka 50
Tsutsui
95
IGA
OWARI
Fuk

Shimazu
605
ŌSUMI
Shimazu
Shikoku
Masuda
200
YAMATO
ISE
Tomita
100
Tanaka
100
Okazaki
Mi

Ito
57
Obi
KII
SHIMA
Ho
Tad

Tanega-
Shima
Island

force to strike deeply through Korea with little opposition. After this initial success the entire operation ground to a halt near the Chinese border, as well-armed ships of the Korean navy sank Japanese troopships and cut the army's lines of communication. With little support from home and in the face of fierce attacks from China, which had rallied to Korea's defense, the Japanese were driven back to the southern tip of the country, leaving small garrisons behind while peace talks went on.

It can only have been as a result of mental imbalance coupled with growing megalomania that led Hideyoshi to launch a second invasion in 1597. This was even less successful than the first, but the samurai were spared a long war by Hideyoshi's death in 1598. The troops were recalled immediately.

Hideyoshi shares with Nobunaga the distinction of being the guiding light of the cultural flowering known as Azuchi-Momoyama. Like Nobunaga, Hideyoshi's undertakings in the field of art and architecture were on as grand a scale as his military campaigns. The two pivotal buildings, the Jurakudai – or 'Mansion of Pleasures' – and Fushimi castle, no longer survive but sufficient architecture has been preserved to indicate the scope of the flamboyant

Momoyama taste. Among these examples are the karamon gate in the Daitokuji temple, to where it was transferred on the destruction of Fushimi, and the interior screens and walls of the Jurakudai which are to be found in the Nishi-Honganji. The most noticeable feature is the lavish use of gold. The extant examples are splendid but manage to avoid the vulgarity of works such as Hideyoshi's tea room in Osaka castle where the shelves and even the tea utensils were of pure gold. A characteristic medium in Momoyama art was the painted screen, notably those painted by the Kano school, where brilliant color is used so skillfully

Above: *The site of the Battle of Sekigahara, 1600.*

Right: *A felon is apprehended by the use of dark lanterns. The dark lantern contained a source of light on a swivel, and the inside was highly polished.*

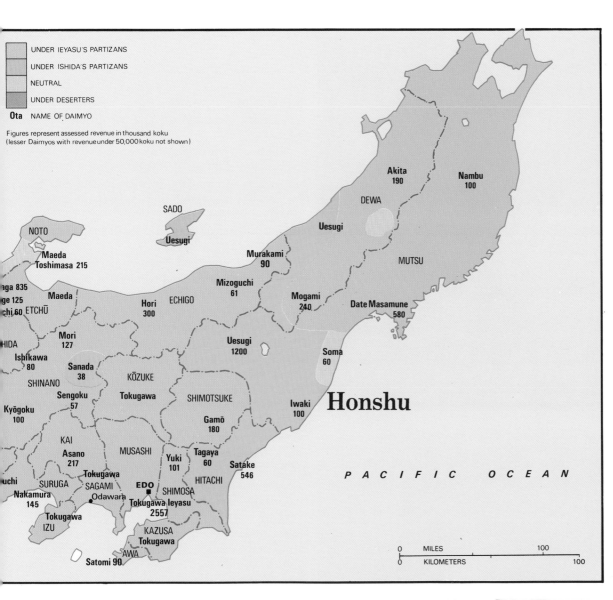

UNDER IEYASU'S PARTIZANS
UNDER ISHIDA'S PARTIZANS
NEUTRAL
UNDER DESERTERS

Ota NAME OF DAIMYO

Figures represent assessed revenue in thousand koku
(lesser Daimyos with revenue under 50,000 koku not shown)

Akita
190

Nambu
100

DEWA

SADO
Uesugi

NOTO

**Maeda
Toshimasa 215**

Murakami
90

MUTSU

aga 835

ge 125

chi 60 ETCHŪ

Maeda

Mizoguchi
61

Hori
300

ECHIGO

Mogami
240

Date Masamune
580

HIDA

Mori
127

Uesugi
1200

Soma
60

Ishikawa
80

Sanada
38

KŌZUKE

SHINANO

Tokugawa

SHIMOTSUKE

Iwaki
100

Honshu

Kyōgoku
100

Sengoku
57

Gamō
180

KAI

Asano
217

MUSASHI

Yuki
101

Tagaya
60

Satake
546

uchi

SURUGA

Tokugawa

EDO

SAGAMI

Nakamura
145

Odawara

SHIMOSA

HITACHI

**Tokugawa Ieyasu
2557**

Tokugawa
IZU

KAZUSA
Tokugawa

AWA

Satomi 90

PACIFIC OCEAN

| 0 | MILES | 100 |
| 0 | KILOMETERS | 100 |

Left: *Japan at the time of
Sekigahara.*

Below: *The battle flag of
Tsugaru Tamenobu, who
fought with Ieyasu at the
Battle of Sekigahara, where
this banner was used. After
the battle Ieyasu increased his
revenue considerably.*

Above: *This form of drum was mounted in a frame and carried on a man's back while another used the drumsticks. The particular example shown here, from Fushimi Momoyama Castle, was used at the Battle of Sekigahara.*

Right: *A Korean helmet, brought back as a souvenir from the Korean War. The 'earflaps' are of red, studded leather, and it is ornamented with a peacock's feather.*

that it enchants rather than repels. Hideyoshi was also lavish in his entertainment. An adept at the tea ceremony, he often let his enthusiasm get the better of its essential simplicity. He was fond of mammoth-sized flower viewing parties, and held a great tea ceremony in Kitano in 1587 attended by hundreds.

The death of Hideyoshi left a power vacuum every bit as serious as the death of Nobunaga had done. Toyotomi Hideyori was only five years old when his father died and although the evidence suggests that Hideyoshi was gradually losing his reason as the end approached, he was sufficiently in control of his faculties to appoint a board of five regents to administer during the boy's minority. The group was soon dominated by Tokugawa Ieyasu, who knew his hour had finally come. All that was needed was some pretext for war and this came in mid-1600

through the plotting of the daimyo Ishida Mitsunari, who formed a coalition against Ieyasu.

The coalition's plan was to draw the Tokugawa away from the Osaka/Kyoto region by a diversionary revolt of the Uesugi in the north of Japan. But Ieyasu's cunning was the equal of any rival. When Uesugi's revolt began he headed north, calmly letting the Ishida faction take control of Osaka. Ieyasu's gamble was based on two strong points. First, he believed that his allies in the north could hold Uesugi in check with no difficulty. This was to prove to be true. Second, as Ieyasu moved north he moved toward his own territories where he could easily organize an army and arouse little suspicion, which would not be the case if he sent summonses from Osaka. The danger was that Ishida would secure such a firm power base in the Osaka/Kyoto region while Ieyasu was away that he could not break it on his return.

Ieyasu's strategy for avoiding this depended upon the lines of communication from the east of Kyoto. There were two roads: the Tokaido, along the coast, and the Nakasendo through the mountains. At their closest, near the village of Sekigahara, the two roads were about 20 miles apart and this jugular vein was guarded by a number of castles. Whichever army held these castles could control the progress of traffic toward the capital.

So when Ieyasu returned from Edo in force his initial aim was these castles. Ishida had to be drawn out of the mighty Osaka, because a pitched battle would give the Tokugawa the best chance of success. As things turned out, the threat to the castles produced the second effect also: not only did Ishida march along the mountain road to meet Ieyasu, he also extended his advance too far. On the night of 20 October he was forced to withdraw to positions on the hills around Sekigahara. There were high winds and driving rain and the morning of 21 October proved to be almost as dark as the night because all of the Sekigahara valley was hidden in thick fog. By 0800 hours the fog lifted to reveal two enormous armies of samurai facing each other. The largest battle ever fought between samurai was about to begin.

In the narrow confines of the valley the battle developed into a huge, muddy melee, in which neither side appeared to have the upper hand. This was dramatically changed by the treachery of the Kobayakawa samurai, who held Ishida's right flank. As the battle hung in the balance they entered the fray on the side of the Tokugawa. It was the decisive factor. Ishida's troops broke, and the Tokugawa professionals won the day. The united country which Hideyoshi had conquered was now Ieyasu's.

Castles: Strongholds of the Daimyo

By far the largest memorials of the age of the samurai left in Japan today are the score or so castles built by the feudal barons, or 'daimyo.' Most have been carefully and lovingly restored to give the visitor a glimpse of life in those bygone times.

The surviving castles are examples of the final and most perfect phase of fortress building in medieval Japan. During the fourteenth century castles were little more than wooden stockades, rather like the forts of the American Wild West. As the need grew to strengthen defenses, stone was incorporated in their buildings, and the sites chosen carefully, such as at the confluence of rivers, or on the top of an hill. By the end of the sixteenth century however, the castle, with its surrounding castle town, was becoming the economic center of the daimyo's territory, so the castle which was built to replace simpler mountain fortresses was situated on the main trade route through a province, and built large enough for the entire samurai army to be enclosed within its walls.

As the sites for these new castles may not have possessed such striking natural defensive features as their predecessors, castles were built high and wide. The central defensive work, the keep, was often raised on a large earth mound, faced with huge blocks of stone, some as long as 10 meters, each fitting closely to the other without the need for mortar. As a result the foundations formed sloped out toward the ground, which had the disadvantage of being fairly easy to scale. This disadvantage could be largely outweighed by incorporating numerous trapdoors through which rocks could be dropped and boiling water poured.

The buildings raised on the stone-faced mound are invariably of wood, designed in almost a fairy-tale manner, with huge sweeping eaves of purest white or somber black, topped with curving roofs of blue tiles, and set off with bronze ornamental dolphins.

Castles served to deter an attacker as much by the wealth they displayed as by their impregnability. This ostentation was continued indoors, with the wealthier castles displaying rich fine woods and painted screens symbolizing the importance of its owner. Nor were military needs forgotten. For example, in the majestic Himeji we find rack upon rack of mounts for spears and guns, and space for storing months worth of supplies should a neighbor be rash enough to try his strength by assaulting such a palace.

Below: A winter's day at Tsuruga castle, scene of one of the final acts of resistance by supporters of the Shogun following the Meiji Restoration. The conflict was finally resolved in September 1868.

Above: *Fushimi Momoyama Castle, rebuilt this century.*

Top: *Matsumoto Castle, built in 1594, and the seat of the Ishikawa and Toda daimyo, among others.*

Top right: *An engraving, probably Dutch, giving a good indication of the size of*

Hideyoshi's immense fortress of Osaka, completed in 1586.

Right: *Hideyoshi's audience chamber, formerly at Fushimi Castle, now part of a Kyoto temple.*

Opposite: *The keep of Osaka Castle looming over the steep sides of the moat walls.*

Above: *This bridge crosses the third and last of the moats that surround Hikone Castle.*

Above right: *The battlements of Kochi Castle, on the island of Shikoku. Note the characteristic tiles, and the loophole for guns or arrows.*

Right: *The keep of Hikone Castle. Hikone Castle, on the shores of Lake Biwa, is among the finest extant specimens of the Japanese castle. It was started by Ii Naokatsu in 1603, and became the residence of his brother Ii Naotaka in 1623.*

Far right, top: *The walls of Himeji Castle, known as 'The Castle of White Heron.' It is perhaps the most magnificent castle to have survived to our day. It was constructed during the period of intensive castle building at the beginning of the seventeenth century, and thereby exhibits an almost perfect defensive system, every gate and passageway being dominated by defensive works above.*

Far right: *The approach to Himeji Castle. Even from this far distance the keep appears to dominate any potential adversary. The castle owes its splendor to Hideyoshi, who captured the original fortress in 1577, and then rebuilt the powerful and graceful edifice seen today.*

CHAPTER 7

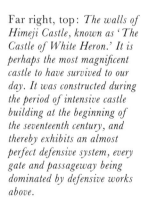

Great Peace Throughout the Land

Previous page: *Justice in Tokugawa Japan. The prisoner kneels in the road as his charge is read. There were different laws for different social classes, but justice was always administered by the samurai. Under certain circumstances a samurai could literally get away with murder, by claiming the right to cut down a lower-class person who had offended him.*

From 1600 until the passing of the samurai during the latter half of the nineteenth century the history of Japan is dominated by one name – Tokugawa. It was the achievement of Tokugawa Ieyasu and his successors to give Japan two-and-a-half centuries of peace and stability. After the years of civil strife that had preceded it, this must be regarded as quite an achievement.

Tokugawa Ieyasu's aim was to perpetuate his family's rule. He therefore instituted a severe but very subtle form of control over rivals that kept them firmly in their place. At the same time he made full use of the institutions of localized daimyo government which had been built up during the Age of War and which were functioning well. The result was a method of government called the *baku-han* system, a combination of *bakufu*, the shogunate, and *han*, the domains of the individual daimyo.

To back up his system Ieyasu had three vital assets: his army, his wealth and his personality. In 1615 the army of the Tokugawa stamped out the last spark of resistance by Hideyori, the son of the late Hideyoshi, with the successful completion of the siege of Osaka castle. The operation lasted for nearly a year and the massive fortress only finally gave way after a spurious peace treaty which led to the defenses being weakened. With Hideyori's death the Toyotomi family was completely destroyed except for two small children, thus leaving no nucleus of former power round which any opposition could gather. In fact throughout the whole of the Tokugawa period there was no organized resistance, any outbreaks that did occur were individual and sporadic affairs. When the collapse of the Tokugawa came about it was the very idea of shogun government that had been called into question, not merely the rule of the Tokugawa.

The growth in Tokugawa wealth had begun in 1590, when Hideyoshi had given Ieyasu the provinces of the Kanto area as a reward for his service at the siege of Odawara. The lands handed over were valued at 2,557,000 *koku*, of which Ieyasu kept about 1,000,000 *koku* for himself and distributed the remaining lands among his loyal followers. He was later to copy this system for Japan as a whole, placing the loyallest men in selected areas where their influence would be to the best advantage. After the Battle of Sekigahara, confiscated territories brought his total holding to nearly 6,500,000 *koku*, about a quarter of the total rice yield of the country. He also amassed considerable quantities of gold and silver. He established his capital at Edo, then a little fishing village, now the city of Tokyo.

His personality was that of a colossus. He was proclaimed shogun in 1603 and during his final years he was treated as an idol. On his death he was deified as Toshogu (Sun God of the East) and worshipped at the shrine built for him at Nikko. His son Hidetada, the second shogun, thus inherited a tremendous moral ascendancy which daunted any possible rebel from attempting to divide the country.

For such a hegemony to succeed there had to be absolute control over the daimyo. To Ieyasu, who saw political issues in clear black and white terms, there were two sorts of daimyo. There were the *fudai* daimyo (Inner Lords), who were traditionally loyal to the Tokugawa, and the *tozama* (Outer Lords), who were not. The former were mostly hereditary vassals of the Tokugawa, or daimyo who had been raised to that station, now defined as 10,000 *koku*, by the Tokugawa. Most were relatively small, holding fiefs of 50,000 *koku* or less, but their loyalty to the Tokugawa was considered absolute. Some, such as Ii of Hikone and Honda Tadakatsu, had been Ieyasu's companions in battle for 40 years.

The *tozama* were the daimyo who had supported the losing side at Sekigahara and submitted to Ieyasu afterward and those who had remained neutral throughout. Many were houses who had received daimyo status under Hideyoshi and thus had no love for the Tokugawa. Others held the same fiefs that their families had maintained for centuries, notably the Shimazu of Satsuma, whose domain had been granted to his ancestor by Yoritomo in 1196. They had progressed from *shugo* to *shokuho-daimyo* and could afford to regard the Tokugawa, for all their claims to descent from the Minamoto, as relative upstarts.

Apart from the *fudai* and *tozama* daimyo there were also a number of houses closely related to

Below: *A soldier in the Tokugawa army seizes a young woman as Osaka castle falls.*

the Tokugawa. Chief among these were the three Tokugawa branches of Kii, Mito and Owari, from whom a shogun was to be selected if the main Tokugawa line died out.

Ieyasu's policy was to treat the *tozama* with generosity but caution, using the loyal *fudai* as watchdogs. He thus began a policy of resettlement that was to carry on long after his death whereby some fiefs were confiscated, others were exchanged, and the daimyo moved round Japan like counters on a board. The object of the exercise was to get a geographical distribution between *fudai* and *tozama* so that potentially hostile *tozama* were split up as far as possible from one another so that coalitions would be difficult to form and maintain. There was also a need to cover strategic routes along which attacks might be launched on Kyoto or Edo.

Above: *The suit of armor worn by Toyotomi Hideyori, defeated by the Tokugawa at Osaka castle. The scales are lacquered gold, and the lacing is red and white.*

good example. Prior to the Tokugawa period Tosa had been the domain of the Chosokabe family, who had ruled the whole island of Shikoku at the peak of their power. In 1585 Hideyoshi had invaded the island and defeated the Chosokabe, allowing them to retain Tosa after swearing loyalty to him. They had remained loyal to the Toyotomi to the extent of siding against Ieyasu at Sekigahara, after which Ieyasu confiscated the domain from the last daimyo, Chosokabe Morichika, who retired from military life and became a monk in Osaka.

The recipient of the former Chosokabe territories was Yamauchi Kazutoyo, a *tozama* daimyo who had joined the Tokugawa side shortly before Sekigahara but had taken no part in the fighting. His grant of Tosa was therefore a generous one, as it raised him from a fief of 50,000 *koku* to one of 240,000. Opposing his official takeover of Tosa were the remnants of what had once been the Chosokabe samurai army. Some were the remainder of the full-time band of samurai which Chosokabe Morichika had been building up in Kochi at the time of his defeat. But the majority of the Chosokabe retainers were *ichiryo gusoku*, who had been the basis of the Chosokabe rise to power. By 1600 they were about 9000 strong.

To quell these rebellious spirits Yamauchi had only 158 mounted samurai, with about 10 *ashigaru* to each samurai. Ieyasu therefore sent reinforcements under Suzuki Hyoe and they besieged the Chosokabe castle. After some fighting, as evidenced by the 273 heads Suzuki sent back to the mainland as proof, the resistance was quelled. This was largely owing to the fears of the senior Chosokabe retainers for their former lord, who was virtually a hostage of the Tokugawa in his monastery in Osaka. With the collapse of resistance the senior retainers were exiled, and the *ichiryo gusoku* classified as farmers.

To be merely classified as a farmer may strike one as a very mild act of retribution compared to exile. However, it was very serious because it meant that the *ichiryo gusoku* were no longer samurai. They were disarmed, separated physically from the samurai that Yamauchi Kazutoyo had brought with him and sent out into the countryside from whence they had come. This process on a national scale completed the trend that had been set in motion by Nobunaga and Hideyoshi, the separation of the samurai from the soil.

The Tokugawa made a sharp definition between samurai and farmers, and extended the keenness of the definition down the class system, so that everyone in Tokugawa Japan literally knew his place, and because he knew his place he knew precisely his function, his geographical location, even his mode of dress.

Above: *The handprint of Tokugawa Ieyasu. The hand of Ieyasu made an impression upon two and a half centuries of Japanese history.*

Right: *A chiselled decoration, called* horimono, *on the lower half of a long spear blade owned by Kuroda Nagamasa (1568–1623).*

Previous page: *A painted screen showing the fall of Osaka castle, 1615. This magnificent work of art was commissioned by Kuroda Nagamasa to commemorate the part he played in the siege, an action which was to become the last major clash of arms in premodern Japan. Thousands of figures are shown in minute detail, giving a dramatic picture of the violence and confusion that marked the military triumph of the Tokugawa war machine.*

Consequently central Japan was dominated by shogun lands, and the three Tokugawa branches were placed one on either side of Edo, and the other south of Osaka. The *tozama* found themselves strung out on the extremes of the Japanese islands with *fudai* dotted around near them. In fact the location of these *tozama* turned out to be a fundamental weakness of the policy as some, like the Shimazu, had merely been left in their hereditary fiefs where they had already established such a degree of independence that changing one overlord for another was not likely to make too much difference.

There thus began a complex and lengthy business of moving house. In the archives of the Ikeda, the daimyo of Okayama in Bizen province, there still exists a map of Okayama in which all the houses are labelled with the names of the samurai residents. Over each name is pasted a slip of paper on which the incoming daimyo has written the names of his retainers, their quarters having been carefully allocated according to rank. There were many complications, particularly among the *tozama*, and some daimyo had difficulty in actually taking possession of their new domains. The transfer in Tosa province is a

In fact a person's life from cradle to grave was clearly defined according to rank. Apart from courtiers, priests, doctors and 'nonhumans' (*eta*), who had function but no clearly delineated class, everyone in Tokugawa Japan was either a samurai, a farmer, an artisan or a merchant. The broad functions of each are reverently explained in the following passage by a contemporary of Ieyasu:

'. . . the samurai is one who maintains his martial discipline even in peace . . . the farmer's work is proverbial from the first grain to a hundred acts of labor, like so many tears of blood. Thus it is a wise man who, while partaking of his meal, appreciates the hundred acts of toil of the people. . . . the artisan's occupation is to make and prepare wares and utensils for the use of others . . . the merchant facilitates the exchange of goods so that the people can cover their nakedness and keep their bodies warm. . . .'

In nearly every aspect of life there was an emphasis on the difference between the classes. Even the law was different for different classes and included the fearsome right of *kirisute-gomen*, which stated that, 'Common people who behave unbecomingly to members of the military class or who show want of respect to direct or indirect vassals may be cut down on the spot.' Mercifully, it was a privilege carried out on rare occasions, but the two swords thrust through the samurai's belt were a potent symbol of an unquestionable authority. Yet for all their superiority, the samurai always remained numerically inferior to the rest of Japanese society. Working from the most reliable figures it can be shown that never in the Tokugawa period did the samurai constitute more than seven percent of the total population, yet the class system held as long as the Tokugawa system itself. There was, naturally enough, a growth of interdependence between the classes as the years went by, as will be shown in future chapters, but for the whole of Tokugawa Japan the 'merchant class' or 'the farmer class' has a defined meaning.

There were subdivisions within each class. Within the samurai class such divisions were a decadent reminder of military rank, being intended as the rank which the owner would be given if there were any other battles, hence the amusing description of a desk-bound senior administrative official in, say, a daimyo's finance department as an *umamawari* (mounted guard). Each rank received lands of an appropriate *koku* rating, except for the lower ranks who were not granted lands but instead received a direct stipend of rice from the daimyo's lands. This method of salaried payment eventually became practically universal for samurai, until this too

was phased out in favor of a cash payment to the supposed market value of the rice. It was a trend that tended to strengthen the class system still further as the samurai ceased even to be nominal landowners and instead became salaried officials.

The Yamauchi of Tosa are a good example of the subdivisions within the samurai. They recognized 10 ranks, five 'upper samurai' and five 'lower samurai.' The highest under the daimyo were the *karo* (elders), with lands of between 1500–10,000 *koku*. On the battlefield they would be generals and in the days of peace headed the major administrative departments. They were allowed to use the Yamauchi family name and served their daimyo in the same way that the most trusted of the *fudai* served the house of Tokugawa. The four ranks beneath them, the officer class in wartime, had lands of 50–1500 *koku* depending on rank.

There was some mobility between these ranks, but little between them and the five ranks below, which extended down to the *ashigaru* (light feet), the foot soldiers Nobunaga had made into a disciplined fighting force. They were kept on a subsistence level with a stipend of between three and seven *koku*, and in peacetime served largely as laborers.

There was a similar system for most daimyo. The highest ranks of the shogunate were staffed by the *fudai* daimyo, who had the privilege of administrative service to the Tokugawa. Below them were the *hatamoto*, a name which literally means 'under the standard,' that being the position which they would occupy in battle. The lowest ranks were called *go-kenin* (honorable-housemen). The *hatamoto* tended to occupy the general staff positions in the Tokugawa administrations, for which they received payment in the form of a rank grant, either lands or stipend, and an extra payment for the office. The majority of the *hatamoto*, however, were employed in the Tokugawa army, split up into guard groups or specialized units, garrisoning the major Tokugawa castles such as Edo, Nagoya and Nijo (in Kyoto).

As well as this regular army, every samurai in the service of the Tokugawa was expected to keep himself in combat readiness at all times, and to supply men and weapons when required by the shogun. Detailed regulations were issued stating precisely how many troops, with what weapons, were to be supplied by various income levels. For example, according to the schedule of 1649, a samurai (*hatamoto*) with an income of 2000 *koku* would be expected to supply personal service, plus eight samurai of *go-kenin* rank, two armor bearers plus one reserve, five spearmen plus one reserve, four grooms, four baggage carriers, one sandal bearer, two *hasamibako* bearers plus one reserve (the *hasamibako* was a

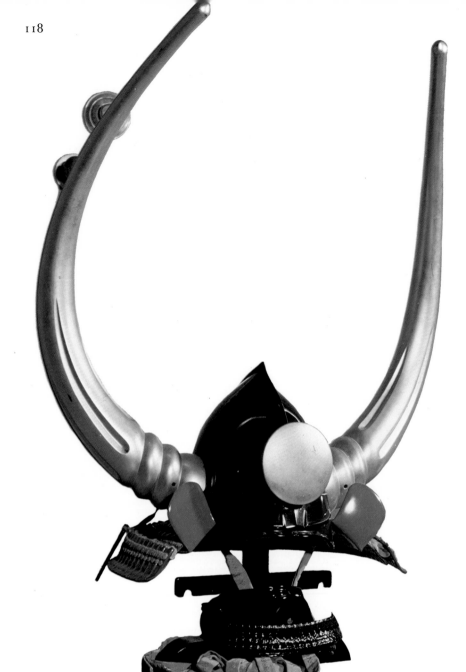

Above: *Helmet of Kuroda Nagamasa (1568–1623). The suit of armor of the Momoyama and early Edo Periods was essentially a simple, functional battle dress with the minimum of decoration. One way, however, in which it could be made more dramatic was to wear an ornately designed helmet, and many examples have survived to our day. This is one of the finest, set off with enormous gold-lacquered wooden buffalo horns.*

fiscation of domains and so forth).

Housebands evolved in two ways: by a powerful daimyo defeating a neighbor and enlisting the defeated lord's samurai into his army or by a daimyo attracting followers as he rose to prominence. The Ikeda are an outstanding example of the latter. They began in a similar fashion to the Ukita. Ikeda Nobuteru's first independent command was as leader of a company of 30 samurai in Nobunaga's army in 1560. By the time his son and heir Terumasa had died in 1613 rewards, commands and grants of land had swollen the original 30 samurai to 6000, five of whom had been members of the original 30. The numbers continued to grow during peacetime as the Ikeda domain grew by resettlement and absorption and, inevitably, the relationship between the daimyo and his houseband changed. Whereas once they had been dependent upon him in the military sense of following a trusted leader into battle, the gradual replacement of land grants by rice stipend meant that they were now economically dependent upon him too, as early housebands had been in the 1540s.

By the time of Ikeda Mitsumasa (1609–1682) the relationship between daimyo and houseband had ceased to be a personal one and was conducted through formal bureaucratic channels and the oaths of allegiance which it had been customary for a newly acquired retainer to take became replaced by oaths of office. The loyal retainers of Ikeda were to Mitsumasa no more than a list of names, or anonymous faces in a parade. Utterly dependent upon their lord for quarters and stipend, the samurai packed together in the castle town of Okayama developed a sense of comradeship to one another, but by the end of the Tokugawa period their real loyalty lay to their service as a samurai which the daimyo represented, rather than a fierce personal attachment to the daimyo himself. Thus in the years leading up to the Meiji restoration the conflict of loyalty which many samurai were to feel was to be more easily resolved, as the bond of service was transferred from one focus to another.

The houseband of samurai with *ryo* (territory) and *tami* (the common people) comprised the daimyo's *han* (domain). It was the achievement of the Tokugawa to turn this basically military institution of a 'petty kingdom' into a system of local government under the *baku-han* system. Ieyasu and his successors were sensible enough to realize that a mere geographical redistribution of potential enemies would not be sufficient to guarantee stability. As a result the shogunate formulated several ingenious laws for controlling the daimyo, most of which were enshrined in the *Buke-sho hatto* (Rules for

travelling case carried on a pole), one archer, two harquebusiers, two fodder bearers, one *no-dachi* bearer (the *no-dachi* was an extra-long sword) two *ashigaru* leaders and one rain-hat carrier. All the soldiers in the 'servant' categories would be fully armed samurai of a lower, that is *ashigaru*, type.

It is interesting to see how the relationship between a daimyo (or the shogun) and the samurai who were notionally to follow him into battle had changed since the wars of the sixteenth century. They were still, in every sense, his samurai. 'Houseband' is probably the best word to describe them. 'Clan' is wildly inaccurate for this period, though there was a sort of clannishness at the very upper reaches of the houseband, the *karo* (elders), who tended to marry into the daimyo's family, and retain a hereditary position. By Tokugawa times every samurai in Japan was either a member of someone's houseband or a *ronin* (literally a wave man, the name given to a samurai without a master through death and extinction of a line, or con-

Above: *The keep of Nagoya Castle. Nagoya Castle was built in 1610 as one of the strategic fortresses of the Tokugawa. The Owari branch of the family lived there from 1610 to 1868. The original building was destroyed during World War II, but has since been completely restored, including the golden dolphins on the roof.*

Left: *A samurai residence. This house of a well-to-do samurai of the Edo Period is preserved in Kanagawa.*

Above: *A common sight on the highways of Japan during the rule of the Tokugawa was one of the many processions by the* daimyo *as they made their way to and from Edo. In this print by Hiroshige a daimyo's retinue marches through Suruga province, with Mount Fuji as a splendid backdrop to the scene.*

Governing Samurai Houses) which was read out to an assembly of daimyo in 1615, and never fundamentally altered. It is a long document, which is not particularly original considering the house codes of the Age of War. It states 13 basic rules which were to govern the behavior of the samurai class for the whole of the shogunate's existence:

1. The study of literature and the martial arts must be practiced at all times.
2. Drunkenness and lewd behavior must be avoided.
3. Lawbreakers must not be hidden in any domain.
4. Daimyo must expel any samurai charged with treason or murder.
5. Residence in a fief is to be restricted to men born in that fief.
6. The shogun authorities must be informed of

any intended repairs to castles. All new construction is forbidden.
7. Any plots or factions discovered in a neighboring fief must be immediately reported.
8. Marriages must not be privately contracted.
9. Visits by daimyo to the capital (Edo) are to be in accordance with regulations.
10. All costumes and decorations are to be appropriate to the wearer's rank.
11. Commoners (that is, the nonsamurai classes) are not to ride in palanquins.
12. Samurai are to live a frugal and simple life.
13. Daimyo must choose men of ability to advise them.

One is first of all struck by the omission from the list of one obvious way of controlling the daimyo – taxation. The daimyo were never directly taxed, instead the shogun contrived to wring as much money as possible out of them by more subtle means. Rule 6 forbade castle building, instead the daimyo were invited to donate money, labor and materials for building the shogun's castles, an enormously expensive business. The process began in 1604 with the building of Edo castle, to which all daimyo were ordered to contribute. The moats and ramparts of the castle, in the style of the times, were faced with enormous blocks of stone brought by sea from the quarries of Izu. The stones were so large that only two could be carried by each ship, and each needed 100 men to manhandle them. For every 100,000 *koku* of their income the daimyo were required to send 1120 of these stones. They also had to supply one man for every 1000 *koku* for the work of levelling the area where the castle was to be built, a large civil engineering project on which 10,000 workmen were eventually engaged. Inclement weather added to the expense. On one occasion several hundred ships carrying stones were sunk in a storm on their way to Edo.

Of all the control systems none was more bizarre than the *sankin-kotai* (alternate-attendance) system. It had long been a custom among the samurai to show proof of their loyalty to a distant overlord by sending wives and children to the lord's castle as hostages. Ieyasu himself spent the first 10 years of his life as a hostage. What the Tokugawa did was to institute such a hostage system on a grand scale, and to combine it with a ritual of visits to Edo to pay homage to the shogun. Under the *sankin-kotai* requirements, which were made a legal obligation in 1633 under the third Tokugawa Shogun, Iemitsu, the wives and children of all the daimyo were required to reside permanently in Edo. The daimyo themselves, accompanied of course by a splendid and expensive retinue, were required to reside alternately one year at Edo and one year

in their castle town. *Fudai* daimyo in the Kanto area alternated every six months while certain distant daimyo had a reduced responsibility, such as the So, on the island of Tsushima between Japan and Korea, who only had to reside in Edo for four months in every three years. At the time of the threat of Russian expansion from the north the daimyo Matsumae of Hokkaido was actually exempt, but this was the only exception ever made. The result of the alternate-attendance system was that the shogun's potential rivals spent a large part of their lives either marching to Edo or marching away from it. On a more serious note, it kept the shogunate well informed of what was going on in outlying areas, and they would have had not the slightest hesitation about slitting the throats of the entire family of any rebel. For the same purpose intercourse between fiefs was discouraged and travel between them made difficult by barriers and passports and the simpler method of letting bridges fall into disrepair. Passport officials were ordered to be particularly on the lookout for *de onna, iri deppo* (literally, 'women going out, and guns going in').

The injunction to daimyo to report anything suspicious in a neighboring fief was backed up by a huge and efficient spy system, personified by the notorious *metsuke* (the all-seeing eyes). The practice of someone watching someone else's business was so common that an amusing incident was caused by the arrival of the first British consul to Japan in 1858, Lord Elgin. He soon noticed that his every move was being watched and reported back by the vigilant *metsuke*. What the Japanese could not understand was that such an important person as Lord Elgin did not have his own *metsuke*, sent by Queen Victoria no doubt, watching him. After a while, however, the consul was observed by a *metsuke* signing documents using his full title of Elgin and Kincardine. The mystery was solved. Kincardine was Elgin's *metsuke*, and what a fine *metsuke* he was too, to render himself invisible!

The marriage laws set out in the *Buke-sho hatto* were designed to ensure that alliances were not made between daimyo, and also between daimyo and courtier. The aristocratic families (*kuge*), numbering about three hundred, were kept, like the emperor, virtual prisoners in the imperial palace in Kyoto. They were supported by modest grants and restricted to ceremonial and ritual duties. Across the road from the palace wall stood the Tokugawa fortress of Nijo castle where a Shogunal official was based. His job was to inform the divine emperor of the will of his temporal servant, the shogun. Daimyo visits to Kyoto were carefully prevented and, as long as the emperor could be controlled, the legitimacy of the shogun was assured.

In addition to the laws that governed the samurai were separate laws for the farmers, the artisans and merchants. On the face of it it looks a harsh, uncaring system that compartmentalizes people, and relies for its control on hostages and spies. It was, however, a system based on an ancient and respected system of ethics, the teachings of Confucius. Confucianism postulated an ideal socity in which each individual occupied his particular place in a natural order. It also stressed the moral nature of authority, the respect which authority should command from the governed and, especially, filial piety. These ideals were well-suited to the shogun's aim of maintaining a stable social and political order. Confucianism was therefore given great support and under Tokugawa patronage developed into a humanistic and pragmatic philosophy. Behind society there was reason and moral order, and government was the business of achieving this moral order among mankind. Filial piety could easily be extended to cover the loyalty that a samurai has to his lord, as well as the loyalty he has to his father. Confucian ideals such as these were to become the basis for the moral code of the samurai, *bushido*.

One concrete effect of Confucian thought on the samurai was the banning in 1663 of the practice of *junshi* (suicide in order to follow a lord in death). *Junshi* belonged to a past age when the bond between a daimyo and his houseband was very close, and the argument for it was that a samurai could not serve two masters and therefore when his lord died he must end his own life. It was, however, entirely inappropriate in Tokugawa times, and led to the loss of several great men. When Shogun Iemitsu died in 1651, 13 senior Tokugawa officials committed *junshi*. Once banned, it was strictly enforced by punishing surviving relatives, such as in the case of the *junshi* of a samurai of Okudaira Tadamasa following the latter's death in 1688. The samurai's children were executed,

Above: Another scene from a daimyo's progress under the 'Alternate Attendance' system. These attendants carry harquebuses, a reminder that these processions were a decadent survival of the military activities of an earlier day. Note particularly the respectful attitude of the commoners at the top of the picture.

other relatives were banished and, as an example to other daimyo, Okudaira's heir was transferred to a smaller fief.

Official patronage of Confucian thought by the Tokugawa tended to be limited to orthodox teaching, mainly that of the Chu Hsi school. In addition, there were several unorthodox approaches, one of which, the teaching of Wang Yang Ming (1472–1529), had enormous influence on later generations of samurai.

Wang Yang Ming's approach was intuitive and individualistic, and bears a similar relationship to orthodox Confucianism as Zen does to mainstream Buddhism. It lays great stress on

Below: The bronze dog-shaped foot warmer of Tokugawa Tsunayoshi, the notorious 'dog shogun.'

practical action rather than academic achievement, and its antischolastic, individual bent made it seem sufficiently subversive to Tokugawa eyes to be banned in 1790. In contrast to the Chu Hsi form, which taught that one must first acquire knowledge and then act upon that knowledge as appropriate, the followers of Wang Yang Ming insisted that to know without acting meant that one does not know. A moral truth must be immediately transformed into action, so that knowledge and action become one. It was the philosophy of the rebel, rather than that of the loyal samurai, and when the definitions of both were brought into question in the nineteenth century Wang Yang Ming was rediscovered and used.

Official Confucianism, at any rate, went hand in hand with the development of the *baku-han* system. The application of Confucian principles to government produced a trend toward *bunji-seiji* (government by moral persuasion) following the ideals of 'benevolent rule' enshrined in Confucian thought. The other trend visible in samurai rule is a clear movement toward bureaucracy. The first article of the *Buke-sho hatto* stressed that the literary and martial arts were always to be practiced, but under peaceful conditions the former became more necessary than the latter. One of the achievements of the Tokugawa is that the samurai class entered the period as an unlearned, partially literate

group of military officers, but came out of it as skilled civil administrators.

Unfortunately for the holders of these offices, their financial rewards did not keep pace with the growth of their new skills. The *Buke-sho hatto* states that samurai should live frugally, and a fixed stipend in an age of rising prices and a shift to a money economy ensured that they stayed that way. In the face of growing poverty many samurai turned to small handicrafts as a way of earning extra money, a practice that was forbidden to the shogun's samurai (the *hatamoto* and *go-kenin*), but positively encouraged by several daimyo, who had considerable financial problems of their own.

The *baku-han* system thus survived for two and a half centuries and, although reviled by the leaders of Japan who were to emerge after it as being a 'dark age' of stagnation, corruption and espionage, achieved its aim of 'Great Peace Throughout the Realm.' Its internal organization system for the shogunate, where the *karo* formed a senior council, at least ensured that things ran as smoothly as possible when the incumbent shogun was a minor or, as sometimes happened, thoroughly incompetent. One of the strangest denizens of this office, though he can scarcely be called incompetent, was Shogun Tsunayoshi (1680–1709). A monk suggested to Tsunayoshi that the reason he had no male heir was because he had taken life during a

previous reincarnation. So Tsunayoshi decided that he must devote his energies to the protection of living things, especially dogs, as Tsunayoshi had been born in the Year of The Dog according to the Chinese calendar. As a result in 1687 numerous orders were issued for their protection, including the death penalty for anyone caught wounding a dog. The most outlandish regulation of all was that dogs should be addressed using honorific terms, usually reserved for superiors. Accordingly the inhabitants of Edo had to address dogs *O-inu sama* (Honorable Mr Dog). In 1695 the Edo authorities tried to reduce the

124

Above: *A notice Prohibiting Christianity. It reads: 'Notice – although the Christian sect has been repeatedly prohibited, yet at every change of ruler it is right to issue a decree that rigid scrutiny must be made without cessation. Of course every suspicious person must be informed against. For their betrayal the following rewards will be given: Foreign priest – 500 pieces of silver; Native priest – 300 pieces of silver; Exiles who again believe this religion – 300 pieces of silver; Catechists – 100 pieces of silver; Even catechists or members who inform against the foreign priests, or members of their own class, will be given 500 pieces of silver, according to the value of their information. In case of concealment, not only the guilty persons, but the headman of the village, and the whole company of five, together with all their relations, will be punished. Signed by the Magistrate, Chief of the Christian Extermination Commission. PS On account of my determination to exterminate this wicked religion, I will duplicate the reward offered by the government to anyone who will give information against those found believing this religion under my jurisdiction. – Yennosuke, Village Headman.'*

effect of these restrictions on its citizens by building kennels for the four-legged samurai in the suburbs, where in the following two years 50,000 dogs were kept and fed at enormous expense. Tsunayoshi's eccentricities had their serious side, however. It was under Tsunayoshi that the shogunate experienced the first of several financial crises, largely due to the shogun's lavish expenditure.

In contrast to Tsunayoshi was Shogun Yoshimune (ruled 1716–1745) who died in 1751. He and his advisers attempted several reforms, and also led the way in attempting to revive the martial arts among the samurai. Even though enshrined in the first article of the *Buke-sho hatto*, the practice of military skills was becoming as rusty as much of the samurai's armor. Under Yoshimune's patronage mock battles and maneuvers were held on the plains under Mount Fuji.

One aspect of Tokugawa Japan has yet to be mentioned. This is that for the whole of the Tokugawa period Japan was a nation isolated from the rest of the world, a country which foreigners were not allowed to visit, and which its own citizens were forbidden to leave. Although the ban was not totally enforced, it had a profound effect upon Japanese society.

At the time of the founding of the Tokugawa Shogunate the opposite attitude toward foreign relations had been dominant. Tokugawa Ieyasu had encouraged foreign trade and issued numerous licenses under his seal for Japanese expeditions and trading voyages. By the 1630s Japan traded with most countries of the East as far as Burma, and Japanese settlements were to be found in Taiwan, the Philippines, Borneo, the Malay peninsula and Siam. One of the most successful of these adventurers was Yamada Nagamasa who, at the time of his death in 1633, was a trusted adviser to the King of Siam, where Japanese samurai had helped to quell a rebellion.

Three factors brought the desirability of foreign contacts into question. The first was the shogun's prime aim of internal security. Several of the great *tozama* daimyo frequently traded abroad which threatened the Tokugawa's control over them. Also, the shogun desired to gain

a monopoly of foreign trade. The Edo area had never proved attractive to foreign vessels, in spite of attempts by Ieyasu to persuade them to trade through Uraga rather than Nagasaki, which was much nearer to China. The third factor was the fear of Christianity.

Christianity had come to Japan by the offices of Saint Francis Xavier in 1549 and had attracted large numbers of converts, particularly in the island of Kyushu. The conversion of a daimyo to the new faith was enough to ensure that his entire *han* became Christian. Oda Nobunaga had encouraged the missionaries, partly because they were very useful in his attempts to control the Buddhist clergy and their warrior monks. In Nobunaga's day it was quite common to meet armies of Christian samurai, who bore the cross on their banners.

Persecution of Christians began under Hideyoshi, largely as a result of his suspicions of the activities of Spanish missionaries, whom he accused of preparing the country for a takeover by the Spanish Empire. The Tokugawa, spurred on by Dutch-versus-Catholic rivalry, shared Hideyoshi's fears about this potentially subversive philosophical system, which could not be allowed to challenge the Tokugawa supremacy. When it was realized that some *tozama* daimyo had remained Christian in spite of the previous edicts by Hideyoshi and that even the loyal *fudai* had Christian converts among their number, the edicts against Christianity were reissued (this was under Hidetada, the second shogun) and all persons ordered to give up the foreign religion. One daimyo, Takayama Ukon (1553–1615), was exiled to Manila because of his Christian beliefs and from 1618–21 a large number of Japanese Christians were executed. In 1622, 'The year of the Great Martyrdom,' over 100 were executed, including, for the first time, foreign priests.

The efficient Tokugawa espionage system now went into action against Christians who continued to practice their faith in secret. Those who were caught, and would not abandon their faith, were horribly tortured, resulting in scenes of the utmost courage and bravery in the face of the cruellest of punishments. In 1629 a special method of discovering hidden Christians was adopted. Anyone suspected of being a Christian was ordered to trample on a religious picture, called a *fumi-e*. Those who refused were assumed to be Christians and summarily dealt with.

During the 1630s the authorities took the final steps toward a tight seclusion policy. In 1633 a memorandum was issued to the governors of Nagasaki. There were three main points:

1. No vessel without a valid license must leave

Above: *After the expulsion of the Portuguese the only foreign trade allowed was with the Dutch. In this painting on silk we see them making the best of their virtual imprisonment on the island of Deshima.*

Below: *Shimabara Castle, scene of the Shimabara Rebellion of 1638.*

Japan.

2. No Japanese subject may leave for a foreign country.

3. Japanese who return from abroad shall be put to death.

The seclusion order was finally tightened after the Shimabara revolt of 1638, when several thousand rebels, *ronin*, farmers opposed to tyranny and many Christians, shut themselves up in Hara castle on the Shimabara peninsula. They managed to hold out against the Tokugawa samurai for several weeks. Their resistance was desperate and well conducted, they even ambushed supply columns for more weapons. The shogunate went so far as to use Dutch ships to bombard the castle from the sea, whereupon the defenders shot messages by arrows into the camp ridiculing the Shogunate for having to rely on foreigners. The length of time it took to crush the rebellion, which was largely conducted by nonsamurai, was an alarming portent of the samurai's military decline. However, with the fall of Shimabara the Christian movement in Japan was all but extinguished, though small bands of believers were occasionally found. Incredible as it sounds, when Christianity was again made legal under the Meiji government in 1869 small groups of 'hidden Christians' were discovered, who had maintained their faith in secret for 200 years.

In 1639 the Portuguese were expelled from Japan, and when a Portuguese mission arrived the following year its members were executed. From this time on, the only foreign trade allowed was with the Dutch, and they were confined to the little artificial island of Deshima in Nagasaki harbor. The Chinese had a concession through Nagasaki itself. Apart from these exceptions Japan had isolated itself from the world and the four classes, samurai, farmers, artisans and merchants, were now confined to the benevolent care of the Tokugawa prison.

CHAPTER 8

The Sword and the Abacus

Previous page: *The seppuku of Oishi Yoshio. The leader of the faithful Forty-Seven Ronin prepares to make the fatal incision, while a second stands by to cut off his head.*

Below: *The samurai of Tokugawa Japan was essentially an urban creature. He lived his life in a castle town, and many of his duties would be connected with urban affairs. In this print a samurai approaches the premises of a sword polisher.*

The metamorphosis of the samurai in the Tokugawa period, from sword-wielding warrior to sword-bearing bureaucrat, was a transformation carried out so gradually and so successfully that it is easy to overlook the context in which it happened. From the first establishment of the castle town and the growth of already important centers such as Osaka and Edo, the city became a major factor in Japanese society, so that it is necessary to view the samurai in the Tokugawa period as being essentially an urban creature. That this should be necessary at all was something of a paradox. City-living samurai are in direct contradiction to the land-based ideal of the Tokugawa system, whose philosophical basis was the Confucian model. This stressed the

nobility of agriculture and the right of the samurai to govern, while assigning the lowest place to the archetypal town dweller, the merchant. Yet one effect of the urbanizing process was to produce a strong but uneasy alliance between the samurai and the merchants. It was a relationship forced by economic reality, and eventually reached the stage of interdependence. It also had very important consequences for the samurai in terms of their function, their daily life and the view which they held of themselves.

The urbanization of the samurai can be traced back to the period of large-scale castle building between 1580–1610. Although many of these castles were built on the site of former fortresses they were all essentially new foundations, replacing numerous small-scale castles in a daimyo's territory with one massive, central structure, placed strategically at the heart of communications of the han. The castle, separated from the land, thus became the physical embodiment of the four-class system, with each daimyo's capital being no more than a small-scale model of the shogun's metropolis of Edo. The pattern was uniform. The daimyo lived in the keep. Around the keep, within the inner walls, were the residences of his highest ranking members of his samurai houseband. The lower ranks occupied a band further out, with temples and shrines placed at the extremities as an outer line of defense.

The one exception to this physical grading of social scale was the location of the merchants. According to the four-class system one would expect to find them on the very perimeter. Instead they were inside the town itself, under the castle walls, a visible proof of the samurai's need for the merchants' services.

Some merchants, known as *goyo-shonin* (charter merchants) were particularly privileged, enjoying a certain degree of tax exemption and living closest to the castle. Many were ex-samurai who had specialized in the handling of military equipment and supplies for the years of war. Now they became an essential tool for the years of peace, as the castle town developed from a garrison to an administrative center, to a consumer center. As the population developed the ratio of castle town inhabitants tended to be 50 percent samurai and 50 percent *chonin* (townspeople), the merchants, artisans and servants who supplied their every need. In some towns the percentage of samurai was frequently greater. In Sendai, the castle town of the Date Han, the figure seldom fell below 70 percent and as late as 1872 the census figures reveal that out of a total population of 50,000, 29,000 were samurai. In Kagoshima, castle town of the independently minded Satsuma province (the

Shimazu daimyo), samurai constituted 8o percent of the population.

The town merchants, therefore, had the
advantages of patronage on a lavish scale, and
the utmost protection against the unlikely
event of an uprising. All commerce in a han was
limited to the central castle town or, in a few
exceptional circumstances, to an additional
town that had functioned as an urban center
before the establishment of the castle town. The
villages of the countryside were confined to
agriculture and handicrafts.

The merchants' services consisted of bridging
the gap for the samurai between the world he
had left and the new urban environment in
which he found himself. The merchants acted
as wholesalers, accumulating produce from the
han territories and acting as distributive agents.
They were the link between the economy of the
han and the economy of the nation as a whole.
Under the *baku-han* system every daimyo was
encouraged to make his han self-sufficient and
prosperous – and the merchant was a vital
factor. This does not, however, imply that the
samurai had abandoned their traditional scorn
for the denizens of the fourth class. In fact, perhaps to inflate their supposed importance, the
samurai hedged the merchant round with innumerable petty restrictions. These were, after
all, the days of the Tokugawa, where there were
rules for just about everything, from the type of
clothing appropriate to one's station, to regulations governing the carrying of umbrellas, but it
turned out that as the merchants grew in
importance so did the attempts to regulate them.
In part this was the result of a growing interest
in Confucian ideals. The merchants found their
early freedom, when they were welcomed into
the inner confines of the castle town, being replaced with supervision and the protection that
had seemed so welcome became akin to the
protection of a prison. Each city block in a castle
town, the *machi*, had its own guards and gates.
With the closing of the country in 1649 foreign
trade became a monopoly of the shogun, thus
closing the one loophole the merchants had for
independence.

Yet the one point in the merchants' favor was
that they were there because the samurai could
not do without them. The question is how did an
armed military elite, growing in literacy and
administrative ability become so dependent?

At the wholesale level, the dependence on the
merchants was fairly straightforward. Things
got complicated when the daimyo had to conduct
trade with one another or with the shogunate.
This was largely because the basis of wealth of a
han was rice. The wealth of a daimyo's territory
had been assessed from the beginning on the
amount of rice which the land could produce,

Left: *The haughty samurai,
wearing through his belt the
two swords that he alone was
permitted to wear, was the
physical embodiment of the
Tokugawa class system. As
the years went by, however, the
status of samurai became
somewhat less prized as its
proud members sank into debt
to the growing merchant class.*

measured in *koku*, one *koku* being the amount
considered necessary to feed one man for one
year. Rice is a perishable commodity, dependent on harvests and affected by storms and
floods. The merchants role therefore became to
convert such a volatile asset into something
more permanent, such as money. In the case of
the samurai of the Tokugawa, for example,
their salary of rice was deposited in the storehouses in the shogun capital of Edo, having been
brought from the farms. It was distributed to the
samurai three times a year, in the second, fifth
and tenth months, at the proportions of a
quarter, a quarter and a half respectively. In the
early years the samurai would go to collect his
rice personally, which was the nearest he would
get to its production before it ended up in his
bowl. However, gradually this duty was given
to the merchants, who would act as rice brokers,
either delivering it to the samurai, or paying him
the equivalent in coin and keeping the rice. It
was a logical step for the merchant to advance
the samurai a loan against the forthcoming
rice stipend, thus opening up another potential
avenue of profit.

This need to convert rice into cash was a problem felt at a higher level that that of the individual samurai. In fact the expenses incurred by the alternate-attendance system caused the practice to be adopted on the scale of the entire han. The daimyo therefore found it worthwhile to maintain their own rice storehouses in Edo or Osaka, so that it could be shipped directly there for buying by the merchants. The Osaka rice market developed a complexity comparable to modern commodity markets. The merchants would advance huge loans to daimyo on rice that had not even been sown, having calculated risks of typhoons and other weather conditions. To the daimyo it was a way of spreading out the income from one harvest a year. To the individual samurai it was a source of convertible funds for the expenses involved in maintaining himself as a samurai in the face of rising prices and a fixed stipend. To the merchants it was profit. Moneychanging was another profitable business, as the coinage system did not help stability. The rates of exchange between coins of gold, silver and copper varied throughout the period, and were subject to short-term fluctuations. Most retail trade was conducted in copper and wholesale trade in silver or gold, so moneychangers were found in every castle town, armed with their ledgers and their *soroban* (abacus), which a skilled operator could employ at a speed that would not have disgraced a modern electronic calculator.

Osaka and Edo thus became the centers of a national economy through which the individual han economies were unified. In time, even the supervision of han warehouses in these cities was given over to trusted merchants. In their role as financial agents the merchants advanced money to daimyo on a very large scale, often equivalent to several years of rice production. In 1761 it is estimated that there were over 200 commercial houses, each with capital equivalent to over 200,000 *koku* of rice, the equivalent of many daimyo. The most notorious was Yodoya Saburoemon. His property was confiscated in 1705 by the shogunate when his outstanding loans to daimyo are said to have totalled over 100,000,000 *ryo*, which is several times the total national income of Japan at the time. This is undoubtedly an exaggeration, but it serves to show the wealth the merchants accumulated and the precariousness of the position of some of them.

Confiscation of property was one way in which the shogunate, and thereby the samurai class, could hit back. Other ways included the arbitrary cancelling of debts by decree and the forced loan. These measures were legitimized by the official Confucian line that the merchants merely absorbed the samurai's stipend and were

thus useless destroyers of grain. Even as late as 1727 an essay by Ogyo Sorai makes such points, a statement completely contradictory to the reality of the times. Later writers did take a more sensible view. Dazai Shundai (1680–1747) a pupil of Ogyu Sorai, argued that the acceptance of a money economy was no more than a legitimate extension of economic growth. It was Kaiho Seiryo (1755–1818) who was to make the most telling point, writing that a samurai who converted his rice stipend to money at a profit was no different from a merchant. Nor, for that matter, does he see the merchant as being significantly different from a samurai, since the profit he made was equivalent to a stipend. The samurai, after all, did not work for his stipend.

A merchant's life was governed by house codes as strict as any devised for the samurai. They stress frugality, the need to work diligently, to obey authority and to protect the good name of their houses. All these were necessary virtues

Above: The samurai frequently had to organize the fighting of fires. As buildings were constructed largely of wood and packed closely together a minor conflagration could spread rapidly. The samurai on horseback is wearing a special fire helmet, to which is attached a long hood as a protection against sparks.

Right: A street scene in Edo. All contemporary accounts speak of the noise and bustle of the town scene at the time of the Tokugawa. Note the colorful shop signs, evidence of thriving commerce.

world. Even the heights of the upper class were not totally denied him for an impoverished samurai could quite easily be persuaded to sell samurai status. This could be done by adopting a merchant son into a samurai family or a poor samurai might take the opportunity of getting his son into a merchant family. Several attempts were made to prohibit it, notably under Shogun Yoshimune, but the practice was so widespread that there were standard rates for the transaction, normally 50 *ryo* of gold for every 100 *koku*, rates were doubled if the case was urgent.

The wealth of merchants may have been a great attraction for the samurai, but another powerful lure was the culture which had grown up around them. The *chonin* enjoyed a new bourgeois culture as they shared in the merchant wealth. To a samurai brought up to take his entertainment in fields appropriate to his status, the *ukiyo* culture (the 'floating world' of the cities), was a huge temptation. When the merchant was not tending his ledgers a wide world of pleasure awaited him. All these pleasures were prohibited to the samurai, and all were indulged in by the samurai on as large a scale as they could manage. First was the geisha, the professional female entertainer, adept in her part of pleasing men. It was, and still is, a profession largely misunderstood by Westerners who tend to regard the geisha as no more than a prostitute. In fact she was in a very real sense an entertainer and companion, skilled in conversation, music and etiquette. The geisha of Tokugawa times derived from the courtesans and dancers who had formed part of the world of aristocratic society. With the growth of merchant wealth she became available to a wider social class.

in a climate in which one's fortune could be confiscated. Yodoya's property was confiscated because he was 'haughty and presumptuous.' One house code puts it succinctly:

'The master samurai will never fight until he has prepared for his possible defeat. It is only at this stage that he will take his bow and arrow and do battle. But because he has prepared he will keep his lands and his followers even if he is defeated in the fight. The reckless samurai ignores such considerations and thinks only of gain. He fights recklessly, and if he loses, forfeits all his lands and his own life . . . if you think only of making more money and so leave no money for the house . . . you will squander your family's fortune in a day. Plan carefully therefore what you would do if you were to suffer a great loss.'

The merchant was thus master in his own

The culture of the 'floating world' reached its apogee in the Genroku Age (1688–1705), when Kyoto and Osaka were the main centers. A century later, between 1804–29, the Bunka-Bunsei period, Edo led the way in another flowering of creative talent and popular taste. Literature flourished, particularly tales based on the world of the geisha. One of the foremost successful popular writers of the Genroku period was Ihara Saikaku (1641–1693), who was himself a merchant of Osaka. He achieved great success with novels about sex, but these were banned by the shogunate, so Ihara turned to the more uplifting task of recounting the lives of successful merchants, virtuous farmers and loyal samurai.

At first sight it is somewhat surprising that the art form associated with the *ukiyo*, the *ukiyo-e* (woodblock prints), were in their time regarded as having little artistic merit. In the light of Japanese art traditions it is perhaps less remarkable as a long tradition of producing restrained and subtle works with much left to the imagination of the viewer would inevitably regard something produced by the hundred for a playbill, or an illustration of a famous actor, as ephemeral and vulgar. Various *ukiyo-e* artists specialized in different topics. Of the illustrators of samurai, a popular subject, few came near the quality of Kuniyoshi. Even though he dressed ancient heroes in the armor of his own day his creations exemplify the spirit of the samurai. They are brave, and very fierce. Battle scenes showing massive armies in action are depicted with enormous vigor. But it is his

individual portraits of snarling, staring samurai that are most evocative of the times.

Of all the *chonin* pleasures none was more spectacular or gaudy than the *kabuki* theater and none was less akin to the notion of what entertainment was proper to the samurai class. Nor was any other form of entertainment so persistently, and ineffectively, banned. Under the Tokugawa class system *kabuki* came off

Above left: *Wooden netsuke carved in the form of a demon mask for the* noh *theater.*

Above: *A streetfight in the rain, from a print by Shigeharu.*

Above right: *One of the strangest sights in Tokugawa Japan was the* komuso,

theater. It dealt with the real world as experienced by the *chonin* and was depicted in a medium at once flamboyant and exaggerated.

The main attraction for the audience in the early years of *kabuki* (1603 is given as the year of the first *kabuki* performance) were the actresses. They were adored by the men, and their ways copied by court ladies. Fights broke out between samurai rivals for an actress's affections. A contemporary wrote of the actresses that, 'Men threw away their wealth, some forgot their fathers and mothers, others did not care if the mothers of their children were jealous . . .' An incident in 1628 involving a fight between samurai led to a ban on women *kabuki* performers. They were banned again in 1629, 1630, 1640, 1645, 1646 and 1647. The final ban was properly enforced and the manager of the offending theater was thrown into prison.

However, there was an alternative to actresses. Since 1612 in some *kabuki* groups all the parts had been played by men, and the *onnagata* (female impersonators) had reached a sophisticated level of skill. The banning of women from the stage made *onnagata* more popular than ever and inevitably attracted a different clientele, prepared to fawn over the beautiful youths as readily as their counterparts had for the actresses. Even though the government saw the theater as an evil influence, its fascination could not be denied. Under the Shogun Tokugawa Iemitsu (ruled 1622–1651) troupes of *kabuki* actors gave command performances at Edo castle. However, the government of the succeeding Shogun Ietsuna viewed *kabuki* with great concern. Women's *kabuki* had been banned because it 'disturbed the country, caused deterioration in various ways, and was the cause

wandering monks who played the shakuhachi *(bamboo flute). They wore a large basketwork hat that completely covered the face. This is the theme behind this titillating print, as the courtesan can see the* komuso's *handsome features reflected in the water.*

badly on two counts. First, it was performed for the townspeople and second it was performed by actors, and actors in Tokugawa Japan were ranked lowest of all, except for the *eta*. The actors in the *noh*, the stately theater of the aristocracy, fared better. So did their art, as it was the one form of theater thought appropriate for samurai. Where the *noh* was restrained and classical, *kabuki* was unashamedly popular

of calamities.' Youth's *kabuki* promised to be even more serious, a threat not only to the morals of the samurai, some of whom were noticeably infatuated by the actors, but also to their morale, as their fighting qualities decreased under the influence of idleness and pleasure.

In an attempt to make the *onnagata* less physically attractive, the authorities ordered the compulsory shaving of the forelock, thus making the actor's hair style identical to the fashionable samurai style of a half-shaved head. The forelock had to be measured periodically to ensure that the actor was not letting it grow again. As a result, *onnagata* took to wearing wigs for women's parts, an abuse against which the shogunate seemed to have no ready answer.

If *kabuki* was so deleterious to public morality, why was it not banned outright? The answer is probably because it was seen, like prostitution, as a necessary evil. It was, after all, an entertainment for the merchant classes and as, in the official view of samurai chauvinism, the merchants were hopelessly corrupt and vulgar anyway, *kabuki* helped to keep them out of

Left: *Few* ukiyo-e *artists came near to Kuniyoshi's skill in depicting the fierce individual samurai warrior. Prints such as these, produced in large quantities, served to make the samurai image a romantic one, and to spread knowledge of samurai values among all classes.*

Above: *Another example of samurai action.*

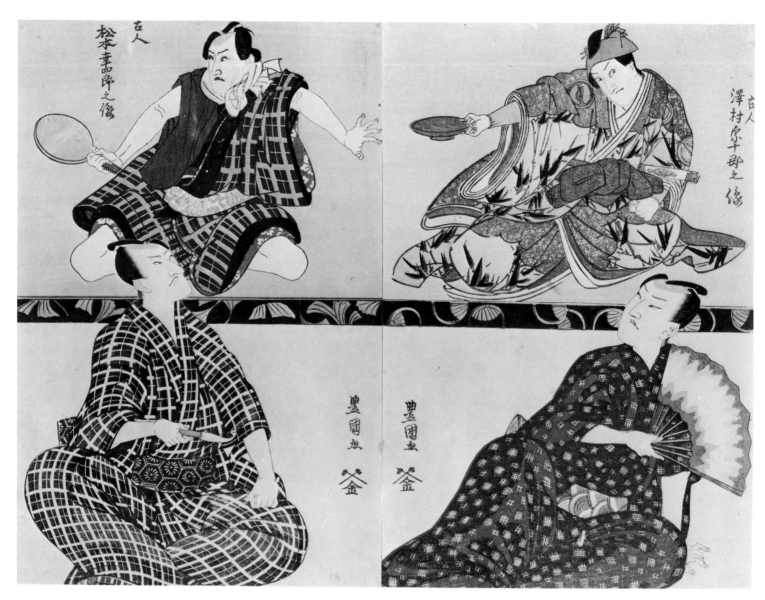

Above: *Although theoretically the lowest of the low in the orthodox Tokugawa class stratification, actors in the* kabuki *theater had a widespread, if somewhat clandestine, following among the samurai class. In this print two top actors in the* kabuki *contemplate portraits of themselves in role.*

mischief. So most of the ordinances aimed at *kabuki* were passed for the samurai's benefit. An example of the hold *kabuki* had on the samurai is the story of a rich young daimyo who met his favorite actor at a temple and insisted on giving the object of his adoration any present he cared to name. The actor replied in jest he would like the pine tree growing in the temple courtyard where they were standing. Such was the affection for actors and such was the power of a daimyo, that two days later the actor was awakened by the sound of workmen knocking a hole in his garden wall. The tree had arrived.

The other enduring theatrical art to date from this period was the puppet theater, now known as the *bunraku*, which used puppets which were two-thirds of full size. Chikamatsu Monzaemon (1653–1725), one of Japan's leading playwrights, wrote many of his finest works for this medium. The puppets had three operators, whose skill imparted incredible realism. From the perspective of the history of the samurai it is interesting to note that some attempt was made at political satire through the puppet theater, and to a lesser extent, the *kabuki*. It became a convention that when Hojo Tokimasa (1138–1215) appeared in a play, then Tokugawa Ieyasu was really indicated. One of Chikamatsu's most successful antishogun satires was his play *The Sagami Lay Monk and the Thousand Dogs*, a barb aimed at the 'Dog Shogun' Tokugawa Tsunayoshi.

The *kabuki* and puppet theater, along with storytellers, sword swallowers, prostitutes, sumo matches, itinerant preachers, sake shops and noodle stalls, comprised some part of the diverse life of the urban samurai. As to the towns themselves, by about 1700 Kyoto had a population of 400,000, Osaka 350,000 and Edo 500,000. Edo was a busy, bustling city whose population was swollen by the residence of the wives and children of the daimyo, kept as permanent hostages by the daimyo. The daimyo themselves were attended by a vast retinue during their regular periods of residence. Numerous craftsmen, merchants and laborers were drawn to the city by the opportunity to serve this vast array of consumers. Contemporary descriptions mention how the narrow streets were thronged with people. There were messengers carrying letters and money, porters carrying goods on the backs or slung on poles, townsfolk shopping, visiting friends or local temples, and all the personnel of business.

Occasionally the *chonin* would be rewarded by the highly entertaining spectacle of a samurai duel. Such incidents were most common in the early half of the seventeenth century, when the end of civil wars had thrown many *ronin* on to the streets. The problem of *ronin* reached its peak in 1651 with an attempted coup led by a *ronin*, Yui Shosetsu. He made his living by giving instruction in the martial arts, as the shogunate wanted its samurai to maintain their prowess. The plot consisted of setting fire to Edo, which was not at any time a difficult thing to do, and seize the castle under the confusion. The plan was betrayed by one of his associates who caught fever and babbled the secrets in his sleep. Yui Shosetsu committed hara-kiri. But such uprisings were few in number and were of less concern than individual *ronin* who would get drunk and start arguments, or even attack defenseless *chonin*, claiming the right of a samurai to cut down any member of the lower classes who insulted him.

Many samurai of far more respectable rank got involved in street violence. Some of *hatamoto* rank, the Tokugawa's own retainers, became bored with garrison life in Edo and joined gangs to rob and murder. They were known as *kabukimono* (eccentrics) from their habit of growing long side whiskers and dressing in fanciful clothes. They called their gangs by outlandish names, such as the *Daisho-jingi-gumi* (Band of All the Gods). To protect themselves, the *chonin* youths organized themselves into groups opposing the samurai gangs. As lower-class warriors fighting samurai on their own terms they attracted quite a following from the writers of *kabuki* and puppet dramas, who called them *otokodate* (brave men who stand up to injustice) and wrote popular plays about noble commoners outwitting samurai. In reality they were probably just as disorderly as the samurai gangs, but in the climate of the times it took little to make any townsman into a hero.

This period also shows the beginning of what may be termed the 'cult of the sword.' Tokugawa Ieyasu, who was certainly no stranger to the potential of a good sword in the right hands, was also a connoisseur of the finer points of a blade that went far beyond its capacity to kill. Swords would be presented to him for his comments, and were much prized as gifts or rewards. In his 'Legacy,' a collection of instructions to his successors, Ieyasu compares the use of the sword in combat to the correct employment of

Above: *The most celebrated performers in the* kabuki *theater were the* onnagata, *the female impersonators. Here two* onnagata *fight with staves.*

military might and power:

'The right use of a sword is that it should subdue the barbarians while lying gleaming in its scabbard. If it leaves its sheath it cannot be said to be used rightly.'

Further on in the text he makes the classic allusion:

'The sword is the soul of the samurai. If any forget or lose it he will not be excused.'

In the Tokugawa Period a whole new system of sword etiquette came into being. To touch another's weapon or to bump into the scabbard was a serious offense, and to enter a friend's house without leaving the sword outside was a breach of friendship. Those whose position required an attendant would leave the sword with the servant. It was customary to wear two swords, the *katana* (standard fighting sword) and the shorter *wakizashi*, which was acceptable to wear indoors. If the *katana* was taken in at the host's wish, it was placed on a sword rack on the right-hand side of the guests so that it could not be drawn and used. It was never placed on the left side unless there was an immediate danger of attack.

To exhibit a naked blade was considered insulting unless a connoisseur wished to show

someone a prized possession. In this case the sword would be handed to the guest with its back toward him, and the weapon withdrawn from its scabbard inch by inch, but not to the full extent unless the owner pressed his guest to do so. If he did, with much apology, the blade would be drawn and held upward and away from the other persons present – a strict rule of sword handling maintained by connoisseurs to this day. Similar etiquette was the rule when examining another's suit of armor. It was considered improper to look inside the helmet, but comments such as that the suit of armor 'looked very brave' were fully acceptable as a gesture of appreciation.

Such niceties of behavior make a pleasing contrast to tales of gang warfare and forbidden pleasures, and lead to a full consideration of the samurai's code of behavior, the famous bushido (Way of the Warrior). The evolution of a written warrior's code can be traced back to the house codes of the sixteenth-century daimyo, and much earlier to the 'House Instructions' of Hojo Nagatoki. The first systematic exposition derives from the writings of Yamaga Soko (1622–1685). The stimulus for Yamaga Soko was very different from those of earlier writers. Hojo had been concerned with his son's leadership and his behavior at court. Chosokabe had needed to rule a domain, and unite his samurai in a wartime situation. Yamaga Soko was concerned by the deterioration of the samurai in times of peace. In the opening passage of his study of bushido, Yamaga sets out his dilemma, and his aim:

'The samurai is one who does not cultivate, does not manufacture, and does not engage in trade, but it cannot be that he had no function at all as a samurai. He who satisfies his needs without performing any function at all would more properly be called an idler. Therefore one must devote all one's mind to the detailed examination of one's calling.'

Such a detailed examination, according to Yamaga, will lead the samurai quickly to a conclusion:

'The business of the samurai consists in reflecting on his own station in life, in discharging loyal service to his master if he has one, in deepening his fidelity in associations with friends, and with due consideration of his own position, in devoting himself to duty above all.'

Duty above all, that is the essence of bushido, a principle which, Yamaga later makes clear, applies equally to all classes of society. So why the 'Way of the Warrior,' why not the way of the farmer, or of the merchant, or even the way of the female impersonator in the *kabuki* theater? Yamaga explains that as these classes have no leisure from their occupations, they cannot constantly act in accordance with these moral obligations and thus serve as a moral example. The samurai, freed from the need to work at a trade, may confine himself to the 'Way of the Warrior.' He alone can uphold it and chastise offenders against it. To be a good samurai, therefore, one should be conscious of one's calling as a samurai. Yamaga Soko thus leaves us with an ethical and speculative approach, but no practical guide to how the 'Way of the Warrior' might be achieved. This deficiency is made up by the great classic of bushido, *Haga-kure* (Hidden behind leaves) which was completed in 1716 and begins with the chilling yet confusing declaration, 'The way of the samurai is found in death.'

Above: *A fully armed samurai fastens his helmet cords.*

Below: *A duel with wooden swords. Two samurai are fighting what appears to be a friendly duel, but each retains the shorter of his pair of swords in his belt.*

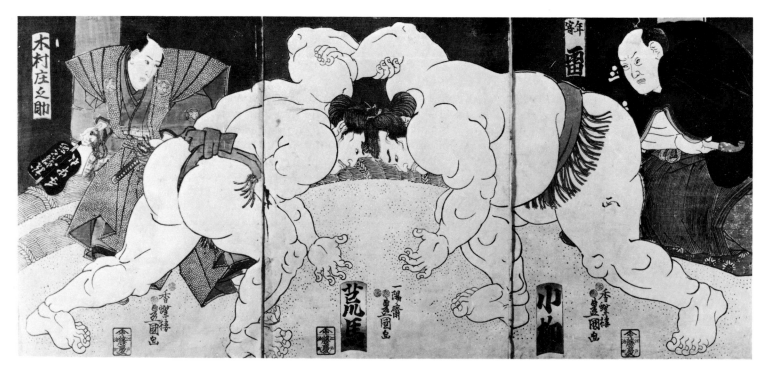

Above: *A print by Kunisada showing sumo wrestlers. The umpire, holding a baton, looks on nervously as the colossal wrestlers strain against one another.*

It is a vastly different approach from Yamaga's. This is to some extent explained by the circumstances in which it came to be written. *Hagakure* was composed by Yamamoto Tsunetomo, a senior retainer of the daimyo of Hizen province in Kyushu, the Nabeshima family. On the death of the third daimyo, Nabeshima Mitsushige, in 1700, Yamamoto expressed the desire to follow his late lord in death. By this time *junshi* had been outlawed by the Tokugawa, so instead Yamamoto retired to a secluded hermitage, where in the following seven years he produced *Hagakure*, a collection of anecdotes, essays and mystical writings put together in a haphazard but sincere manner. The book became a favorite of the samurai in the Nabashima han for use in training their samurai spirit. Where Yamaga Soko appealed to the intellect, Hagakure appealed to the heart. After the shock of the opening sentence, the exposition continues:

'If the choice is given between life and death, the samurai must choose death. There is no more meaning beyond this. Make up your mind and follow the predetermined course. Someone may say, "You die in vain if you do not accomplish what you set out to do." That represents an insincere approach of the Kyoto people to bushido. . . . if he misses his objectives and continues to live, as a samurai he must be regarded as a coward. . . . If he misses his objectives and chooses death . . . this must not be regarded as a shameful act. It is of utmost importance for bushido. Day and night, if you make a conscious effort to think of death and resolve to pursue it, and if you are ready to discard life at a moment's notice, you and the bushido will become one. In this way throughout your life you can perform your duties for your master. . . .'

Again we see the emphasis on *giri* (duty, obligation or debt of gratitude). In the narrow sense of the term it is the loyalty that a samurai must show to his lord. The other classes, as Yamaga Soko wrote, have other ways of fulfilling duty, but identical responsibilities to express it. To Yamamoto such duty will be seen in its purest expression when the samurai dies for his lord, when the way of the samurai really is found in death. But there is duty required before that particular moment of truth. By accepting his master's stipend the samurai was committed to the ultimate duty, but any obligation undertaken by a samurai required a willingness to undergo any sacrifice in order to repay a kindness, or honor a commitment. It was said that the samurai 'had one word.' Once he had pledged his word he was bound by it, and nothing would dissuade him from fulfilling the duty he had undertaken.

In the same way the samurai was expected to put himself above all material reward, especially money, hence the official contempt for the merchants. The samurai must also work constantly at his prowess in the martial arts, and cultivate a 'fearless spirit' the better to serve his lord. His own reputation must also be kept unsullied. Therefore he must avoid bringing disgrace upon himself and observe all due proprieties in his dealings with others. If his name is blackened, it must be cleared of all insults, real or imagined.

Thus the concept of duty was almost identical to self-respect, and in fact the two were regarded as complementary. However, such a quest for honor out of insult in a peaceful society inevitably led to bloody fights to the death over trivial matters such as an accidental clash of swords on a street corner. The exponents of bushido were aware of this and they therefore qualified their exhortations by reminding the samurai once again that his duty was to his lord and that his life was therefore the personal property of his lord, so that it should not be wasted in a petty quarrel. The saddest aspect of bushido is that it was felt to be needed at all. In an age of war, it may be argued, such values would not only be vital but also be perfectly natural. To set them out for the bored bureaucrats who constituted the samurai class of Tokugawa Japan is almost an admission of failure, a desperate attempt to rally a demoralized elite.

The intriguing question is, of course, to what extent did the samurai take bushido seriously? It is a particularly relevant question with regard to the events of the mid-nineteenth century, when the tremendous political upheaval of the Meiji Restoration was accompanied by an equally dramatic rearrangement of loyalties. This will be discussed further in a later chapter, but it is worth noting at this stage that the central notion of bushido, that of duty, was never questioned by the samurai who eventually overthrew the shogunate. With them the only matter was to decide where their duty lay, and seeing their immediate superiors abandon their duty, the conclusion was not that duty was wrong, but that the duty they were required to render was due to a higher level, which ultimately led to the emperor.

The irony of a martial code in a nonmartial era was not lost on the popular writer Ihara Saikaku. In his book *Buke Giri Monogatari*, 'Tales of Samurai Duty,' published in 1688, Ihara, an Osaka merchant, takes the samurai class and the notion of bushido with his tongue firmly in his cheek. According to Ihara, the merchant lives solely for profit, the samurai for duty. From this deliberate oversimplification he develops the theme that such a self-sacrificing attitude on the part of the samurai, so noble when compared to a money-grubbing merchant such as himself, could itself be the path to riches. The samurai is antimaterialistic and loyal, but only so because it is the way to success. In one of his tales the father of a boy killed in a duel adopts the boy's victor as his own son because he is better at the martial arts than his own son was. Now it was clearly in a samurai's interests to have the finest heir, but such calculated opportunism is so exaggerated that Ihara's only purpose can be to ridicule the samurai.

One of his most telling satires is found in a story set at the time of the Shimabara rebellion. A young samurai is ill and cannot join his comrades in battle. As they prepare to set off for the fight he bewails his plight until his

Below: A scene from the classic tale of samurai honor and vengeance, the Forty-Seven Ronin. Here the gallant Forty-Seven break down the shutters of Kira's mansion, ready to take his head.

Above: *The tombs of the Forty-Seven Ronin, at the Sengaku-ji Temple in Tokyo. The last resting place of the heroes has become something of a shrine to the samurai virtues, and attracts numerous visitors.*

comrades are so tired of hearing him that they make fun of him, and suggest that he would be better served using what little breath he has left in his lungs chanting invocations to Buddha. This infuriates the invalid, who prays, like Samson, that he might be given back his strength for one last effort. His prayer is answered and he stands up and puts on his armor but instead of setting off for Shimabara his duty demands that the stain on his honor from his comrades' insults be avenged. He thereupon challenges them, kills all three, and then commits hara-kiri, thus depriving his lord of four samurai for the coming battle. As in all cases of conflict of duty, the duty itself is never questioned, merely the direction in which it must be applied.

No such conflict of duty existed, however, in the minds of the famous Forty-Seven Ronin of Ako, the ultimate warriors whose revenge for the death of their master shocked contemporary Japan into realizing that some samurai did take bushido seriously. The loyal forty-seven were retainers of Asano Naganori (1667–1701), of a cadet branch of the Asano, who possessed a fief of 55,000 *koku* based in the town of Ako in Harima province. In 1700 Asano, together with Kira Yoshinaka, was commissioned to entertain envoys of the emperor at the court of the 'Dog Shogun,' Tokugawa Tsunayoshi. Kira held the office of 'Master of Ceremonies' in the shogun court, and it was the custom that his colleague should give him some presents in order to get instruction from him and thus avoid any error of etiquette. However, Asano brought no gifts and Kira, deeply offended, spared no opportunity to scorn his colleague. One day he went so far as to rebuke him in public. Asano lost his temper, drew his *wakizashi* and wounded Kira on the forehead. Even to draw a weapon in the presence of the shogun was a very serious matter, so Asano was banished and 'invited' to

commit hara-kiri. His han was confiscated, thus making his former retainers *ronin*. The chief of these former retainers, Oishi Yoshio, retired to Kyoto where he began to plot a secret revenge with the forty-six others who pledged to remain loyal to the memory of their dead master. Suspecting a plot, Kira sent men to watch Oishi but found only a man addicted to drink and given to pleasure. It was a front which Oishi kept up for nearly two years, until on a snowy night in December 1702, the loyal forty-seven, wearing armor secretly manufactured, came together in a raid on Kira's mansion. Oishi Yoshio cut off Kira's head and placed it on Asano's tomb in recognition of duty fulfilled. One of the *ronin* had been killed in the raid, so it was the remaining forty-six who went to the authorities and proclaimed what they had done.

The government had thus been placed in a nice quandary. Oishi Yoshio had been a pupil of Yamaga Soko, whose exposition of bushido as being 'duty above all' had earned the highest regard from the leaders of samurai. The forty-six had fulfilled their duty. The government did not know whether to punish them for murder by vendetta or reward them for behaving more like true samurai than any for a century. The decision reached was that the law must be upheld. The possible consequences of giving official approval to a vendetta were too ominous to contemplate so the *ronin* were ordered to commit hara-kiri, a course of action for which they had been prepared from the start.

No other act of samurai duty was to have such an effect as the exploit of the forty-seven *ronin*. With their deaths they became martyrs to the cause of bushido and even though the years leading up to the Meiji Restoration were to see many such assassinations none would produce adulation, nor spawn plays, stories, wood-block prints and mementoes by the score.

There is a little-known sideline to the story which neatly illustrates the theme of 'the sword and the abacus.' When the sentence on Asano Naganori was passed Oishi Yoshio hurried back to the castle in Ako, covering the 400 miles in five days. The reason for his haste was that the Asano Han, in common with many other daimyo, had issued currency notes. On examining the Asano treasury he found that their gold only covered 60 percent of the note issue, so he had the notes converted at this rate. This enabled the holders to recover something before the confiscation order descended, and incidentally deprived the shogun of a sizable sum of money. From this Oishi went on to his better known-form of revenge. Bushido may have had its duty, but even in this classic account of its execution the abacus is never far behind the sword.

Weapons and Modern Fighting Arts

One consequence of the dominance of the samurai during the Tokugawa Period was that the lower classes were disarmed. The characteristic two swords were the samurai's alone, and no weapon was allowed to those beneath him. Now an overweight, desk-bound ex-warrior may not have posed much of a threat to a commoner, particularly as the samurai's sword might well have been made of wood (the real thing being in pawn), but to be confronted by a hungry, desperate *ronin*, turned to crime by poverty and maintaining his martial valor, was not a prospect which an unarmed merchant or farmer would have relished. The result was the development of a series of combat arts, using ordinary implements, or even bare hands, which have come down to us as modern *budo*, and are spoken of colloquially as 'samurai fighting arts.' Perhaps 'antisamurai fighting arts' is more accurate.

One such is jodo, the art of fighting with a staff. Though less well-known than judo, karate and so on, fighting with a staff was developed to a very high degree – so much so, in fact, that the comment has been made

Below: Minamoto Musashi, the best-known samurai of the Tokugawa Period. He was a superb swordsman and master of the art of fighting with a sword in each hand, as shown in this print by Kuniyoshi.

Above and left: *Examples of the* jitte *in combat. The official use of the* jitte *was restricted to police officers in the feudal era.*

Left: *Another example of the* jitte *in combat. An expert user could snap a* katana *in two.*

Right: *An idealized version of an* iai *draw. In reality, when evenly-matched samurai met with this weapon, both would be killed.*

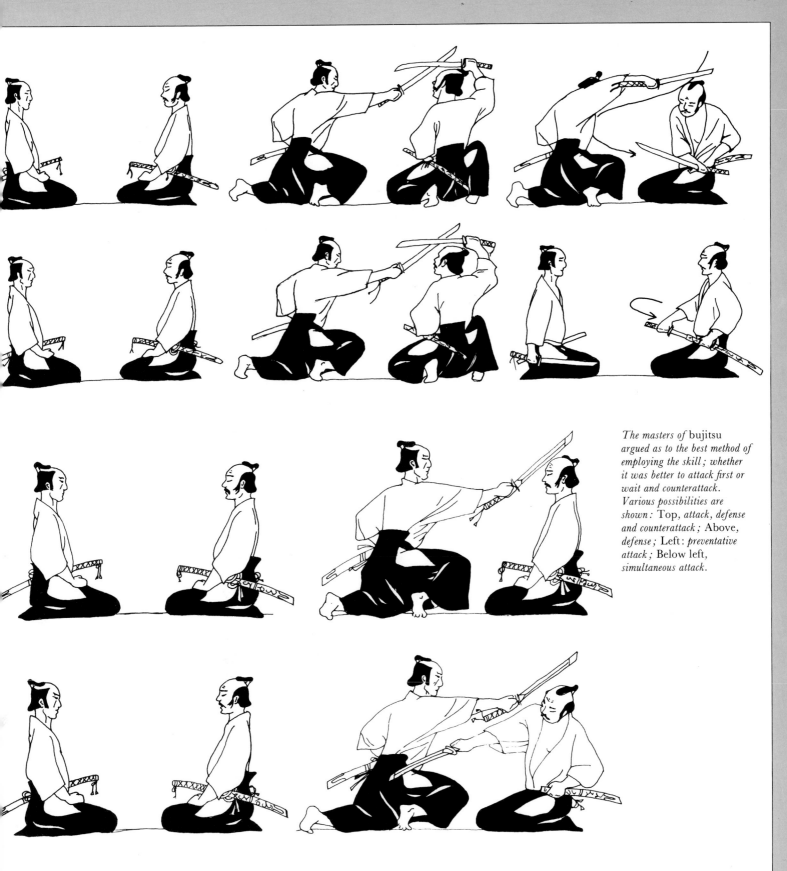

The masters of bujitsu argued as to the best method of employing the skill; whether it was better to attack first or wait and counterattack. Various possibilities are shown: Top, attack, defense and counterattack; Above, defense; Left: preventative attack; Below left, simultaneous attack.

that a trained practitioner with the staff could easily defeat a swordsman, perhaps by the classic jodo stroke, the thrust with the point of the staff to the side of the temple. If the idea of a trained samurai being overcome by a stick sounds fanciful, it is worth remembering that such arts were developed specifically for dealing with such defensive situations. The same would probably be claimed for such arts as *aikido*, itself a pure defensive art, and such exotica as the *Kusari*, a sickle with chain and weight attached to the handle, and various sword

catchers, and so on.

Arts such as *kendo* (fencing) and *iai* (drawing the sword) of course have purely samurai origins. Naginata fighting is now a branch of *kendo*, using a wooden replica, similar to the *kendo shinai*, of the terrible glaive of the warrior monks. *Kyudo* (archery) is also very popular, being regarded as an excellent training for the mind, with considerable overtones of Zen, laying emphasis on 'the way' in which it is performed, the characteristic approach which has colored all *budo* up to the present day.

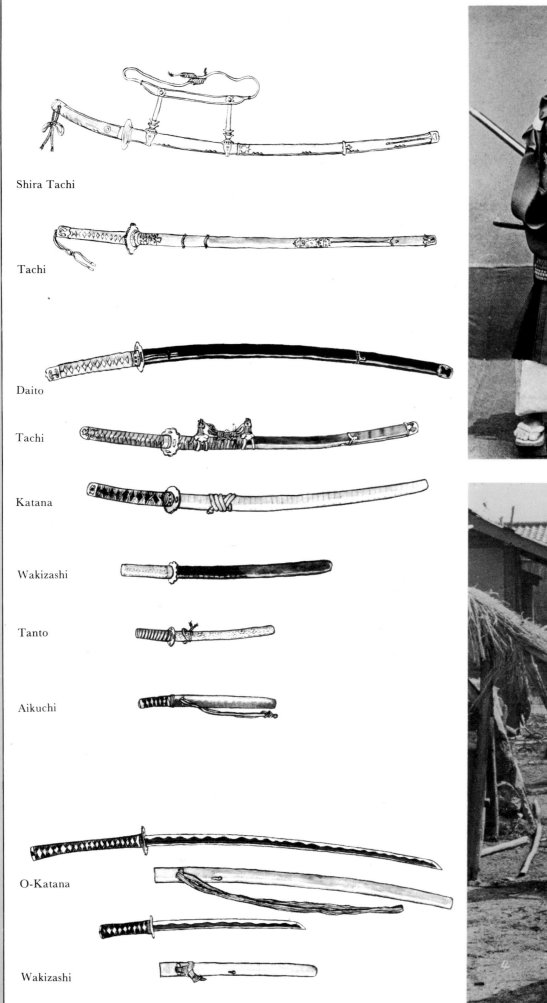

Shira Tachi

Tachi

Daito

Tachi

Katana

Wakizashi

Tanto

Aikuchi

O-Katana

Wakizashi

Far left: *A model of a warrior monk, one of the inhabitants of the temples of Nara and Kyoto. These monks lived in an almost constant state of warfare.*

Center left: *Armor typical of the sixteenth century. In fact by this time bows were rarely used.*

Left: *This type of armor is typical of the Ashikaga Shogunate. The quiver is protected from rain by a cloth.*

Below and below left: *These two shots from a Japanese movie give an impression of the sword in action.*

CHAPTER 9

Decline and Opportunity

Previous page: *A European ship firing guns. The decisive realization of the samurai class in the nineteenth century was that Japan would not be able to resist a threat from the West.*

Opposite: *A Tosa School impression of a court,* circa *1800. The apparent tranquility of the rigid Tokugawa world concealed turmoil beneath.*

Below: *A scene from a Japanese film. Many films on samurai themes, notably the famous* Seven Samurai, *contain a profound statement about the society in which the samurai lived, and his relations with the lower orders.*

The last century of Tokugawa rule was a time of crisis for the samurai. At a national level the supreme realization of their class was that the Japanese nation, which for all relevant purposes meant the samurai, was incapable of either meeting or resisting the military threat posed by the Western nations, whose incursions into Japanese waters were to increase greatly in frequency from the end of the eighteenth century. The acceptance of this unpalatable truth inevitably led to a questioning of the capability of the purely samurai government, the shogunate, whose reaction to the Western threat was characterized by indecision and irresponsibility. The failure of the samurai to govern led to a questioning of the need for such an unproductive military elite as a ruling class at all. This consideration was examined on a far more basic level by the lower orders, who came to regard the samurai not only as an unnecessary nuisance, which was no new conclusion, but, in the light of *kokugaku*, as a nuisance of comparatively recent vintage. No group felt the weight of the samurai more keenly, or questioned their rule

so forcefully, as the farmers, so it is to this class that we must now turn.

The greatest compliment that Hollywood has ever paid to Japan must surely be the remaking of Kurosawa's masterpiece, *Seven Samurai*, as the classic Western, *The Magnificent Seven*. On the heroic level *Seven Samurai* is the tale of how a village recruits seven *ronin* to defend its population against attacks by bandits. The film also makes a very subtle yet forceful statement about the society in which the action takes place and the relationship between the samurai class and the farmer class. It is a statement summed up in the closing sequence when the farmers are planting rice. 'We have won,' says one of the surviving samurai, as he surveys the scene of peace which their sacrifice has brought. 'No,' replies his companion, gazing at the farmers, 'they have won.' The point is that this samurai has realized what the villagers have known all along, that the bandits were samurai too and therefore the gallant seven were no more than a temporary necessary evil, hired in order to destroy their own kind. The exploitation of the farmers by the bandits was merely a small-scale instance of a centuries-old phenomenon. One daimyo is recorded as saying that farmers were like sesame seeds, the more you squeezed them, the more you got out of them. It may be stretching the comparison, but it is perhaps relevant that the farmers in *The Magnificent Seven* are Mexicans. In other words, the only way that a Western film could show such a gulf of supposed superiority as that between the samurai and the farmer was to make the farmers in the Western a different racial group. The despised farmers were the Atlas that supported every other member of Japanese society on its shoulders but, in a society that regarded farming highly but farmers lowly, farmers never received the recognition they deserved.

The agreed aim of the samurai class with regard to the farmer was twofold: to keep the farmer on the land and to increase production. On the whole the latter aim proved more successful than the former. Improvements in agricultural techniques, particularly the uses of fertilizer, led to a doubling of cereal production between 1600–1730 and the introduction of many new crops. Land-reclamation projects were also encouraged, in some cases to the extent of rewarding successful pioneers with samurai status. One of the main stimulli for increased production was the growing urban population and the development of a money economy, which influenced quickly the rural areas closest to castle towns as farmers were forced to obtain agricultural machinery.

This growing need for money led many farmers to the door of the usurer, where the

farmer had to offer his land tenure as security, though, of course, it still belonged to the daimyo. If the farmer failed to repay a loan then the tenure of the land fell to the usurer, who thus became a landlord, a nominal cultivator and a taxpayer. The new 'landowner' therefore tried to increase the farmer's yield so as to pay the tax and also leave himself with a profit. The result was that as the years went by the farmer class gradually split into different levels based on wealth. There had always been hierarchies in the village system, but these became more pronounced when allied with a new landlord class, which, in many cases, was one and the same person as the village *shoya* (headman).

The decisive factor in the increasing power of the *shoya* was the moving of the samurai class to the towns. Rural administration became the prerogative of the headman, the lowest unit of han administration. He organized the local assessment and collection of taxes and was responsible for all government functions within his assigned area, including festivals, livestock sales, police work and public morality. *Shoya* were in general very efficient, and incredibly proud. In fact toward the 1850s they were so convinced of their innate superiority to samurai that they pulled no punches when it came to complaining about maltreatment at the hands of their supposed betters. It was no longer felt necessary to begin a petition by affirming the

acceptance of samurai priority. In a significant move the *shoya* included in their petitions records of the evolution of their group from pre-shogun times, showing how the role of the *shoya* 'the head of the commoners' was honored by Imperial Commission, and far more ancient than the institution of samurai 'the feet of the nobles.' They explained their various functions and responsibilities, of which the few listed above are but a small sample, and demanded certain privileges – the most common was a demand for samurai status.

The important thing about the *shoya* in the decline of the samurai is not merely that they were not afraid to say outright that the samurai were an unnecessary hindrance, but by ruling the country wisely and well they actually proved that the administrative needs of 95 percent of the Japanese population could be met without the efforts of the supposedly governing class.

One fundamental difference in the relationships between the samurai and the farmers, and the samurai and the other classes, was that the samurai had once been farmers. By 1800 the change from samurai/farmer through fief-holding vassal to stipend receiver was almost universal, but the nostalgic yearning for the old days of the samurai/farmer were kept alive by such writers as Kumazawa Banzan (1619–1691), who wrote:

'When the old system of farmer/soldiers is restored and a tribute of only one-tenth is paid, wealth will be widely distributed and the people's hearts will be won . . . When the samurai become farmer/soldiers, the martial spirit of the nation will be greatly strengthened and it will deserve to be called a martial country. Ever since the samurai and the farmers became separate classes, the samurai have become sickly and their hands and feet have grown weak. . . .'

Yet the establishment of castle towns had seen to it that such a return would be unlikely, and that the samurai lifestyle would continue to be that of a man who lived in a hotel and never paid his bills.

In some areas, however, something a little nearer to the farmer/samurai ideal than the urbanized bureaucrat did already exist. In Tosa, for example, one way adopted by the Yamauchi for pacifying the old Chosokabe retainers had been to give them the rank of *goshi* (country samurai). In 1644 the practice was widened considerably and used as an incentive for land reclamation. Any applicant who could prove descent from a Chosokabe retainer, and had reclaimed fields of a minimum yield of 30 *koku* per year, was eligible for *goshi* status. In time the requirement of descent was

Below: *The simple straw cloak and sedge hat are almost symbolic of the despised farming class, on whose toil the samurai depended. The cloak was in fact very efficient and was often used by samurai, particularly those of lower rank, to keep their armor dry.*

dropped, and eventually so was the need to have existing samurai rank. Thus in 1763 merchants became eligible and in 1822 *goshi* rank was put on free sale. Consequently the rank of *goshi*, the highest bracket of the lower samurai ranks, was infiltrated by wealthy farmer/landlords and merchants who had bought their way into the samurai class by a legal and eminently more sensible method than paid adoption. The *goshi*, therefore, represented a segment of the samurai class divorced from their upper-class brethren in the castle town. With their closer relationship with the affairs of the countryside they had more in common with the *shoya* than with the samurai. This group were to make serious demands for change that were to have a devastating effect on the samurai in the 1850s.

Whatever the nature of the samurai's relationship to the land or to those who worked it, the fundamental fact was that Tokugawa Japan was based on an overwhelmingly agricultural economy and was, therefore, particularly susceptible to natural disasters. Crop failures, poor harvests, droughts and peaks in population all produced terrible consequences – famine was the most common and the most tragic. The samurai aim of squeezing the peasant, which meant attempting to keep him at the subsistence level, coupled with the growth of landlordism, meant that the new class of landless farmer, the hired laborer forbidden by law to leave the land, became the first victim. Between 1675–1837 there were 20 recorded large-scale famines. The one in 1732, for example, caused the near starvation of over 1,500,000 people. Even the very fear of possible famine was enough to lead certain sections of the population to resort to measures such as infanticide or abortion.

The more enlightened samurai officials attempted to relieve the suffering in times of famine by the distribution of rice. As a large part of the hardship was due to the clumsy and

insensitive bureaucratic system the samurai represented, the lower classes scorned their charity and took to direct action to bring their grievances home to their masters. Peasant uprisings, which had been significant in the fifteenth century, came back into prominence in the later Tokugawa period, when some type of mass riot occurred on average once every 10 years. Most of these riots took place in the countryside, but as the population of the cities and castle towns grew, they too became the scene for demonstrations and riots, usually set off by rising prices or shortages. The bulk of their support came from the new urban proletariat who had emigrated to the towns to escape the miseries of the countryside. City life, of course, gave the opportunity to make riots that much more dramatic. There were the houses of the rich merchants, the moneylenders and the wealthy brewers to attack and loot, in the periodic surges of violence known as *uchikowashi* (smashings). Osaka, the center of the rice trade, suffered many such smashings as the fury of the mob was directed against those who made profits from the nation's staple diet.

The responsibility for controlling agrarian riots at the local level was at first placed squarely on the *shoya*. As the most respected members of the community, they were ordered to calm things down and the distant samurai, in a dramatic illustration of their uselessness, could wash their hands of the matter until tax collecting time came round again. If a *shoya* succeeded in heading off a revolt he would be rewarded with a surname and two swords, if he failed he was dismissed.

Large-scale urban riots were clearly out of any *shoya*'s hands, and were met by direct samurai action and severe reprisals, faster and more decisive than any steps they ever took to relieve the suffering which had caused the trouble in the first place. Sometimes the

Above: An uchikowashi *(smashing) directed against the premises of a rice merchant. The straw bales containing his stock are ripped apart and the rice scattered, while hungry people attempt to gather some of the spoils. Urban riots such as these became more frequent during the 1830s.*

efficient *metsuke* were able to tip off the authorities before a revolt began. The ringleaders were then punished, often by crucifixion.

The final years of the long reign of Shogun Tokugawa Ienari (ruled 1787–1837) were marred by a series of calamities, both natural and

manmade. Crop failures were widespread from 1824–32. There was a famine in the north of the country in 1833 and a nationwide famine in 1836, when the rice yield was more than halved. The price of rice steadily increased and the effect was noticed most of all in the cities, which

Above: *Ships entering harbor. Under the Tokugawa roads and bridges were deliberately kept in bad repair to discourage contact between territories that might lead to rebellion. Most transport of rice and other*

天保山
万船
入津の
図

五岳

culminating in an attempted uprising in 1837 which shocked the shogunate and surprised everyone owing to the fact that it was led by a samurai, Oshio Heihachiro. The story is worth telling in some detail because it reveals the strength of feeling against the shogunate, and also the lack of ability to control events successfully, in this case shown on both sides, in the strangest assault on the shogun's powers since Shimabara.

Oshio Heihachiro was a samurai scholar and had formerly served as a magistrate. His philosophy was that of the neo-Confucian Wang Yang Ming school, which linked knowledge with action. It was a philosophy which Oshio followed to the letter, stimulated as he was by the famine which he saw around him in Osaka. Disgusted by what he regarded as the government's lack of action to relieve the suffering, Oshio petitioned the local officials to release rice from the government storehouses for famine relief, and also approached the large merchant houses for money. For his pains and idealism Oshio was threatened with prosecution when he attempted to submit a direct petition to the shogun officials. It was the time to link action with knowledge, so Oshio sold his vast library and used most of the profits to aid the poor. Not all, because some he secretly used to purchase a cannon, swords and guns, and hired a gunnery expert to train his followers.

Oshio's aims were clear, but his plans for achieving them were not, He envisaged a massive uprising against corrupt officialdom, and its replacement by men of virtue, such as himself, without going so far as the complete overthrow of the shogun and the Tokugawa hegemony. The program would be continued until justice had been obtained for the people. The uprising would begin in Osaka, where the farmers, under Oshio's leadership, would break into government offices and destroy the tax records, killing any corrupt official who tried to stop them. This would be a signal for an enormous uprising from the countryside. Merchants' stores would be destroyed and food distributed to the starving. His plans stopped here, for future developments were as vague as the ways in which these grand schemes would be carried out. The revolt was to begin by attacking two high officials who were due to make a tour of inspection on 25 March 1837. Immediately afterward there would be attacks on rice merchants and the distribution of food. The fires from burning buildings would bring in the contingents from the countryside.

Once again, in the long catalogue of failed revolts there was a traitor in the camp, or maybe a *metsuke* planted by a suspicious secret policeman. Anyway, the plot was discovered.

supplies therefore had to go by sea. The threat from foreign ships exposed this practice as a fundamental strategic weakness. Eventually, Japan was forced to adopt Western technology.

were teeming with displaced peasants seeking work. Emergency measures were half-hearted and further handicapped by the enormous drain on the Tokugawa finances caused by Ienari's reckless and indulgent overspending. Smashings became a frequent phenomenon,

Above: Samurai of the Tokugawa Period. The model for this photograph wears an authentic kami-shimo, *a garment consisting of a winged jacket and wide trousers. His hair is tightly drawn back into the obligatory queue, and his bow and arrows are neatly arrayed behind him.*

Right: During the period of seclusion the only outside learning that came the way of the Japanese was provided by the Dutch, as exemplified by this treatise on anatomy.

Oshio was warned that his plans were known, and decided to act immediately. His followers marched out from his house carrying banners inscribed with his motto, 'Save the People!' As they spread out round the city they systematically set fire to the houses of officials who were known to be corrupt. The flames spread quickly, and by the time they, and the rebellion, had been brought under control two days later, a quarter of Osaka was in ruins.

So, too, were Oshio's ideals, for his lofty scheme for 'liberating' foodstuffs soon degenerated into wholesale looting, with no attempt being made to distribute the rewards to the poor. Drunkenness made his followers even harder to control as they attacked the brewers and drank their fill, and in spite of their special training they proved largely ineffective when it came to fighting the shogun's troops. There was, however, a slight moral victory when the report from Oshio's cannon so scared the horse of their opponents' commander that the beast reared up and threw its rider. This incident provoked numerous malicious jibes from the townspeople in the time to come. As the full force of the shogun's army was turned upon them, Oshio fled from Osaka to the mountains of Yoshino. He returned to the city after a few days wandering and finally committed suicide.

Oshio's rebellion was thus a dismal failure, but it caused such a sensation in the country that other revolts by poor farmers, or the poor of the cities, broke out under leaders calling themselves 'the disciples of Oshio Heihachiro' sworn to destroy the 'robbers of the people.' These revolts, like all the others, remained isolated and sporadic incidents. There was true grievance and call for reform but nothing that could in any sense be called an organized protest movement. Such reforms as followed upheavals were aimed largely at restoring the shogunate's prestige by cutting consumption or breaking monopolies, rather than any drastic overhaul of the system. The 'Tempo' reforms of Mizuno

Tadakuni, introduced in 1841, attempted a wide range of tasks and failed miserably in nearly all. They ended with Mizuno's dismissal in 1843, largely because no class in Japan would accept a lower standard of living.

The rulers of Tokugawa Japan have been seen by historians as guardians of a social and economic system which they had received intact and were determined to pass on similarly undisturbed and it is possible to view their subjects as like minded. The Tokugawa had after all given them 250 years of peace and there was no obvious replacement for them. The intellectual current of the 1830s served largely to support this outlook. Confucian morality tended to reinforce the idea that the established order was true, just and fully legitimate. Such intellectual dissent as existed was more in the line of theoretical opposition to the rule of the shogun, rather than any planned system of argument against it. Of such, potentially the most damaging to the shogun's prestige was the study by scholars of the Shinto tradition, and its theories of the divine nature of the emperor. They could demonstrate how the emperor had ruled alone in antiquity, which led to the obvious conclusion that the shogun was a usurper of the divine monarch. Certain aspects of Confucian studies also supported the primacy of the emperor over the shogun, but as long as there was no rift between the imperial court in Kyoto and the shogun's court in Edo then the label of usurper could not be applied, as the shogun ruled by the commission of the emperor. It would require times of

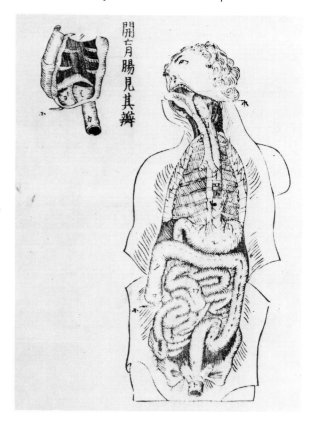

crisis, situations when the Tokugawa practice of decision making by examining precedents did not work, to substantiate any misgivings. Otherwise they were doomed to remain purely theoretical.

Further 'theoretical opposition' came from those who questioned the wisdom of the continuing policy of seclusion. Many were the followers of 'Dutch Studies' provided by the traders on the artificial island of Deshima in Nagasaki Harbor, Japan's only contact with the outside world for two centuries. Every new visitor to Deshima was plied with questions by the inquisitive Japanese, whether in the fields of medicine, astronomy or military science. It was the latter, in particular, that attracted the attention of those in power. Several far-sighted samurai were able to discern Japan's comparative weakness in military terms from descriptions of foreign weaponry and sightings of foreign ships. Sakuma Zozan, a samurai from northern Japan, devoted his life to military science, especially artillery. In 1841 he presented a study on national defense to the shogun in which he and others urged the adoption of Western-style armaments. He was eventually found guilty of an offense under the seclusion laws and jailed until 1862. Honda Toshiaki (1744–1821) turned from defense to offense, urging Japan to conquer a wide empire and establish a new capital in Kamchatka. These ideas did differ from the established order but in no way were they subversive. Even such a sweeping plan as one for the abolition of feudalism and its replacement by a centralized, authoritarian state, which was put forward by Sato Shinen in the early nineteenth century was little known and little read.

So all these undercurrents of intellectual formulations, ideas of imperial divinity, Western learning, economic and agrarian distress were independently contributing to a potential demand for great change. It required some dramatic development, some extraordinary, external and entirely new problem to bring all these dissatisfactions to the surface. In 1853 that challenge came when Commodore Matthew Galbraith Perry of the United States Navy arrived in Japan. His arrival was a problem that the shogun could not solve, and, like Perry himself, it was a problem that would not go away. Perry's arrival marks the start of the modernization of Japan, and between 1853–57 Japan overcame its three levels of crisis: the national, governmental and personal. The rapidity of the change, coupled with the active part which Japan itself played in the transformation, makes the development unique in world history.

The greatest ally Japan had had for maintaining its seclusion policy for so long was its geography. It was the Asian country furthest away from Western Europe. It was separated from Russia by the half-explored wastes of Siberia, and in the days before the development of California the growing power of the United States was as far away as Europe. By the end of the eighteenth century it became obvious to far-sighted members of Japanese society that such conditions could not last for ever. The seclusion policy had been adopted against the old colonial powers of Spain and Portugal. The nations who now threatened them were a completely unknown quantity.

Russia was the first of the new powers to come to the attention of the Japanese. A profitable fur trade with China led Russian explorers to move down the island chain of the Kuriles toward Hokkaido. Hokkaido, then called Ezo, was in Tokugawa days little explored as it was the last refuge of the Ainu. However an important supplier of marine products, a trade supervised by the daimyo Matsumae, whose role was regarded as being of such importance that the Matsumae were exempt from the requirements of alternate attendance. Worries about Russian intentions caused alarm, ranging from speculation about a Russian attack to Honda Toshiaki's call for Japan to move its capital to Kamchatka as a base for world domination.

The problem came into the open in 1792 when Lieutenant Laxman, acting as an envoy of Catherine the Great, anchored off Hokkaido, and presented a request for trade relations to the Matsumae daimyo. After consideration by the shogun the request was turned down, but permission was granted for a Russian ship to enter Nagasaki. Meanwhile the shogunate reacted speedily to the threat which Laxman's visit had posed. In 1798 Hokkaido was officially mapped, and encouragement given to settlement on the island. In 1802 the Matsumae han was taken over by the shogunate and a commissioner was appointed with responsibility for development and defense. In the next 10 years there were a number of Russian raids on Japanese defense posts in Hokkaido. The forts of Hakodate, incidentally, were defended with Dutch cannon, imports obtained through the loophole of Deshima. They were clearly of a fairly primitive model, as one Russian who saw them commented that their explosion might put savages to flight, but did nothing to terrify Europeans.

By that time, however, Russia was firmly embroiled in the Napoleonic Wars, leaving the field free to the British. By the early nineteenth century British interests in the Far East had moved beyond India to China, and in 1808 the Royal Navy saw an opportunity to test Japan's seclusion. At this time Holland had been taken

Above: *A grandmother with a samurai grandson. This reconstruction represents the ancient ceremony of 'tying up the hair,' performed when the child was three years old.*

Above: *Men exercising with staves, circa 1815. The weapons, illustrated in detail at the side of the picture, appear very similar to the modern* shinai, *used in kendo.*

over by Napoleon and was thus technically at war with Britain. After Britain took over Java, Sir Stamford Raffles conceived of a plan for Britain to replace the Dutch as the only European trader allowed into Japan. Accordingly, in 1808 HMS *Phaeton*, flying a Dutch flag, forcibly entered Nagasaki. It finally left without bombarding the town, an action the captain had threatened, but the Nagasaki magistrate felt so disgraced at allowing such a breach of the seclusion policy that he committed suicide. Two more British ships returned in 1813 but the commander of the Dutch factory refused to give in to threats, and succeeded in keeping Deshima as the only place in Japan where the Dutch flag was flying in 1813. In 1824 there was an armed clash between foraging British sailors and local inhabitants near Kagoshima, an incident which drove the shogunate to a dramatic decision in 1825 – the issuing of the *Uchi-harai-rei*, a declaration that any foreign ships which violated Japanese waters would be attacked and driven off without a second thought. The shogunate thus made antiforeign agitation official government policy, a decision that was to cause it much embarrassment in the years to come.

British intentions had by then switched from Japan back to China. The seizure of Singapore in 1819 and the growing trade in opium made China a far more attractive prize than little Japan. In particular the Opium War of 1839–42 gave Japan a breathing space and also an opportunity for them to see the possible fate of their nation. No amount of censorship or suppression could hide the truth about China's humiliation from critics of the shogun's policies. Sato Shinen (1769–1850), showed a firm understanding of the international situation and proposed that Japan should seize a foothold in China as a bulwark against British advance. Sakuma Shozan (1811–1864) also urged vigilance against Britain and, like Sato, was highly critical of the shogun's neglect of military defenses. He urged that Japan should study Western techniques via the Dutch, or suffer the fate of China.

In 1842 the shogunate, fearful lest an incident sparked off by a foreigner testing the *Uchi-harai-rei* should start a war, relaxed the edict and permitted foreign ships to be refuelled and victualled in certain ports. It was a complete reverse in policy, and brought down the wrath of the growing antiforeign element which the shogunate had itself encouraged. To their cry of '*Joi!*' (Expel the Barbarians!) was now added '*Sonno*' (Revere the Emperor) as the attack switched to the shogun himself. He was culpable, in their eyes, of disrespect for the emperor by pandering to the aliens.

The gap left in Japan's dealings with the outside world by Britain's preoccupation with China was soon filled by the United States. This young and vigorous country had been running Britain a close second in the tonnage carried by its ships, and with the acquisition of California in 1848, and the development of San Francisco as a major port for the China trade, American interest turned toward Japan. The rapidly increasing American whaling industry raised the problem of shipwrecked sailors and the need for provisions, so while Britain, France and Russia were busy fighting in the Crimea, America took a serious look at the possibility of opening up treaty rights. As Commodore Perry wrote before he set off for his fateful voyage:

'. . . the Japanese and many other islands of the Pacific are still left untouched by this (that is, British) government, and some of them lie in the route of a great commerce which is destined to become of great importance to the United States. No time should be lost . . .'

Perry was a far-sighted man, and so was his country's foreign policy, which included plans for Taiwan and the Ryukyu islands. Perry's was not the United States' first attempt to open up Japan. In 1837 a merchant ship carrying Japanese castaways had entered Edo Harbor and been driven off by cannon fire. In 1846 Biddle had attempted to land, but balked at the idea of using force. Finally, on 8 July 1853, Perry's squadron of four 'black ships,' two of which were steam frigates, anchored off Uraga and Perry presented a letter from President Fillmore addressed to the Japanese 'Emperor,' which went to the shogun.

Perry's arrival sent the city of Edo into an uproar. In all directions mothers were seen flying with children in their arms to a background of tolling temple bells and parades of samurai determined to resist the 'foreign invasion.' A coincidental meteor in the night sky, which was inevitably interpreted as unlucky, added a lurid glare to the scene.

It is not generally known, but the shogunate had been aware for some time that Perry's mission was coming through the good offices of their Dutch friends on Deshima. The matter had been kept very quiet simply because the government did not know what to do. Now that Perry had arrived they still did not know what to do. The message from the president was handed over, in a short ceremony preceded by a scene which makes one regret that a camera was not among the equipment on Perry's ships. 'Old Bruin,' as Perry was called, had marched to meet the Japanese representatives at the head of a marine band, flanked on either side by row

upon row of motionless samurai in full armor. The visitors left on the morning of 17 July and Perry recorded in his journal that '. . . to a maritime people, the contrast between their weak junks and . . . our powerful vessels must have made a deep impression.' Exactly what impression would be discovered the following spring, when Perry was to return to collect an answer to his demands.

The winter of 1853/4 thus proved a true winter of discontent for the shogunate. Its coastal defenses, which had been criticized for decades, had been proved hopelessly inadequate in repelling a breach in seclusion. As most of the

rice for Edo arrived by sea it was also clear that Perry's 'black ships' could constitute an effective blockade if his demands were not met. The differences in opinion which had been tossed about since the easing of the *Uchi-harai-rei* in 1842 began to crystallize into two opposing factions. On the one hand were those who felt that the shogun should abandon the seclusion policy and meet the Americans halfway. In violent contrast were the advocates of '*Sonno-joi*' (Revere the Emperor and Expel the Barbarian). One of the most outspoken critics of the shogun, and the staunchest *Sonno-joi* supporter, was Tokugawa Nariaki, of the Mito branch of the

Above: *A European making love to a courtesan. A color woodblock print by Eisho.*

Above: *A cannon of Japanese manufacture. This particular example, preserved at Mito, neatly illustrates the efforts of Tokugawa Nariaki, Lord of Mito, to arm his country ready to expel the foreigners.*

Below: *Townsend Harris, the first United States Consul to be appointed to Japan.*

Tokugawa house. Nariaki advocated nothing less than a war to drive the foreigners from Japan's shores, and called on the shogunate to lead a reawakening of the Japanese spirit to resist the foreign effrontery.

The president of the shogun's council, the *roju*, was at that time Abe Masahiro, a skilled administrator and sufficiently wise to see that no matter how desirable it may be to drive the Americans away, Japan did not at that time possess the strength with which to do it. Abe, however, lacked the power to make such a decision alone, and so did the shogun. Confronted by a problem without precedent, he circulated a letter throughout all the daimyo, including the 'Outer' *tozama*, and made a report to the imperial court at Kyoto. That any shogun decision should be made open to discussion, and particularly that the emperor should be approached, was a major show of weakness on the government's part.

The overwhelming majority of the answers received advocated rejection of Perry's demands. Seven daimyo answered in support of Tokugawa Nariaki's call for all out war. Having received such a drastic rejection of his own better judgment Abe Masahiro decided to move carefully. The result was a very cautious compromise.

The shogunate would agree to Perry's requests hoping thereby to satisfy the Americans before their demands became excessive, and at the same time take every possible step to build up Japan's defenses until they were strong enough to expel the Barbarians. Then they would strike.

The first part of the plan resulted in the signing of the Treaty of Kanagawa on Perry's return in 1854. The treaty provided for the opening of Shimoda and Hakodate to foreign trade, the good treatment of shipwrecked sailors and the eventual appointment of an American consul to reside in Shimoda. The second part set in motion a frantic session of rearmament, which dug deeply into the shogun coffers. Tokugawa Nariaki was chosen to lead the strengthening of the defenses, a job he must have relished.

The decision to rearm inevitably involved the Dutch, and Dutch influence in Japan reached its peak. Warships and armaments were ordered from Holland in 1854 and new forts were built to guard the ports. In 1855 20 Dutch naval instructors arrived to set up a training school in Nagasaki. Their first reports indicated some dissatisfaction at the progress of their students. They found the Japanese were incredibly rank conscious, resulting in high-ranking samurai finding the routine of command below their dignity, while forbidding their lower-rank comrades from practicing with any sort of firearms. Drummers' instruction was the favorite activity. Yet from these unpromising beginnings the modern Japanese navy was to emerge.

Knowledge of the military ways of the West was as important as training, so in 1857 the Bansho Shirabesho (Institute for the Investigation of Barbarian Books) was opened. Scholars to staff it were drawn from all over Japan, making the institute one of the major centers for Western study in the country.

Japan thus presented the paradox of an unparalleled interest and respect for the knowledge of the West, conducted for no other aim than the eventual expulsion of the West. In 1856 Townsend Harris, America's first consular representative, arrived in fulfillment of the clause in the Treaty of Kanagawa. He argued the benefits of trade with Hotta Masayoshi, who had succeeded Abe to chairmanship of the *roju* in 1855. A consultation with the major daimyo convinced Hotta that the mood was favorable for a further treaty, which he proceeded to draft with Harris. The new suggestions included the opening up of more ports, the residence of foreigners and certain matters dealing with trade which many saw as disadvantageous to Japan. Not surprisingly, the proposals met fierce opposition from the *Sonno-joi* faction, especially Tokugawa Nariaki, whose furious efforts for the past few years would be instantly outmaneuvered if the treaty went through. Harris had friends in high places and on 7 December 1857 received the unprecedented honor of being received by the shogun in person at Edo castle.

Frustrated by the intransigence of the *Sonno-joi* group, Hotta decided to go above their heads and went to Kyoto to obtain imperial support. It was not granted, but Hotta's action pulled the emperor into the forefront of politics. Almost at the same time, the house of Tokugawa was split into two competing factions on another issue. In 1858 the shogun Tokugawa Iesada had died without an heir. The *roju* and the *fudai-daimyo* favored Tokugawa Yoshitomi, daimyo of Kii, as successor. The *tozama* and the other Tokugawa branch families supported Hitotsubashi Yoshinobu, the son of the antiforeign Tokugawa Nariaki, who had put himself on record the previous year as suggesting that Townsend Harris ought to be decapitated. The greatest powers in the land were thus divided over two issues, forcing the *roju* to action. They decided that a strong hand was needed so they appointed as *tairo* (great councillor), with a mandate to settle the chaos, one of the staunchest supporters of the shogunate, Ii Naosuke. Ii could trace his lineage back to one of the first

Above: *Ii Naosuke, the shogun's 'strong man,' who was to cause an uproar by signing treaties with the West, and his suppression of opposition voices.*

Tokugawa shogun's closest comrades at Sekigahara, and had been one of only two daimyo to advocate ending seclusion in 1853. With the authority given to him by the *roju*, Ii acted. He settled the succession dispute in favor of his nominee, Tokugawa Yoshitomi, and then proceeded to sign the American treaty. Within months he had negotiated and signed five treaties with different nations: America, Britain, France, Holland and Russia. The *Sonno-joi* factions were furious at Ii's high-handed approach to the problems. Ii counterattacked with the directness of a medieval daimyo. Tokugawa Nariaki was placed under house arrest. So were Hitotsubashi Yoshinobu, the daimyo of Owari, Tosa and Satsuma, and several others. Numerous shogun officials who had sympathized with the *Sonno-joi* opinion were dismissed, and intellectual critics of the shogunate, such as Yoshida Shoin, were executed. The treaties had been signed, the barbarians were not to be expelled, and the shogunate, with the strong hand of Ii behind it, was once again a force to be reckoned with.

Men of High Purpose

There was nothing unusual about the morning of 24 March 1860, except, perhaps, the weather. Bitterly cold sleet and rain lashed at the faces of the samurai as they attempted to maintain as much formality in their parade as the squelchy mud underfoot would allow. The tall spears, their blades hidden in ornamental scabbards covered with black cock's feathers, swayed in the wind as they proclaimed to the cloaked and muffled onlookers that in the palanquin that followed, a square, box-like sedan chair lacquered in black and gold, sat probably the most powerful man in Japan, the Tairo Ii Naosuke, the shogun's strongman. In the two years that had passed since he had pulled off his two great coups – the signing of the American treaty, and the successor of his choice to the shogunate – Ii had seen other treaties signed, a great increase in foreign trade and settlement, and the successful stifling of opposition following his purge. The shogun, through Ii, was at last acting in the decisive manner of which the great Ieyasu himself would have approved, and the cries of 'Joi!' were no longer heard outside the territories of the *tozama-daimyo*, in the far corners of Japan.

Ii was on his way from his residence in Edo to the shogun's castle in the center of the city. It was a journey he took every morning as it was part of his duty as the equivalent of the shogun's prime minister. As his procession was about to step on to the Sakurada Bridge, the first of three they would have to cross, one of the seemingly innocent bystanders ran out in front of the spear bearers. As the guards ran forward to seize him, 17 other onlookers flung back their cloaks to reveal themselves as armed men. With the guards' attention momentarily taken away from the palanquin by the decoy, the samurai struck. The palanquin bearers were felled and as their burden crashed to the muddy ground, its door was wrenched open and the head of the Tairo speedily sliced from his body. The assassin who made the final cut ran off with the head and, as a further gesture, committed hara-kiri outside the mansion of a member of the senior council. Of the 18 assailants, two were from Satsuma province. The others were all from Mito, and returned to Tokugawa Nariaki, still confined in the house arrest where Ii had placed him.

They reported an operation that to them was not merely revenge but the execution of a traitor who had committed a crime against the whole Japanese nation by violating the most

Below: *The murder of Ii Naosuke. The savage assassination of the shogun's chief minister launched a series of terrorist attacks by the shishi, the 'Men of High Purpose.'*

sacred law of all, that forbidding the admission of foreigners to Japan.

The death of the Tairo Ii Naosuke marked the opening of a terror campaign against pro-foreign statesmen, and soon also against the foreigners themselves. It was also the first indication that a new force was abroad, taking the slogan '*Joi!*' to its logical and savage extreme. Indeed, it was more than a new force. It was the emergence of a whole new breed of samurai from the shadows into the front-line of Japanese politics. They called themselves *shishi* (men of high purpose).

There is a more permanent record of the appearance of these new samurai above that provided by contemporary descriptions, for during the 1860s Japan began her passionate and enduring love affair with the camera. Among the earliest subjects to pose stiffly for the long exposure required by the early machines were the *shishi*. The photographs that resulted give a picture of the samurai as menacing and yet as incongruous as any pulled from a wood block as a print by Kuniyoshi. These men, or at any rate those of them who survived their own fanaticism are seen in later pictures also. Gone are the swords and the wide *hakama* trousers in favor of frock coats and medals. The faces once shown off by carefully maintained coiffure now sport mutton chop whiskers as flamboyant as any of Queen Victoria's ministers. The role played by these men in Japanese history, and in particular their metamorphosis from swordsmen to statesmen, is one of the most fascinating stories behind the tumultuous events that make up what is known as the Meiji Restoration – the upheaval that was both revolution and reformation and encompassed the collapse of the Tokugawa Shogunate, the restoration of the emperor, the modernization of Japan and, ultimately, the disappearance of the samurai themselves.

The above description of the assassination of Ii Naosuke will have made it abundantly clear that, for the period from about 1850 onward at least, the picture of the samurai as an idle bureaucrat, whose notions of bushido came from popular literature, and to whom a daring exploit meant going to a *kabuki* play and not getting caught, was at the very least only partially true. The regular daimyo procession, of course, still had to be made to Edo. Small handicrafts still had to be undertaken if the samurai was to survive on his stipend. Yet, among all the bureaucracy and outward pomp, something had been stirring, a movement that seemed to be throwing the samurai decline completely into reverse, in a similar way that the forty-seven *ronin* of Ako had, a century and a half before, shown that a spirit was still alive which many had given up for dead. But this

time there would be no *kabuki* plays, wood block prints or puppet shows to immortalize the murderers of Ii Naosuke. This particular manifestation of duty, loyalty, honor, call it what you will, was part of a process directed not at a rival in favor of a wronged lord, but at the very center of power itself, the Tokugawa Shogunate.

It is, therefore, not surprising that the *shishi* came, in the main, from the four great *tozama* han of Japan. One of Tokugawa Ieyasu's most decisive acts in controlling the daimyo had been his resettling of the *tozama-daimyo* (who had been his enemies, or his half-hearted allies at Sekigahara), where they were both separated from each other and could be watched by the *fudai-daimyo*. Of these *tozama-daimyo*, the most influential were those four whose territories were almost as far from Edo as possible. The provinces were Satsuma, in the extreme south of Kyushu island, where the ratio of samurai to commoners was an incredible one to three (the national average was one to 17) and from where, it was said, no Tokugawa *metsuke* had ever returned alive. Choshu, at the extreme Western tip of Honshu and guarding the straits of Shimonoseki through which many a Western ship passed was another. Hizen, in Western Kyushu, which included within its bounds the harbor of Nagasaki, the one contact Japan had had with the outside world for two centuries was the third, and Tosa, at the southern edge of Shikoku island, where the Yamauchi suffered the difficulties of resettlement after doing very little at the Battle of Sekigahara, was the other.

The *shishi*, therefore, came from areas characterized by strategic importance, long-standing enmity against the Tokugawa, and in the years from 1853 onward, active involvement by the daimyo in the discussions on ports, treaties and the admission of foreigners. Their social origins were varied, though it is significant that many came from the lower ranks of the samurai, in particular from the *goshi*, or country-samurai class, whose forebears had achieved samurai

Above: *A doctor treating a samurai. Doctors were one of the few groups of people in Tokugawa Japan who were regarded as being outside the class system.*

status by grants of land. The antipathy of samurai of the *goshi* type to their betters in the castle towns, who had a vested interest in the continuation of the idle life, has already been noted. It was in fact these very class differences that dissuaded many in the upper ranks of the class from joining a movement toward which they had some sympathy.

Further characteristics of these young men – for their youth in a country which revered the wisdom of age was a notable feature – were their high levels of education and military skill, the latter being a particular product of the threat from the West. Saigo Takamori of Satsuma, for example, was a fine military commander who rose to lead the han forces while still only young.

Their intellectual armament was largely the Confucian values, modified by the needs of Japan. Like Wang Yang Ming, they believed in the unity of knowledge and action, and even if they may not have used the word bushido, and unified their concepts of morality under its convenient umbrella, the ideas of duty and loyalty were very clear in their minds. To the *shishi*, loyalty was part of his duty, but he was also subject to what the Confucian philosophers called *taigi meibun* (supreme duty). Supreme duty set these new samurai apart from the 'armchair bushido' of their predecessors. As they were largely country samurai, the loyalty toward one's lord, which is usually taken as the duty of the samurai, was to them a very tenuous feeling. There was, in a sense, a loyalty gap, and here the intellectual and political trends of the mid-nineteenth century came most admirably to the rescue. By the 1850s national Shinto studies had rediscovered the idea of a divine emperor who ruled the sacred land. The shogun, of course, saw no reason to do anything but encourage such studies as long as it was appreciated by all that the ruling of the land was being done by him on the emperor's behalf, following the ancient commission of 'Barbarian-Suppression' enshrined in title of shogun which had been entrusted to Minamoto Yoritomo and his

descendants in 1192. So long as the shogun continued to exercise that function correctly then no *shishi* would dispute his right to rule, and would show loyalty in the correct direction up the feudal ladder.

Japan in the 1860s was not like that. In the past decade shogun had allowed the sacred country to be violated by the barbarians. What had been pure was no longer so. Now in such a case a high-ranking samurai might weigh up the political and military considerations, and decide that because of Japan's weakness a thoroughly antiforeign stance was impracticable whatever one's personal feelings might be, and realize that the foreign problem had to be met with compromise. Ii Naosuke had reached this conclusion and he had paid for it with his head. To a young, vigorous, politically conscious and bitter *shishi* such a situation would point clearly to his *taigi-meibun*. This supreme duty would dictate a course he had to follow even if it was taken in defiance of accepted discipline, duty and personal safety. It could lead him to rebel against his daimyo, to leave his province and become a *ronin*, to join a secret society, to attack innocent foreigners. All that was needed to carry the supreme duty along was courage, and here the *shishi* excelled as strikingly as any of their class since the days of Nobunaga and Hideyoshi. It was as if, in response to the opening up of Japan, the cult of the romantic samurai had sprung up from the pages of bushido texts and puppet plays to achieve rebirth in these frightening young men.

The aims of the *shishi* were therefore clear: to preserve their sacred land from foreign impurity and to revere the emperor, the essence of purity. To this extent then the *shishi* represented a Loyalist movement, if not yet a specifically Restoration movement. If the shogun expelled the foreigners, he need have no fears over his position. The idea of abolishing the shogun had not even been considered necessary.

The response of the *shishi* varied from man to man and from area to area. Some remained in their daimyo's domain, where their youth and vigor suited them well for the arduous tasks ahead, involving secret diplomacy between distant fiefs, such as Satsuma and Tosa, or Mito and Hizen. There were journeys to be made and agents of the shogun to be avoided. Others left their han to become *ronin*, and to be able to use their swords without embarrassing their masters. So many chose this hazardous and illicit life that the problem of *ronin*, thought solved in the 1650s, became a fresh consideration for the Tokugawa administrators. Here we find the most fanatical of the *shishi*, who soon turned their swords directly on to the hated foreigners. Henry Heusken, secretary and interpreter to Townsend

Above: *A warning against mixed marriages! The inscription tells that to the amazement of the parents and the neighbors a Japanese girl bore a child to a white sailor. The little boy was bearded and excessively hairy, and although newborn could stand and displayed great strength.*

Harris, was cut down by two *ronin* as he rode home late one night in January 1861.

This was an outrage that sent shock waves through the foreign community and the representatives of Holland, Prussia, France and Britain, only recently arrived in Japan, left Edo for the comparative safety of Yokohama. Only Harris remained in the shogun's capital, convinced that to move away from the center of power was simply to play into the hands of the *shishi*. Harris was fully aware that the shogunate were afraid of the *shishi* as much as were the foreign residents. Harris, therefore, weathered the storm and when the crisis was over the other

legations returned.

During 1862 the *shishi* as members of a definable, antiforeign movement began to gather more strength. *Ronin* were gathering near Kyoto, Satsuma and Choshu were on the move and the *shishi* of Tosa, not to be outdone by any other han, killed Yoshida Toya, a prominent local sympathizer of foreign trade. Further fuel was added to the flames as the economic effects of imported goods made an impact on rural producers, convincing ordinary people of the inequality of the treaties. The assassination of leading political figures continued with increased vigor, and 15 *shishi* launched a furious attack against the British Legation in Edo, which was fought off by the residents, armed with revolvers and rifles. This incident led Sir Rutherford Alcock to make a disparaging and incisive comparison between the abilities of the attackers and the guards provided for them by the Tokugawa shogun. At the time of the attack there were no fewer than 150 samurai supposedly guarding the legation. Every one of them had been caught asleep by the *shishi*.

With so little to stop them the *shishi* went from outrage to outrage, and as the prestige and power of the shogun's police faded so the *shishi* grew in violence. Both real and imagined enemies were cut down. Officials believed to have been connected with Ii's purge of 1858 were murdered in broad daylight. In case any should doubt their intentions, the *shishi* began displaying the heads of their victims in the Kyoto streets together with placards listing their supposed crimes and a statement which invariably included the phrase *tenchu* (heavenly punishment).

It was not long before the swaggering *shishi* of Edo and Kyoto turned toward the wealthy merchants to fund their cause. Terror tactics were an obvious way, but the mindless fanaticism shown by certain of the movement betrayed their original idealism of 'supreme duty.' Nowhere is this better shown than in the suggestion made in all seriousness by one *shishi* leader to his followers. Faced with a refusal by a merchant to make a donation, the *shishi* should immediately commit hara-kiri. No merchant, suggested the leader, would be able to resist more than three suicides.

As its conventional police forces had failed to control the *shishi* the shogunate decided to 'set a *ronin* to catch a *ronin*.' Shogun agents began to infiltrate the ranks of the *shishi* and report on their movements, while Tokugawa murder squads were organized and trained to kill *shishi* in their own merciless manner. A celebrated account of one such operation is the attempt on the life of a prominent *shishi* called Sakamoto Ryoma, from Tosa, and his friend Miyoshi Shinzo. It is such a splendid tale of samurai action that it is hard to believe that it took place as late as 1866, except for Sakamoto's use of a revolver to supplement his sword! He and his friend were going to bed in an inn called the Teradaya in Fushimi, near Kyoto, when they fancied they heard footsteps and the rattle of staves. At that point a maid raced upstairs and warned them that men with spears were coming to get them. The comrades pulled on their *hakama* trousers, seized their swords and crouched down in a corner of the room to meet the attack. Twenty or so samurai were ascending the stairs and moving into an adjoining room. As they entered the room where the two *shishi*

were concealed Sakamoto brandished his revolver, at which the leaders withdrew, but others came against them and soon the fight grew fast and furious. One samurai leapt at Sakamoto out of the darkness and cut his left hand but, making good use of the six shots in the pistol, and their sharp swords, the two managed to drive them temporarily out of the room. Sakamoto tried to reload his pistol, but the wound on his hand made it difficult, and all the while the enemy were to be heard outside. As he fumbled in the dark Sakamoto dropped the bullet chamber and could not find it. His companion was for rushing into the midst of the enemy in good old samurai style, but Sakamoto suggested that they look for a way out. Fortunately the rear of the building was unguarded, so the two companions slipped down a ladder into the rear courtyard.

As the courtyard was enclosed there was no direct way out except through one of the buildings that surrounded it. All the shutters of the house next to them were locked, so the only way of escape was to literally bash their way through the entire house. This they proceeded to do with gusto. After smashing through the outer wooden shutters they found themselves in a bedroom, occupied by several rather startled inhabitants. Believing that the shortest distance between two points was a straight line, the two *shishi* drew their swords and headed for

Above: The British Legation in Edo. This was the scene of one of the fiercest shishi attacks on foreigners, when, in 1862, a group forced their way into the building, catching the Shogun's appointed guards asleep.

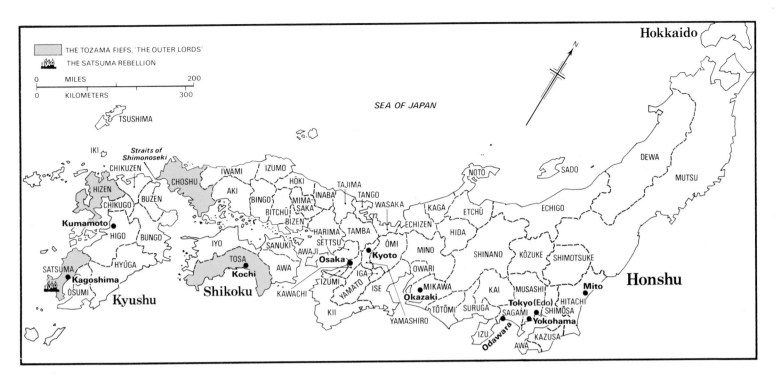

the open street, cutting through each *shoji* (sliding wood and paper walls that act as room dividers) as they came to them. The house proved to be rather large, so by the time they made it out into the street Sakamoto and his companion had cut and kicked their way through several rooms, leaving a succession of irregular holes behind them.

As well as trying to catch *shishi*, the government made a dramatic gesture to the loyal daimyo in a drastic restructuring of the alternate-attendance system that stopped just short of total abolition. The idea was that the money the daimyo would save could be spent on defense measures. Instead it flung Kyoto into the center of the political stage. With their hostage families safely with them, the daimyo could play at politics on a grand scale, adding yet another dimension to the anarchy that daily threatened.

Amid all the confusion the foreign residents, the cause and object of the troubles, made a brave show of 'business as usual.' The stage was set for the cause célèbre of antiforeign incidents, a murder that was to have far greater repercussions than any since the death of Ii Naosuke.

In the forefront of the drama were Shimazu Hisamitsu, the daimyo of Satsuma and a conservative in his attitudes toward *shishi*, and Charles Richardson Esq, businessman, presently of Yokohama, whose attitude toward the Japanese had already been recognized as high handed and insensitive. In the autumn of 1862 Richardson was out riding with three friends when they happened to meet head on the vanguard of the procession of the Satsuma daimyo, who was returning from Edo having negotiated certain reforms with the shogun. Ignoring the scowls and gestures of the leading samurai, Richardson rode on and only reined in his horse by the side of the road when he was level with the elaborate palanquin of the daimyo.

His inquisitive stares (the accepted position when met by a daimyo's procession was to squat on all fours and place one's forehead tightly to the ground) enraged one samurai, who lunged at Richardson with his sword. As if it were a signal, the street became a dusty tumult as other samurai slashed at the four Britons. Three of them, though badly wounded, managed to escape. Richardson tried to get away, fell from his horse and was left for dead. As he stirred and began to drag himself to the side of the road another samurai finished him off.

Tempers rose so high that evening among the foreign residents that, had reason not prevailed, they might well have pursued Shimazu and launched a full-scale attack on the Satsuma

Above: A view of the coast of Choshu near the Straits of Shimonoseki, at the extreme Western tip of Honshu.

Top: Japan in the nineteenth century, showing the location of the principal tozama *fiefs.*

Opposite: A samurai giving a cup of water to a wounded comrade. There was great loyalty between the shishi, *as shown in this print from Yoshitoshi's* Kwaidai Hyaku Senso.

Above: *Sir Harry Parkes, the far-sighted British diplomat who saw the weakness of the shogunate, and dealt directly with the outer lords, particularly Satsuma.*

daimyo's entourage. Instead the cumbersome machine of British diplomacy was left to sort out the business and decide on suitable punishment. After several months the conclusion reached was that the shogun should pay an indemnity of £100,000, that the Satsuma daimyo be ordered to execute the samurai responsible in the presence of English witnesses, and that the Satsuma daimyo should also pay a further £25,000 as compensation to Richardson's relatives.

The shogun was given 20 days to comply. If not, the British warned, coercive measures would be taken. After many delays, and the approach of a sizable British naval presence, the shogun's bill was finally paid on 24 June 1863. This was a particularly unfortunate coincidence of dates for the shogun as he had already been coerced by the Loyalist opposition, which by mid-1863 had matured somewhat from random assassination to a powerful political lobby, into setting 25 June as a final deadline for the expulsion of all foreigners from Japan. That this threat was not taken seriously by the British was shown by the squadron anchored off Yokohama. It collected £100,000 in silver bullion instead of refugees. Gunboat diplomacy had finally hit Japan.

However, Choshu, the han that covered the straits of Shimonoseki, did take the deadline seriously. On 25 June it opened up a private war by shelling foreign shipping that passed through the straits. The guns used, incidentally, were those purchased during the phase of rearmament of 1853. Some damage was done, and the *shishi* waited eagerly for the enemy to hit back. But Choshu would have to wait a while for foreign retaliation, for the Royal Navy squadron was now steaming leisurely toward Satsuma to present an ultimatum to Shimazu to pay up his £25,000, which he had consistently refused to do.

Meanwhile there had been further developments on the *shishi* front in Kyoto. The virtual ending of the alternate-attendance system meant that the major han now had activists, if not actual armies, in and around the capital. Most of the han, too, were firmly in *shishi* hands. In the spring of 1863 the shogun had visited the emperor, a thing unheard of for 250 years, and even though his retinue had consisted of 3000 men it was still an admission of weakness. There could well have been a coup there and then, but there was not. This was largely because the *shishi* of various han were suspicious of each other. Their supreme duty may have been the same, but rivalry between han kept them from acting in unity. Satsuma and Choshu were particularly jealous and suspicious of each other's motives, and each accused the other of plotting to set up a new shogunate. In 1864 they

actually came to blows. In February a Satsuma ship was shelled in the straits of Shimonoseki. Shortly afterward Choshu men attacked and burned another Satsuma ship in Beppu, a port of Kyushu, and almost Satsuma home territory. In July the shogun's 'murder squad' destroyed a group of Choshu and Tosa plotters in Kyoto, and later used Satsuma troops against an attempted coup by Choshu.

It was a breathing space for the shogun, but it was not to last. The shogunate knew that if ever Satsuma and Choshu united against them there would be a civil war. The longer the *shishi* could be kept apart, the better the shogunate could strengthen its defenses, not against the foreigner any longer, but against the *tozama-daimyo*.

Yet in the past year the incident had already occurred that was to unite the Satsuma and Choshu against the shogun. The haughty daimyo of Satsuma had steadfastly refused to pay his share of the compensation for Richardson's murder. Accordingly, in August 1863 the British bombarded Kagoshima. It was not an entirely one-sided affair. In fact the Satsuma gunners managed to get several shots in first at the flagship HMS *Euryalus*, with their Dutch-supplied cannon, but the bombardment that followed was devastating. Kagoshima was pounded by heavy guns and set on fire by rockets. Not long afterward Choshu received similar treatment from an allied naval force.

The foreign navies sailed away, satisfied that a good job had been done. It certainly had, but not in the way that the foreigners had expected. The sheer power of the bombardments brought home to these arrogant *shishi* one vital factor that had been appreciated by men like Ii Naosuke 10 years before, yet had been denied by the supposedly stronger domains. This was that compared to these nations, Japan was weak, and that whatever the demands of supreme duty the foreigners could never be driven out by force. To the *shishi* of Satsuma and Choshu it was a salutory experience. With the appreciation of the strength of the foreigner came a complete change of heart, however grudgingly or bitterly it was made, and the *shishi* at last appreciated that they would have to cooperate with the foreigner and learn his ways if they were going to survive the civil war which daily looked more inevitable.

Events began to move rapidly. Sir Harry Parkes, the British Consul General who had replaced Sir Rutherford Alcock, visited Satsuma where he was persuaded by Saigo Takamori, doyen of the *shishi* grown wiser, that the shogun's days were numbered, and that Britain's best interests would be served by dealing direct with the emperor and with the outer lords. The French, meanwhile, in the person of Leon Roches, backed the losing horse and dealt exclusively with the shogun, supplying arms and support in its efforts against the han. It was this, more than anything else, that drove Satsuma and Choshu together.

But what a change had come over the *shishi*! By 1865 the worst savagery was over. Many of the really xenophobic fanatics had been killed off, and any further deeds of violence against foreigners were the isolated acts of men who lacked both leadership and support. The others had undergone a subtle conceptual change. One of the new leaders expressed it by writing that it would indeed be desirable to rise up against the foreigner in revenge for the shame and humiliation which the shogun's officials had inflicted upon the country. But three centuries of softness had made it impossible at this stage, and history must not be hurried. The short-term object must be to cross the seas and master the technology and military science of the West. Then, and only then, could the treaties be renegotiated, new land be conquered, and the disgrace forever wiped out.

So the *shishi* had matured, and so had their battle cry. '*Joi!*' no longer stood for exclusion and isolation, but independence and equality. As for relations with the shogunate, the question was no longer whether there would be a civil war, but when it would begin. Succored by French help for a sweeping program of modernization, the Shogun revived hopes for its own survival and the destruction of the outer lords. Conservatives among the shogun's advisers began to agitate for a further expedition to crush Choshu, in the wake of the successful operation carried out with Satsuma help. There was even an attempt to revive the alternate-attendance system. But times had changed. Choshu was now secure in its alliance with Satsuma and looming on the horizon was the British Navy.

The second Choshu expedition, which began in June 1866, was an unmitigated disaster for the shogunate. It was a war that was lost almost before it began, as shown by a letter written by a senior shogunate official who declared that the shogun's army could not win the war, because Choshu had the backing of Satsuma and Great Britain and that the entire han was 'burning with the conviction of victory.' In contrast, the shogun's army had no desire to fight. Its equipment was poor by comparison with the modern arms possessed by Choshu, and the war was, in his opinion, already lost. The only superior shogun force was their navy. This factor was not exploited to the full because of Great Britain, who barred the shogun's navy from operating in the straits of Shimonoseki on the grounds that it would interfere with foreign shipping! That such arrogance could be displayed by the nation

that had suffered the murder of Charles Richardson only four years before is some measure of the changed climate.

The defeat of the shogunate at the hands of a single han made clear to all that the Tokugawa hegemony was at an end. To some extent the Tokugawa accepted it also, but it was not at all clear what could replace it. Then, in early 1867, two almost simultaneous events brought the political situation to its final crisis. Emperor Komei died, to be succeeded by his 14-year-old son, Mutsuhito, and the house of Tokugawa acquired its fifteenth and last, shogun – Tokugawa Keiki, formerly Hitotsubashi Yoshinobu.

By now the *shishi* had laid aside their swords for the world of political intrigue, constitutional proposals and rivalries. The new shogun continued to work for some form of coalition under the emperor which would retain some element of shogun control. At this point the daimyo of Tosa, wary of the might of Satsuma and Choshu, proposed a solution of his own. Under the Tosa plan, the shogun would resign and return his political authority to the emperor, but retain his lands and act as the emperor's prime minister, working with a council of daimyo. The plan was acceptable to Shogun Keiki and, under the

Above: *Tokugawa Keiki, the fifteenth and last Tokugawa Shogun of Japan.*

Above: *A street scene in Edo. The moon shines down on a view of Old Japan that was so soon to become a memory.*

Right: *The scene in Nijo Castle when Shogun Keiki proclaimed to the assembled daimyo that he was handing back to the emperor his commission of 'Shogun.' The institution of 'Shogun,' which had existed for nearly seven centuries, was at an end.*

pressure of his advisers who warned him that war could not be delayed for much longer, finally summoned all daimyo and important officials to Nijo Castle in Kyoto to receive the proclamation of his relinquishing of power, the handing back to the emperor of his commission as shogun, the 'Commander in Chief for the suppression of Barbarians.' It was the end of an era.

The memorable scene has been preserved in a well-known painting. It depicts the slight figure of Tokugawa Keiki seated on a dais, while in front of him bow the serried ranks of daimyo. Their lines are precise, their feet, in the spotless white divided socks, tucked neatly beneath them. Not a hair is out of place. Yet two in the second row have inclined their faces toward each other as if to mark by some unspoken gesture of understanding that the moment they had fought and plotted for had finally come.

There was one final act to be played in the drama. The Tosa settlement may have been acceptable to the shogun and the majority of the daimyo, but it was not acceptable to the mighty forces of Satsuma and Choshu. In the hours before dawn on 3 January 1868 Prince Iwakura, the Kyoto noble closest to Satsuma, went to the imperial palace to secure the young emperor's approval for the coup that was to be enacted in his name. At the same time, samurai from Satsuma, Choshu, Tosa and other sympathetic han secured the palace gates. A few carefully selected courtiers and daimyo were admitted, and the emperor appeared before them and read a proclamation which announced that all powers had now been assumed by him. There would be no shogun masquerading as a prime minister, and Tokugawa Keiki was to be reduced to the level of a common daimyo. This was the Meiji Restoration, a name taken from the era which now began with Emperor Meiji, as young Mutsuhito became known. Meiji means 'Enlightened Rule.'

There was some resistance, but Tokugawa Keiki had no desire to fight and withdrew his troops to Osaka. He was, however, unable to restrain some of his commanders, and on 27 January an attempt to recapture Kyoto was beaten off by an army of Satsuma, Choshu and Tosa under the command of Saigo Takamori. The han forces of 5000 samurai took only two days to defeat an army three times their number. Two months later the new government army marched into Edo, put down a small resistance at Ueno, and Tokugawa Keiki surrendered. There was some further fighting in the north of Japan, and the Tokugawa Navy actually held out in Hokkaido until May 1869. The Tokugawa resistance was at an end. The *shishi* had achieved their high purpose.

The Floating World

The Floating World is the name given to the culture of the towns and cities, particularly that of Edo and Osaka, during the Tokugawa Period. As the samurai were required to live in the castle towns the *ukiyo* world was a response to their presence. It was not, though, a response to their wealth, for the main patrons of the arts were the wealthy merchants on whom the frequently impoverished samurai were forced to depend.

It is hard to imagine a Japan without such phenomena as geisha, woodblock prints and the *kabuki* theater, yet all these are the creations of the Floating World, and as such have a comparatively short history. By the standards of Japanese art they are also comparatively vulgar, and unexpectedly colorful, but this again is evidence of the influence of the merchant class, whose very existence the samurai affected to despise.

Although the official line was that a self-respecting samurai should have nothing to do with the lower orders, and even less to do with their culture, in practice the entire Floating World was actively patronized and enjoyed by them. Even the shogun and his entourage were known to put on 'command performances' of *kabuki*, and the

Below: *Samurai enjoying a leisurely meal, as depicted on the Shubaron Scroll.*

Right: *A late-eighteenth-century print by Harunoba showing a geisha taking a lantern upstairs. Although by this time it was understood, most Japanese artists did not use Western perspective.*

selection of samurai topics for plots in this and the puppet theater indicate an active interest.

Woodblock prints (the well-known *ukiyo-e*) were produced by the thousand. The technique was for the artist to draw the design on very thin paper with a brush. This was then pasted face downward on to a block of wood so that the design showed through in reverse. The printmaker would then carefully carve round the lines with very sharp cutting tools. The print itself would be built up in stages, first line, then areas of color, each overlay being printed with absolute precision. Several hundred prints could be pulled off one block, and the topics ranged from the glorification of past heroics to the humorous and erotic. In depicting actors of the *kabuki*, two aspects of the Floating World came harmoniously together.

Overall the Floating World represents an almost dream-like time, totally in keeping with Japan's isolation from the outside world. Although not appreciated for its artistic qualities at the time, this age is a unique and precious moment in Japan's long and varied culture.

Far left, above and below:
Bunraku *puppets date from
the Edo Era and have
endured to this day.*

Left: *A print by Otagawa
Toyoharu showing the
interior of a theater with a
kabuki play in progress. The
mon of the actors hang from
wooden beams. The typical
'L' shaped stage produced a
very intimate atmosphere.*

Below: *A noh play in
progress today. Noh is more
restrained and classical than
kabuki. Note the masks worn
by the actors.*

CHAPTER 11

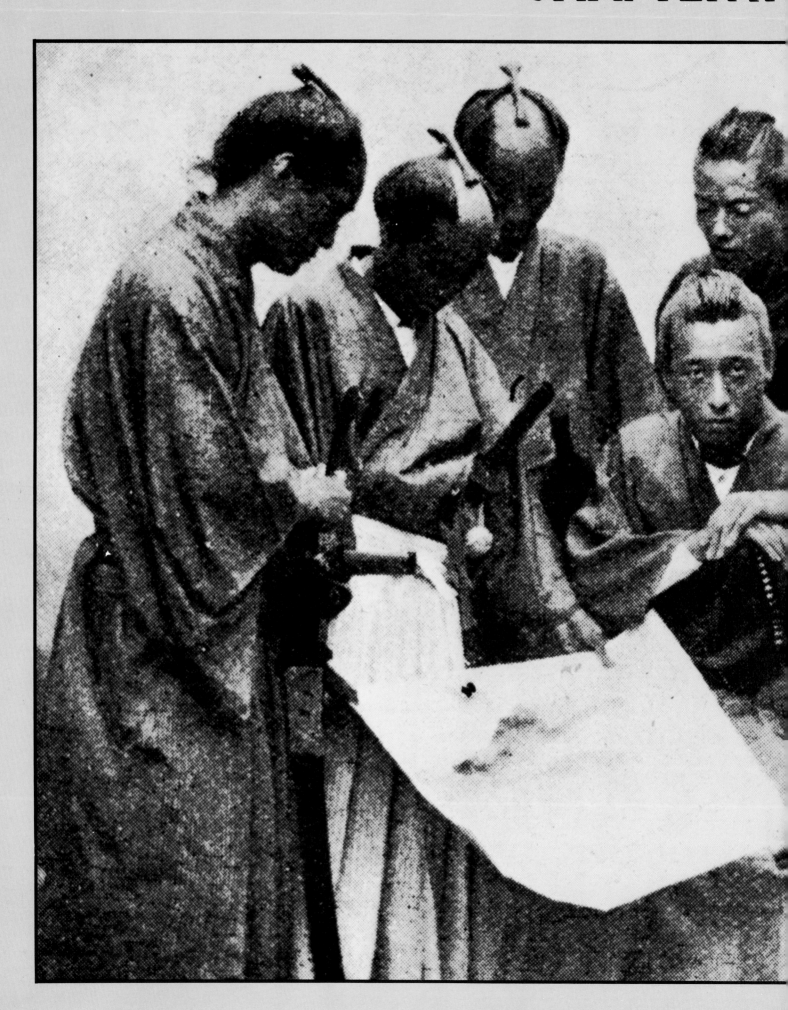

The Last of the Samurai

Previous page: *Samurai of the Satsuma Rebellion. A carefully posed photograph of Saigo's students before they departed for the Satsuma Rebellion. No photograph of Saigo himself was ever taken.*

One of the great advantages that the new men of the Meiji Restoration possessed was that they were acting in the name of something familiar. Because there had always been an emperor they were spared the embarrassing business usually attendant upon revolutions of awakening public respect and loyalty behind an unknown quantity. The Tokugawa regime had been abolished in favor of a concept older by far than that of the Shogun, and also in a very definite sense even more Japanese. That the new emperor was young and vigorous made it a double blessing, and eased considerably the painful road of decision which the samurai would now have to follow, whether they were loyal to the new regime or to their class.

The keynote of the Meiji Restoration was contained in the slogan *fukoku-kyohei* which was adopted as the national goal. That such a strong military aim could be stated so forcefully at the outset of the new regime may seem menacingly prophetic to a generation brought up with memories of recent Japanese militarism, but it reflected keenly the preoccupations and character of the men who were to mold the nation.

Here their attitude to the West was as decisive as it had been 20 years before. By 1868 all had accepted fully the superiority of Western technology. Several had visited abroad, and others had long associations with Westerners in Japan. They further accepted the need to modernize the nation as they had once done for their own han. That the countries of the West were keen to assist in the process was self-evident, yet the fear of the West remained, as it would for many years to come. So *fukoku-kyohei* became more than just a rallying point for modernization.

It also represented a determination to strengthen the country to meet the threat from outside, thus giving the first motto of modern Japan an uncanny parallel with the views of the violently antiforeign Mito Nariaki in 1853.

That such views should be officially adopted does not, at first sight, indicate that the demise of the samurai as a class was either imminent or inevitable. It is, in fact, far from likely that such a decision was ever taken as a deliberate act of policy. Yet a new, modern Japan with factories and railways was totally incompatible with an idle military class, so that if the Meiji state was to be built from the ashes of the Tokugawa, or on its foundations, depending upon the point of view, the samurai would soon be called upon to make a sacrifice far greater than any demanded by their previous masters. 'The way of the samurai,' wrote the author of 'Hagakure,' 'is found in death.' Their new emperor would require one final act of loyalty from his followers, for if the nation was to become great, and the samurai were not to become flotsam discarded by the retreating tide of feudalism, then they had to see themselves as the anachronism they had become, and perform a collective act of social suicide, the hara-kiri of the samurai class.

In many aspects the Meiji government looks similar to the administrations resulting from previous coups in samurai history. One shogunate has been abolished, to be replaced by a coalition of daimyo who control the young emperor and dominate the military life of the nation. But the important difference is this, that no matter how much the Meiji government may have looked like a Satsuma/Choshu shogunate at first, it did not stay that way, but by sweeping

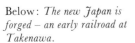
Below: *The new Japan is forged – an early railroad at Takenawa.*

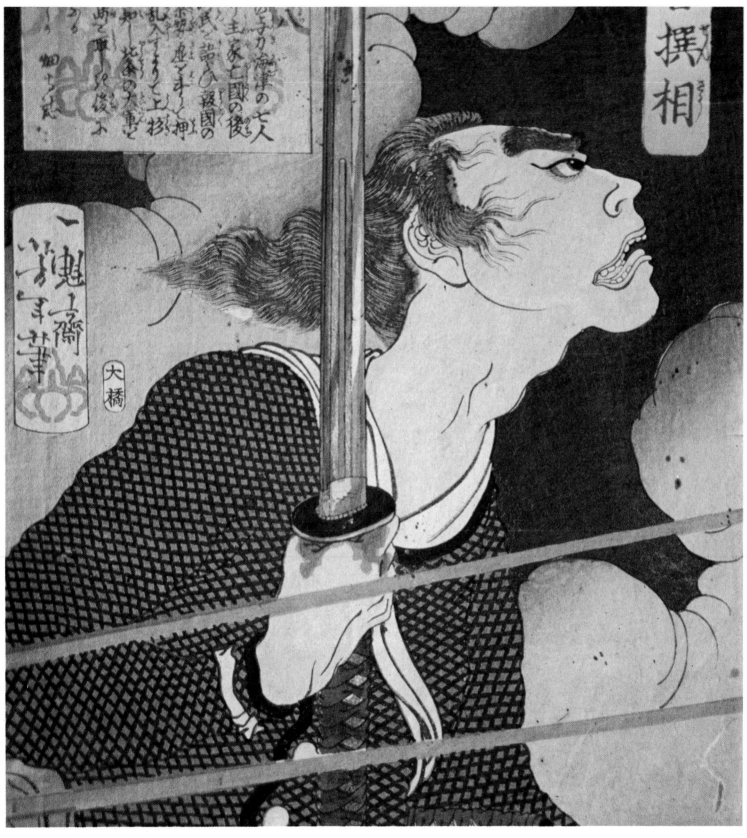

measures changed the whole nature of Japanese politics. The measures began with a simplification of the class system, whereby courtiers and daimyo were classed as *kazoku*, (nobility), the samurai as *shizoku* (gentry) or *sotsuzoku* (soldiers) and all the remaining classes as *heimin* (commoners), who were granted freedom of occupation and residence, and permitted to use surnames. The new rulers then set an example to their peers. Under the leadership and persuasion of Okubo Toshimichi, a man who was to earn the appellation of The Bismarck of Japan, the daimyo of Satsuma, Choshu, Tosa and Hizen handed back to the Imperial government the domain grants they had received from the Shogun, and while the han remained in name, their former masters now became mere governors under a centralization system of administration. During 1869 and 1870 the other daimyo followed suit, so that by 1871 the climate was favorable for a further step in the same direction. After much behind-the-scenes

Above: *A symbolic tour-de-force from Yoshitoshi's* Kwaidai Hyaku Senso, *depicting the lone samurai, sword in hand, facing modern weapons with defiance. Some ex-samurai rebels went so far as to eschew modern firearms entirely.*

Right: *This rare photograph
from the 1870s shows samurai
of old Japan armed with long
bow (center) and pole arms.*

Below: *An engraving shows
that as late as 1862 samurai
still used traditional weapons.*

diplomacy the daimyo/governors were summoned into the presence of His Majesty on 29 August 1871 to hear a decree which ensured the end of the daimyo once and for all. The han were abolished to be replaced by the prefectures which, with some restructuring and mergers, are the units of local government found in Japan today. The castles which had once represented the daimyo's might were confiscated, the private armies which still remained were abolished, and the daimyo pensioned off into retirement.

It is a matter of the greatest credit to the former daimyo, and of the greatest relief to the Meiji government, that such a drastic restructuring of power took place successfully and without bloodshed. Some returned their fiefs voluntarily as an act of loyalty in the new regime. Others had to be persuaded by men like Okubo that such an act was in their best interests, and that there was no reason to resist the transfer of what had become, by 1871, a hollow title to a domain enfeebled by military expenditure. Other more militant daimyo had to be forced to see the writing on the wall, for the military aspect of *fukoku-kyohei* was not undertaken with eyes fixed entirely on potential enemies from across the sea. It was the swords and guns of Satsuma and Choshu that had put Meiji where it was, and no matter how enlightened the Enlightened Rule was to prove, it was military might that would keep it there, whether the opposition was Tokugawa reactionaries or rival han, and behind the ready acquiescence of the daimyo

lurked the threat of armed confrontation. For the first two years of its existence the army of the Meiji government consisted of han forces under central command. In 1869 Omura Masajiro, a Choshu man, was appointed to set up a Department of War and lay the foundations of a Japanese army. Military schools were founded and arsenals established, but the old samurai spirit was still abroad, and his proposal for a national conscription system, whereby recruitment would come from all classes, was rejected. Omura was working on the reorganization of the army when he was murdered, along with five of his officers, in November 1869.

He was succeeded by Yamagata Aritomo, also from Choshu, who further supported conscription in the face of opposition from Saigo Takamori of Satsuma, who was of the opinion that a national army should be formed from, and only from, the existing military class. To some extent Saigo got his own way, for in 1871 an imperial guard of about 10,000 men drawn from Satsuma, Choshu and Tosa was formed and placed under his personal command. With the private armies gone, all weapons and military institutions nationalized, and Saigo's Imperial Guard forming a rather familiar elite, the independent side of the samurai ethos seemed to have quietly, and happily, abolished itself. There was now a Japanese national army soundly based on samurai ideals and personnel, under the leadership of one of the greatest of the shishi, for Saigo was appointed commander in chief of all armed forces in 1872.

But things were not destined to stay that way. Yamagata Aritomo made an inspection tour of Europe, and came back convinced that what Japan needed was a national army on the European model (he chose France as the example to be followed), in which conscription played an essential part. By the end of 1872 plans for the introduction of such a system was well advanced. This time the government was in agreement, and a law was passed in January 1873. Not even the elevation of Saigo to the rank of field marshal could disguise the fact that the days of the samurai as a military elite were now firmly at an end. The practical demands of the conscription law were that all males were to be put on the conscript register at the age of 21. They would have to supply three years active service followed by six years on reserve. A target of 46,000 men was set for the new army, to which all would belong, except for certain categories such as heirs, officials and some professions. But exception was not to be made for lowliness of social class, abolishing at a stroke the distinction between samurai and commoner.

By 1873 other factors reinforced the slight to samurai tradition implied by the new conscrip-

tion laws. In 1871 sword wearing had been made optional, and the impact of Western ideas of fashion had gradually made the traditional samurai costume, in particular the carefully oiled top knot, seem quaintly out of date, but it took a law of as late as 1876 to provide the symbolic tour de force. This was the banning of the wearing of swords by anyone except a member of the armed forces. It was the final indignity, and one that was greatly resented, coming as it did at the same time as a severe economic body blow to the class, the commutation of pensions.

The Meiji Restoration had effectively left the government with nearly 2,000,000 unemployed samurai on its hands, or about 5–6 percent of the total population. It was fortunate for those samurai living in reduced circumstances that the government itself was, of course, composed of ex-samurai, and thus far from deaf to their entreaties. In fact, great pains were taken to find occupations for them. The army was one obvious place, but posts were restricted in number, as were administrative positions. As the vast majority knew no trade other than the minor handicraft skills they had adopted to eke out their stipends the pension with which the government had replaced their salaries was their only support. The problem of pensions thus became one of huge proportions, accounting for about one-third of the government's annual expenditure. This put such a strain on resources that even the most diehard samurai spokesman in the government was forced to advocate phasing out the pensions in favor of a compulsory conversion to bonds, payable in a lump sum and backed by the government, with the samurai living off the interest. It is a mark of the government's economic worries that the process was rushed through and completed by 1876, the year sword wearing was abolished.

On average every samurai household received about 550 yen, which in most cases yielded too little interest for independent support. The samurai were thus cast adrift to fend for themselves in a modern world that had no need for their talents. Again the government tried to help with loans to set up businesses or land reclamation projects. The opening up of Hokkaido for agriculture was undertaken largely as a means of aiding the samurai.

Some projects failed, others were successful. In similar ways some individual samurai managed to adapt well to the changed conditions and prospered. Others fought against the change. They were bitter at what they saw as a lack of reward for their struggles in the war against the Tokugawa. They were warriors and leaders, they argued, and the government should be giving them the opportunity to exercise such

talents. Furthermore, even though the han had been abolished, these ex-samurai knew where their real loyalty lay, and resented members of other han rising to high positions in government circles. The uncertainty of their economic position, coupled with the amazing speed at which the government was showing how little it needed them, provoked them to angry reaction.

But for such resentment to become full-scale revolt there has to be a nucleus to which disaffection can attach itself, and here the Meiji reforms had been most successful. The nucleus for these dispossessed samurai had been the daimyo and his han. Both had been abolished, and whereas the pension arrangements for the majority of samurai had threatened penury, in the case of the daimyo they had been bought off most generously, ensuring for the former lords a comfortable retirement and for the government a secure support. In the absence of such a focus many of the more desperate samurai turned to terrorism as a means of political action. The *shishi* had shown the way in 1858. Now they were the government of the land, and it was their turn to fear the terrorist's sword. Omura Masujiro, the architect of the national army, was an early victim, felled by samurai from his own han. Yokoi Shonan, a prominent member of the government, was killed in 1869 for his liberal views. Iwakura Tonomi, efficient leader of a mission to the Western world in 1872/73, escaped with his life after an assassination attempt in 1874, and even the great 'Bismarck of Japan,' Okubo Toshimichi, was destined to end his days at the hands of an assassin in 1878.

Opposition to the government was also felt from the other end of the social scale. It must not be assumed that the introduction of the conscript law was welcomed by the farmers with open arms. The opportunity to become soldiers may have assured a new social status, but to a class that had long been exempt from the privilege of getting killed in battle the new law was dubbed a blood tax. Added to this was a complicated land reform of 1873, resulting in

Above: *The Imperial Japanese Army. The suppression of the Satsuma Rebellion was more influential than anything else in establishing the new army, and destroying the elite samurai forever.*

Below: *A transition samurai. This photograph, which probably dates from the early Meiji period, shows a curious mixture of traditional Japanese and European styles of military dress.*

Above: *The Satsuma Rebellion. Saigo Takamori called the force sent against him an army of peasant conscripts, yet it was to prove superior to the last of the samurai, even though equally matched in the supply of modern weapons.*

three major changes. First, taxes were paid by the individual, not the village. Second, tax was paid on the assessed land value, not the crop, and finally tax was, of course, now payable to the central government rather than to a daimyo. Rural uprisings reminiscent of the 1830s began again, averaging nearly 30 incidents a year from 1869 to 1874.

But if agrarian riots disturbed the government it was a small matter compared to opposition from samurai, and of this the terrorist was only a small, if deadly, example. The abolition of the han in 1871 had unwittingly demonstrated the near monopoly of government enjoyed by the clique of Satsuma and Choshu. Among demands

for retention of samurai status, and greater representation in government decision making, fundamental differences of opinion arose as to the course of modernization which Japan should follow. Certain statesmen favored the course already being put into practice, that of industrialization on Western lines, accompanied by that internal reconstruction which had by 1876 effectively disarmed and abolished the samurai class. This was the point of view held by Okubo and Iwakura. Others argued for an immediate, forceful expansion of the nation by means of a war against Korea. This opinion, that young Meiji Japan could succeed where Hideyoshi had failed, was given particular support by Saigo

Takamori, the hero of the Restoration War and failed protagonist of an elite, nonconscripted samurai army.

Relations with Korea had been uneasy since 1871, when Korea had behaved churlishly toward a Japanese diplomatic mission. Matters came to a head in 1873, while the main opponents of an expedition against Korea, notably Okubo and Iwakura, were undertaking their lengthy tour of the West. The Koreans broke off trade relations with Japan, provoking the reaction from Saigo and others of a call for a punitive invasion. So serious did the situation appear that the members of the Iwakura mission were hurriedly summoned back from Europe, and, being more convinced than ever that Japan must continue along the path of modernization and internal reform, unanimously rejected Saigo's call for war.

It must not be concluded from the above that Okubo et al represented a major peace-loving faction in contrast to Saigo's bellicose intentions. When the time came for war, 20 years later, they were warlike enough, but their experience of Europe convinced them that Japan was just not ready for such a venture. Saigo, being one of the very few leaders of the Meiji Restoration who had never left Japan, was thus hopelessly out of touch.

For the former samurai class, of which Saigo appeared to have become spokesman, an invasion of Korea had obvious attractions. It would solve their social problems overnight, restoring them to their traditional position of warriors and leaders. To others of more advanced political vision it would represent a defeat for the Satsuma/Choshu clique, as exemplified by Okubo. At any rate the invasion idea was soundly defeated, and Saigo resigned from the government in disgust. He gave up all his official posts except that of army general and returned to his native Kagoshima. For him it was a final break with the Meiji government. His supporters left with him, acknowledging a complete victory by the Okubo faction.

With Saigo out of the way the government could continue unhindered with its reforms described above. Unhindered that is, politically, for the terrorism spawned by disaffected samurai began to show itself on a larger scale. The first major revolt occurred in 1874 and was led by Eto Shimpei, a former vice-minister of education, who had resigned from the government at the same time as Saigo. He led 2000 samurai in an attempt to incite the whole of Kyushu to rebellion. The revolt was short-lived, and Eto, who had rebelled as a protest against the government's Korea policy, fled to Kagoshima where Saigo attempted to dissuade him from continuing. Shortly afterward Eto was captured,

executed and his head publicly displayed as a deterrent to any future rebels. It is a gruesome footnote to the story of Japan's adoption of Western technology that photographs of Eto's severed head were circulated and ordered to be displayed in all government offices throughout the country.

But even though it had been a disastrous failure, Eto's rebellion had shown that the vacuum of protest left by the passing of the daimyo could now be filled by disaffected members of government who possessed military skill and charismatic leadership, and believed passionately that the Meiji Restoration had betrayed the samurai who had died to bring it about.

Such a description fitted Saigo so well that the government thought it prudent to keep a close watch on events in Kagoshima. They had good reason to. With the abolition of sword wearing and the commutation of pensions in 1876 the whole island of Kyushu seemed to become a hotbed of discontent. One of the most dramatic rebellions occured in the town of Kumamoto, where 200 former samurai, enraged by what they saw as the government's abandonment of Japanese traditions for Western ways, formed themselves into a league which they called the kami-kaze, or divine tempest, thus identifying themselves with the destruction of the Mongol invaders in the thirteenth century. In an attempt to act unsullied by the decadent Western technology they refused to carry guns or other Western weapons, and launched themselves in an attack on the Imperial garrison using only swords. They were mown down by the defenders' firepower, and the survivors committed suicide to a man. At the same time there was a rising in Choshu led by a former vice-minister of war, Maebara Issei, under the slogan, 'War with Korea, Restoration of the daimyo, and expulsion of the foreigner.' He, too,

Below: *View from the keep of Kumamoto Castle. Kumamoto Castle was besieged by the insurgents during the Satsuma Rebellion of 1877. The success of the garrison in resisting the ex-samurai rebels added greatly to the morale of the new Japanese army.*

Above: *An unusual photograph of a samurai in the 1860s.*

was seized and executed.

Meanwhile Saigo had not been idle, but had used his retirement to set up private schools in Satsuma for training samurai in the military arts. When he had left Tokyo several of his officers had gone with him to become instructors. By 1876, the fateful year in which samurai were officially denied the symbol of their existence, there were in Satsuma about 7000 student samurai, armed to the teeth.

One factor which gave the government great concern was the presence in Kagoshima of three ammunition depots and two armament plants, dating from the days of Satsuma's arming prior to the Restoration. Although they were now nominally in the control of government officials, their presence in the prefectural capital indicated that, should a rebellion occur, the supply of arms available would make it a far more difficult affair to control than previous insurrections. Accordingly, on 30 January 1877 the authorities attempted to remove the stores in secret and transfer them to Osaka. Saigo was away hunting, but his students got wind of the plan, and attacked and drove off the naval force, which returned empty handed. Saigo was at first angry when told the news. He then congratulated his students and reconciled himself to the inevitable outcome. He was now in a state of rebellion against the government of Japan.

It was the most dangerous upheaval to threaten Japan since the Meiji Restoration. Saigo was stripped of all his military honors and declared an enemy of the Court. His former comrades in arms, Prince Arisugawa and General Yamagata, were appointed to lead the Imperial forces, and left for Kyushu, taking among their force the Imperial Guard, which Saigo had founded.

The Satsuma Rebellion, as Saigo's insurrection is known to the West, was the first major clash of arms to be experienced by the new Japanese army. It was also the last to be conducted against rebel samurai. It is interesting, therefore, to compare the military capabilities of the two sides. The Satsuma Army, as we have seen, was built round a nucleus of Saigo's students, most of whom had fought during the Restoration Wars. Their morale was high, as they were utterly convinced that they were fighting the enemies of the emperor, just as they had 10 years before. They were hardy and well trained. Each man carried the obligatory, and now illegal, sword, but unlike the kami-kaze fanatics did not scorn Western style weapons. There were enough Snider and Enfield rifles, together with various carbines and pistols, to equip the whole army, but only about 100 rounds of ammunition per man. There were also two artillery units, equipped with field guns and mortars. The Imperial Army was a force of 'conscripted peasants,' as Saigo put it, with small arms identical to those of the rebels but with considerably more ammunition and artillery pieces.

On 17 February 1877 Saigo's army marched out of Kagoshima in a heavy snowstorm. Their object was Kumamoto Castle, and it is sad to relate that a rebellion led by the former commander in chief of the Imperial Army should have begun with such an ill-conceived strategy. Kumamoto was one of the strongest castles in Japan. It had been built by the great general Kato Kiyomasa after his return from the Korean War in 1598, and incorporated in its design all that he had learned while campaigning on the continent. In 1877 it was defended by 4000 men under General Tani. We can only conclude that Saigo despised the peasant conscripts so much that he thought they would put up no resistance, for not only did he advance on Kumamoto but also left no garrison behind in Kagoshima.

The first shots of the Satsuma Rebellion were fired on 21 February, when advance guards of the Imperial Army were driven back within the castle. General Tani was now cut off from his headquarters, surrounded by Saigo's 9000 men. At the front of General Tani's mind was the question of morale. The Imperial Army was still new, and effectively untested. Kumamoto had also had to face the wrath of the kami-kaze fanatics in 1876, which had left them shaken. Yet fate took a surprising hand. On 19 February a fire broke out in the castle and threatened to engulf the ammunition store. As the fire seemed impossible to control it was decided to take the risky step of moving the ammunition to a safer part of the fortress. The operation was a success, and the precious ammunition was saved, but of equal importance was the heightened morale among the garrison, and they prepared to face Saigo with a new resolve.

The following days saw furious attacks launched against the castle walls, as the Satsuma samurai, sword in hand, crept over the ramparts to be engaged in rifle fire from the despised conscripts. Soon both sides were running short of ammunition, and each used assault units equipped only with swords. The garrison must have acquitted itself well even in this samurai-style combat, for no impression was made to the defense in spite of the fact that the Satsuma forward outposts were now so close to the castle that insults could be freely exchanged between attacker and defender. By the end of March food was running low, and there was great rejoicing in the castle whenever a horse was killed by Satsuma fire, for the soldiers then had the prospect of fresh meat.

A relieving force arrived on 14 April, and

further showed the potential of the Imperial Army by driving Saigo's force away from Kumamoto and back into Satsuma. Saigo may not have despised his opponents so much had he witnessed an incident that occurred the day before, when a certain Lieutenant Colonel Yamakawa continued to advance against Saigo's withdrawing troops in spite of orders to resist. The individual samurai spirit obviously lived on in the new army.

The next few months saw a long and tortuous pursuit of Saigo's army across Kyushu, which ended back at Kagoshima on 1 September. Only a few hundred men were left with him, of whom no more than a third were properly armed. Over half his original army had been killed, including nearly all his students. He was now surrounded by 30,000 Imperial troops, and withdrew to a little cave near Shiroyama, a hill to the north of Kagoshima looking out across the bay.

The end was near. The final attack began at four o'clock in the morning of 24 September. Saigo was hit in the groin by a bullet as he descended the hill to meet the assault. Beppu Shinsuke, one of his most loyal followers, lifted him on to his shoulders and carried him further down the hill to a spot suitable for the act of suicide. Beppu cut off Saigo's head with one sweep of his sword, then charged down the hill to be killed by rifle fire.

The Satsuma Rebellion was the last armed uprising against the Meiji government. It achieved nothing in terms of political gain, and, in fact, had effects diametrically opposed to what Saigo would have desired. It showed the qualities of the conscripted peasant army, who had held out in Kumamoto and finally defeated the elitist samurai army, showing no little heroism and fighting spirit in so doing. Thus, paradoxically, the Satsuma Rebellion destroyed the samurai ideals more effectively and more thoroughly than any commutation of pensions or antisword law could possibly have done. Saigo Takamori may have been the last of the samurai. He was also the man who finally destroyed them. The *fukoku-kyohei* policy could now go ahead unhindered by civil war, and future opposition to government would be limited to party politics and the odd individual assassination. Within 20 years Japan would be at war with China, a prospect Saigo would have relished.

With his death Saigo Takamori entered the pantheon of samurai heroes, and after a few years was rehabilitated as an example of devotion and loyalty. There is a fine statue of him in Tokyo, showing him as a stocky, resolute samurai.

But why end with Saigo? Japan's age of militarism was certainly not at an end, for the

wars against China and Russia were not many years away, setting a pattern that was to be continued into the Pacific War. The Imperial army had by then grown from the peasant conscripts scorned by Saigo, and took its share of heroism, and exhibited several instances of samurai behavior, notably that of Admiral Togo at the Battle of Tsushima. As an outstanding example of an old tradition we can cite General Nogi who committed *junshi* on the day of the funeral of Emperor Meiji in 1912, so that he might join his master in death.

But such incidents are throwbacks to a former age. Saigo's death marked the passing of the heroic age of the shadow warriors. The Satsuma Rebellion, too, marked the end of an era as it was the last civil war in Japan, a type of combat the nation had suffered, with few exceptions, for 1500 years. It may be argued that the true samurai spirit could only flourish in a civil war context, where there is sufficient respect from the enemy to allow the particular manifestation of samurai heroism the full rein it requires. This is mere conjecture, but if there is any truth in it then Saigo was certainly the last of the samurai.

Above: The spirit of the samurai. The samurai may have been abolished, but in the new Japanese army the heroic spirit was maintained during future wars.

Glossary

Ashigaru Peasant troops; literally 'light feet'

Bakufu Shogunate

Be Occupational groups of craftsmen and workers

Buke Military (samurai class)

Buke-sho hatto 'Rules for Governing Samurai Houses'

Bunji-seiji 'Government by moral persuasion'

Bunraku Puppet theater

Bushido Code of conduct; chivalry; literally 'the Way of the Warrior'

Chonin General term for townspeople

Daimyo The provincial lord; literally 'great name'

Daisho-jingi-guri 'The Band of All the Gods' (streetwise samurai)

Do-maru 'Wrap around'; armor worn originally by the lower ranks

Doso 'Warehouse keepers' and money lenders

Emakimono Painted Scrolls

Fudai-daimyo 'Inner Lords' (The daimyo who actively supported Ieyasu at the battle of Sekigahara)

Geisha Professional female entertainer

Gembuku The ceremony of entering manhood

Giri Duty; obligation, notably to a superior

Go-kenin Lowest rank; literally 'honorable housemen'

Goyo-shonin 'Charter merchants'

Gunkimono The 'military chronicles'

Han The domain of an individual daimyo

Haniwa Pottery figures

Hanzei 'Half rights' (a tax dodge)

Hara-kiri Self inflicted death held in honor by the samurai class; literally 'belly cutting'

Fukoku-kyohei 'a prosperous state and a strong army'

Hasamibako Travelling case carried on a pole

Hatamoto 'Under the standard,' motto of the samurai under the fudai-daimyo

Heimin Commoners

Ichimon Family member (of the clan leader)

Ichiryo gusoku Rustic samurai

Ikki Rural leagues

Jito Officials accountable to the Shogun

Junshi The practice of suicide in order to follow a lord in death

Kabuki Japanese popular theater

Kabukimono 'Eccentrics'

Kakun 'Family Instructions' a written code

Kami Holiness; God; the deities of Japan

Kamikaze 'Divine wind' (The storm which destroyed the Mongol fleet in 1281)

Karma Fate

Karo 'Elders'

Katana Standard fighting sword

Kazoku Nobility

Kebiishi Important appointment, concerned with arrest and punishment of officials

Kenin Non-kin samurai, or 'housemen'; retainers

Kishin Practice of commendation

Kirisute-gomen 'Common people who behave unbecomingly to members of the military class or show want of respect to direct or indirect vassals may be cut down on the spot'

Kofun Burial mounds; ancient tomb

Kuge Noble of the court

Koku Unit of measurement of wealth (about 180 liters) which was regarded as the amount of rice necessary to feed one man for one year

Kokoshu Military guard

Kokugaku Officially sponsored 'national learning' stressing Japan's ancient origins

Kokujin 'Man of the province'

Kyogen Short farces

Machi A number of neighboring city blocks

Metsuke 'All seeing eyes,' the secret police

Mikoshi A huge portable shrine

Mon Badge

Mononobe The hereditary palace guards

Naginata A heavy glaive with a long, curved blade; a long-handled sword

No-dachi A longer sword

Noh Japanese dramas

Onnagata Female impersonators

Otomo The hereditary palace guards (*Mononobe*)

Otokodate 'A brave man who stands up to injustice'

Roju President of the Shogun's council

Ronin Masterless samurai; literally 'wave men'

Ryo Territory; a fief

Samurai-dokoro The office of samurai

Sankin kotai 'Alternative attendance' system, whereby every daimyo was compelled to spend a regular period of attendance at the shogun's court in Edo

Sashimono Banner worn on armor

Shinto Religion; literally 'Way of the Gods'

Shishi 'Men of high purpose,' a new breed of samurai (1853) active in promoting the cause of imperial restoration

Shoen A manor; manorial system

Shogun A Military dictator; a general; a commander in chief

Shogunate ruling body; government

Shizoku gentry

Shoya The headman in a rural administration

Shugo Military governor

Sode (Armor) Shoulder plates

Sohei Samurai monks; a monk soldier

Soroban Japanese abacus

Sotsuzoku Soldiers

Suiboko Monochrome style of painting, ink brushwork

Tami The common people

Tan land measurement

Tenchu Heavenly punishment

Tengu Wood goblins (half man, half bird)

Tozama 'Outer Lords) (those who fought against Ieyasu at Sekigahara, or were otherwise hostile)

Ukiyo 'Floating World'; the transience of human life

Ukiyo-e woodblock prints

Uji Tribe or clan; family name

Wakato 'Officer trainees'

Wako Japanese pirates; literally 'dwarf warriors'

Wakizashi Shorter sword (used for hara-kiri)

Yabusame Mounted archery

Yoroi A style of armor

Index

承之先に次やうやく其らきて御車をよせ信業

らく御車をのせ奉し今は仮所も御るよろ御車を

よう御知し其れ其在んあうら御車をまいらうらる

を西門院へよろ乃ををまいら〜

師仲殿う御をれいまれける信業義経佑

渡やきあ成橋沈より使源光基某語

沚遠便雪へ実小御車を打つらみ大御